The Web of Inclusion

ARCHITECTURE FOR BUILDING GREAT ORGANIZATIONS

The Web of Inclusion

ARCHITECTURE FOR BUILDING GREAT ORGANIZATIONS

Sally Helgesen

For my father, Charles Helgesen

Acknowledgments

First of all, I owe thanks to the many people I interviewed at the five organizations profiled in this book; they were generous with their time and ideas, and provided me with much guidance. There are too many of them to name here, and their eloquent voices speak for themselves throughout the book, but Ric Giardina and Carlene Ellis at Intel and Julie Anixter at Anixter made themselves available in extraordinary ways and engaged with me in long and wide-ranging conversations that helped shape the entire book.

I also spent many hours over the last few years talking with a variety of people about issues of organizational change. Among the many to whom I owe a debt for useful and wise suggestions are Sharon Capeling-Alakija of the United Nations Development Program, Kelly Morgan, Nancy Badore, Lawrence Wilkerson of the Global Business Network, Eric Utne, Brian Arthur of Stanford University, Beth Summers, Nancy Evans, Sarah Beckman of Hewlett

Packer, Mark Barenberg of Columbia University Law School, Rayona Sharpnack of the Institute for Women and the Future, and, as always, my sister Cece Helgesen. I am also grateful to Tom Peters, who was so generous to me with my last book, and to Tony Pappas, who gave invaluable help.

Finally, I must thank those who helped me through the sometimes painful publishing process: my agent, Anne Borchardt, my editors Bill Thomas and Harriet Rubin, and Steve Rubin, President of Doubleday.

CONTENTS

PART I
THE ARCHITECTURE
OF THE WEB

PART II
THE WEB IN OPERATION

"*Electronic circuitry is Orientalizing the West. The contained, the distinct, the separate, our Western legacy—are being replaced by the flowing, the unified, the fused.*"

—Marshall McLuhan

"*What do networks want? The redistribution of power.*"

—Alvin Toffler

PART I

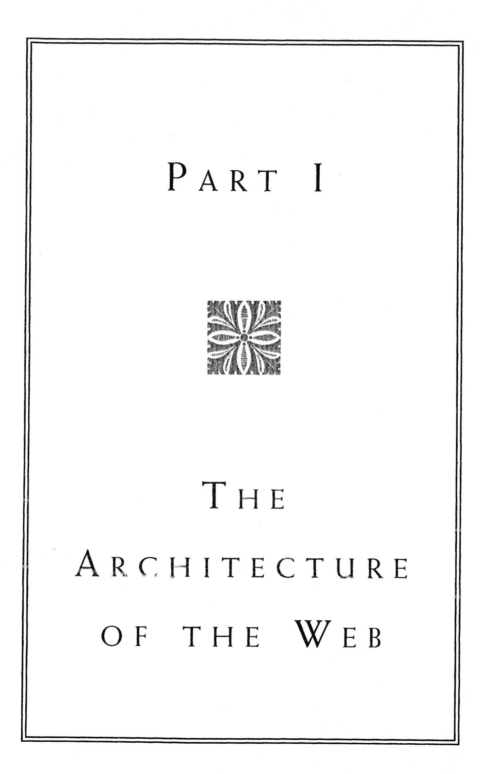

THE
ARCHITECTURE
OF THE WEB

PART I

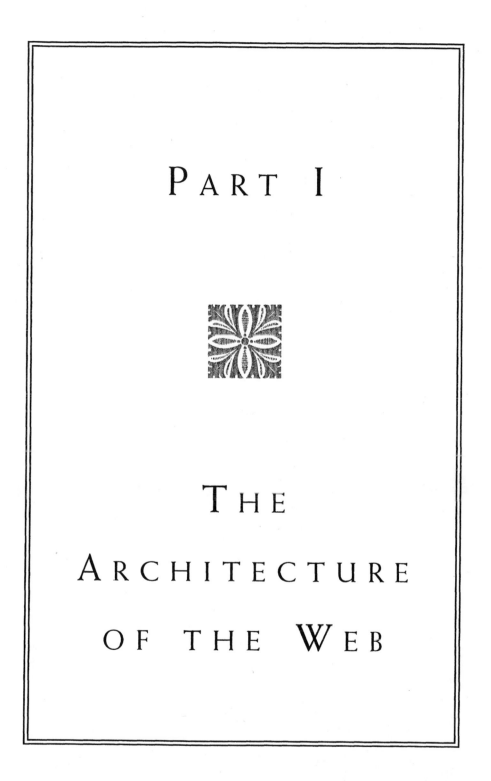

THE
ARCHITECTURE
OF THE WEB

ONE

The Search
for New Sources
of Order

In 1971, I took a job as an assistant at the *Village Voice*, the original, prototypical, and most influential and financially successful example of what was then referred to as the alternative press. The *Village Voice* was in fact a weekly newspaper that covered the goings-on in a particular neighborhood, Greenwich Village, but did so with a depth and perspective that made people in California and Wisconsin and Paris feel during the sixties and into the mid-seventies as if they could not afford to miss an issue. Dan Wolf, the editor, was adamant in believing that, if the paper covered local issues with sufficient originality and intelligence, people who did not live in Greenwich Village would nevertheless see their concerns reflected in some vital way. Thus, long before the nineties injunction to "act locally and think globally" had been enunciated, Dan Wolf recognized the principle and put it into successful practice.

He had started the paper in 1955, along with the psychologist Ed Fancher, the novelist Norman Mailer, and the heir to a pharmaceutical fortune named Wally Lutz. It began as an eight-page foldout that covered the downtown art and theatrical scenes, and sought to break the remnant of the Tammany machine that still controlled local politics in the person of boss Carmine DeSapio. By the time I arrived in 1971, the paper was up to eighty-eight pages, was stuffed with display ads, and had a classified section that was the envy of every weekly and most dailies in the United States. It had put SoHo and Off Broadway on the national cultural map, and been instrumental in enabling a local political group, led by a then little-known Greenwich Village reformer named Ed Koch, to break the Tammany stranglehold.

Yet despite the paper's high profile and evident success, the staff had not grown much since the paper's modest beginnings. There was still one associate editor, one city editor, one layout editor, and a single copy editor. There were no fact-checkers, no department heads except in advertising, few assistants, and never a consultant. Most of the articles were contributed by freelancers, who accepted low fees in return for a wide and influential readership, as well as the freedom to explore their personal obsessions in print with the minimal editing assured by the tiny staff. At any given time, there were only about four or five staff writers, and these tended to be people who had been contributing to the paper on a regular basis, often for years.

There were no staff meetings, ever. Dan Wolf was notorious for hating them. I don't recall ever receiving a memo, either informing me of some change in policy or exhorting me to do something differently. If anything like a management chart had existed, you would have been at a loss while looking at it to identify channels of communication or discover a rational chain of command. And yet I have never worked at a place where communication was so constant, so built into the daily process. Information was exchanged via bulletin board (corkboard, in that pre-computer era), and took the form of both general and specific notices. In part because most staffers were writers —but even more because of the pervasively open and often hotly contentious spirit of the place—most postings elicited scribbled responses that then might result in extended dialogues. Debates and policy discussions raged on the corkboard in a way that made rumor and intrigue difficult to sustain and kept most traumas in the open and so under a measure of control.

But perhaps the most noteworthy aspect of how the paper was run (and in retrospect, the most memorable for anyone who worked there) was the extreme and yet completely unstructured access that people at every level had to Dan Wolf. Dan essentially ran the paper by sitting in his office at the center of the top floor and making himself available, virtually to anyone who walked through the door. You did not make an appointment to see him; he had no secretary, and he disliked the notion of scheduling in any case. You just knocked on his door. If he was busy with someone else, you came back later; if not, you went in and talked about what was on your mind. As he explained to me years later, he kept his time flexible to an extraordinary degree by delegating most of the tasks that keep editors occupied, such as designing the paper beyond the third page. He delegated, gave up great amounts of control, so that he could be free to do what he considered his real job: getting to know his people and encouraging them in their work.

In addition, Dan usually invited someone from the paper out to lunch with him—often, one of the youngest and least experienced staffers. Invitations were spontaneous, and as with the office meetings, the talk was highly personal. Dan tried to find out what interested people, what delighted them or made them angry, and pointed them in the direction of exploring that. Out of these unstructured discussions would evolve ideas for features, series, columns, and sections, as well as influential events such as the Obies, the awards for Off Broadway theater that quickly became a cultural institution. Dan also brought people at the paper together with influential New Yorkers he knew—judges, politicians, established figures in the arts. By freely sharing his contacts, he continually drew more people ever more tightly into his orbit.

In essence, Dan shaped the organization by listening and asking the right questions, eliciting ideas that people hadn't even known they had. His method was classically Socratic, seeming at times to have been lifted directly from the *Apologia,* for as with the Greek philosopher, the main business of his life was holding conversations with those who sought him out. His most abiding belief as an editor was that interesting individuals, if encouraged and left to their own devices, would discover the things that most interested readers. He abhorred the notion of an editor trying to spot trends, insisting rather that an editor's job was to unearth the kind of people who would *create* new directions by following their own instincts, and then giving them the latitude and support they needed to do just that.

The political columnist Jack Newfield once observed that "Dan edited personality instead of copy." He went on to describe Dan's method of leading as "structured permissiveness," while another observer called it "managed chaos." I have come to think of it also as what might be called "interactive charisma," a way of leading that *derives power and authority from being accessible,* since access allows one to shape information as it evolves. Interactive charisma stands in contrast to what might be defined as "the charisma of command and control," which commonly distinguishes leadership in a top-down organization. Command and control charisma is based on position and maintained by distance, as in the military model, whereas interactive charisma is based on influence and maintained by communication. As an interactive leader, Dan Wolf sought to strengthen ties throughout the organization by continually breaking down barriers, which has the powerful effect of making everyone, at whatever level, feel included.

Inclusion worked brilliantly in the early years at the *Village Voice,* creating an intense loyalty that allowed the paper always to operate on a shoestring—an ability that proved crucial during the paper's financially precarious early years. Like many low-overhead operations, the paper was a hothouse for developing talent, but unlike many, it retained that talent beyond what might seem reasonable expectations; those who wanted more money than they could make writing for the paper could always contribute to other publications; contracts were loose, rather than exclusive. Dan Wolf recognized what Anita Roddick, the founder of The Body Shop, articulated when she said that "Money is not the most important thing to people. What most people *really* want from their work is the feeling that they are part of something *important.*" The corollary of this observation is of course that if an organization *fails* to make people feel like a part of something that matters, it will have to pay them more in order to keep them.

The *Village Voice*'s value, in those days, lay in the quality and diversity of its staff, an unlikely mix of individuals who often sharply disagreed. The capacity of the paper to present divergent views made it a forum for debate, keeping things lively for the reader, who never knew what to expect. Dan Wolf understood that a diversity of views was necessary if the paper was to avoid becoming predictable, and he maintained it by resisting pressure from the various factions that were continually vying for ascendancy. He maintained this balance by means of a strategy of inclusion that continually supported individual and dissenting views. This approach made everyone involved with the paper feel like participants in the debate and part of something important and always evolving. A kind of fractious togetherness developed, a good example of what *Inc.* magazine has recently called "emancipation capitalism," an enterprise in which everyone who is part of it feels a sense of ownership—even if, in literal terms, they have none.

In the mid-seventies, a major investor in the *Village Voice* acquired a new partner; the two decided to bring in new management. Dan Wolf and the publisher Ed Fancher resigned, thus beginning a process that would drastically change the character of the paper they had started. Under a flamboyant yet at heart far more conventional editor, the culture of individualism was altered. Almost overnight, the formerly flat structure of the paper became top-heavy with supervisors, managers, editors, and department heads. Every story that came in was scrutinized and edited, often by several people of ascending rank. The staff further ballooned as even occasional contributors were put under contract. Frequent staff meetings became the order of the day.

The changes fostered a climate of uncertainty and suspicion; the public bulletin board was replaced by rumor. In short order, the staff did what would have previously been unthinkable: it voted to unionize, thus institutionalizing an us-versus-them mentality that had previously been held at bay. Many petty decisions had now to be worked out by grievance. Although staff members were soon making far more money than in the past, some of the best were also leaving the paper, as if to confirm Dan Wolf's firmly held view that money cannot buy loyalty.

Soon the paper was sold, then sold again; editors came and went. Deprived of Dan Wolf's assiduous cultivation of individualism and commitment to balanced divergent views, the paper was soon riven by the factions that had always vied to control it. Meanwhile, Dan Wolf transplanted his style of management to City Hall, where he established himself as the alter ego and unpaid first deputy to his former protégé Ed Koch, who had by then become mayor of New York. As Howard Blum, a *New York Times* reporter at the time and close friend of both Dan and Ed Koch, describes it, "Dan ran the mayor's office the same way he'd run the *Voice*—talking to everyone, finding out what was on their minds, leaving his door open, giving everyone access. And access to *him* meant access to the top.

"Essentially, he saw people as equals no matter what their position. You were only as good as your ideas, in Dan's view. He sort of maximized nonconformity, finding unusual people and getting the most from them by freeing them to develop their ideas. Every day, he would ask people to have lunch with him and Ed. Often, they were people who were pretty low level in their jobs, some lowly cultural advisor—but he wanted to find out what they were thinking about." In Howard Blum's view, Dan Wolf's inclusive method worked to instill a kind of sibling rivalry among people in the organization who contended for his approval, creating a family-like atmosphere charged fiercely with loyalty. In contrast to most families, however, approval was granted to those who were most bold about expressing their individual talents and strongly held views, rather than those who conformed to the common family standard.

Meanwhile, at the *Village Voice,* the goal of maximizing profits and rationalizing decision-making by building a chain of command had managed greatly to weaken an institution that had been functioning at its peak. Despite huge increases in staff and overhead, circulation never went much beyond the point it had reached in the last days of Dan Wolf and Ed Fancher, with their tiny staff and tight reign on expenses. A measure of the paper's golden profitability, as well as a good portion of its political and cultural influence, had been squandered in the attempt to "professionalize" its management.

Watching this particular drama unfold provided me with a stark and early lesson in the difference between effective and misguided management. It made vividly clear the direct consequences that each can have, not only upon that abstract entity known as "the organization," but upon the daily lives of considerable numbers of people. Though the lesson was absorbed at a deep level, I did not have much occasion to think about it until years later, when I was researching *The Female Advantage: Women's Ways of Leadership.* In that book, I examined by means of diary studies the day-to-day management style of some of America's best women business leaders.

The women I studied were vividly different, and ran organizations that were wildly diverse—a construction firm, a group of radio stations, a nonprofit enterprise, the training institute for the Ford Motor Company. Nevertheless, I noticed many similarities in their style of leading, their presumptions about what motivates people, their goals, and the ways in which they accomplished their tasks. I also saw similarities in how the women structured their organizations, which were markedly different from any of the companies for which I had worked since leaving the *Village Voice*—companies such as IBM, New York Telephone, and various national newspapers and magazines. The women's structures were also different from those of other kinds of institutions that I had encountered over the course of my life—schools and universities, political and charitable organizations, and perhaps most dramatically, the Catholic Church into which I had been born, and which had so shaped my vision of the world.

In the process of devising ways of leading that made sense to *them*, the women I studied had built profoundly integrated and organic organizations, in which the focus was on nurturing good relationships; in which the niceties of hierarchical rank and distinction played little part; and in which lines of communication were multiplicitous, open, and diffuse. I noted that the women tended to put themselves at the centers of their organizations rather than at the top, thus emphasizing both accessibility and equality, and that they labored constantly to include people in their decision-making. This had the effect of undermining the boundaries so characteristic of mainstream organizations, with their strict job descriptions, categorizing of people according to rank, and restrictions on the flow of information.

In some cases, the structures devised by the women were explicit, codified in organizational charts that were deliberately circular as opposed to being top-down. But more often, the structures were discernible mainly in the daily rhythms of how the businesses were run—how time was used, what titles people assumed, how physical space was allotted, the means by which people talked to one another and reached decisions. There was no recognized name or category for what the women were doing, but because I needed a way to describe their organizations, I began referring to them as "webs of inclusion."

The notion stirred a lot of interest. People from around the country wrote me to describe how they too were using a web-like approach to doing their work and structuring the organizations of which they were a part. Many were inspired to write by pleasure in having a name to describe what they were doing—"I thought it was just *my* style, but now I find it's *a* style" was a frequent comment. I heard from many women, of course—entrepreneurs, executives, teachers, nurses, nuns. But I also heard from men—a lawyer for a high-tech firm, an executive who had left General Motors, the head of a big-city hospital, a black sales executive who felt his experience was mirrored in my book.

I also had a response from the military—a number of naval officers, and a general who taught leadership at the U.S. Army College of War. All were fascinated by alternatives to traditional top-down structures—of which the military is of course the very model and prototype—and intrigued by the role women might play in helping to devise something else. They also wanted me to know that men who had broken away from traditional hierarchical ways of thinking and leading had an enormous contribution to make in what they believed was the inevitable transformation of our major institutions.

The response surprised me. It was fairly easy to see why the women in the diary studies had structured their companies in innovative ways, for they came as outsiders to positions of leadership in the public sphere. Indeed, it is not too extreme to say that all of our major public sphere organizations have been built, structured, reformed, and refined virtually without the input or ideas of women. Thus it only makes sense that women, coming now to assume public leadership for the first time to any degree, would cast a fresh and critical eye at how our organizations are structured and led.

But many men today also perceive themselves as outsiders to mainstream organizations, as my male correspondents were eager to point out. Over the last decade especially, men have begun to feel increasingly alienated from and critical of the top-down hierarchies that have long set the pattern for how we organize our public world. The reasons are many. The demise of the old "Organization Man" era institutions, which promised lifetime security in exchange for loyalty and the dutiful assumption of a predefined role, has meant that men today do not necessarily look upon the organizations that employ them with the unquestioning perspective of the insider. In addition, as the former GM executive who wrote me noted, many men have grown disillusioned with traditional chain-of-command leadership through watching their own companies flounder because of bad decisions made by insulated executives handing down directives from the top. Then too, the blurring of lines between what were formerly men's and women's exclusive domains has made some men more open to learning things from women.

Thus, while it is surely no accident that "the web of inclusion" should have been identified in a study of women's organizations, the structure has a significance and utility that far transcend the bounds of gender. This is particularly true now, when all of our institutions—business, medical, legal, educational, governmental, and religious—are engaged in a search for ways to adapt to a transformed environment. As the new century approaches, organizations of every variety are being challenged to reconfigure in ways that will make them better able to take advantage of innovative technologies and more responsive to a vastly expanded market—*while in the process becoming more satisfactory places for people to work.*

This last imperative is no longer simply a question of being moral or decent, but also of making wise use of a valuable resource. In the knowledge-based economy that Peter Drucker foresees as our future, the real value of an organization will lie in its people's ability to think, to process information, to evolve creative solutions to complex problems. And people simply cannot *think* creatively and well if they do not feel valued, if they do not feel a sense of ownership of their work, if they do not have the freedom to give full scope to their talents. Because the new economy must rely upon well-trained people with high morale, it also demands that organizations move beyond the old Industrial Era mentality that perceived a dichotomy between what is efficient and what is humane.

As Margaret Wheatley observes in *Leadership and the New Science,* we are presently engaged in "nothing less than the search for *new sources of order in our world.*" The architecture of the web of inclusion offers us such a source. The notion of architecture is key here, for the science and art of architecture lie in skillfully relating individual parts to a greater whole, creating a form uniquely appropriate for the exercise of a specific set of functions. The old organizational architecture, with its implicit presumptions of an underlying hierarchical order, its emphasis on rank, boundary, and division, has outlived its usefulness as the metaphor by which we relate individuals to the institutions that employ their labor and shape their lives.

In architectural terms, the most obvious characteristics of the web are that it builds from the center out, and that this building is a never-ending process. The architect of the web works as the spider does, by ceaselessly spinning new tendrils of connection, while also continually strengthening those that already exist. The architect's tools are not force, not the ability to issue commands, but rather providing access and engaging in constant dialogue. Such an architect recognizes that the periphery and the center are interdependent, parts of a fabric, no seam of which can be rent without tearing the whole. Balance and harmony are essential if the periphery is to hold; if only the center is strong, the edges will quickly fray. Thus the leader in a web-like structure must manifest strength by yielding, and secure his or her position by continually augmenting the influence of others.

Because tasks done at the periphery truly matter in the web, those who perform them share directly in the responsibilities and rewards of major undertakings. They thus have far more incentive for full-hearted participation than people in the ranks of traditional top-down organizations, which tend relentlessly to emphasize the importance of those at the top. This aggrandizement of purely positional power leads many organizations to fall prey to a heroes-and-drones syndrome, which deprives those who have not achieved top rank of both autonomy and support. The attitude is reflected in such popular slogans as "Lead, follow, or get out of the way," or, even less appealingly, "Unless you're the lead horse, the view never changes." No organization today can hope to thrive with this demoralizing vision of the options available to the majority of its people—a vision that wastes talent and resources, breeds frustration and cynicism, and fosters an atmosphere of us-against-them.

The web is particularly suited as an architecture for our era because its very design mirrors the structure of our primary technology, the integrated network. In just such a way, the hierarchy reflected the technology of the Industrial Age, which began with the steam engine and continued through the development of the mainframe computer. As Stanley Davis points out in his insightful study of the new economy, *Future Perfect,* electronic information systems "provide a formal method for overcoming the limitations of chain-of-command organizations, by creating channels that permit the various parts of the organization to communicate directly." Transferring expertise onto software, onto an "expert system," makes *anyone in the organization who has access to that system* an expert. And so the very process of adapting to today's information technology destroys an organization's long-held notions of who has sufficient information to make important decisions, and who does not. It takes away the distinctions between heads and hands, between those who think and those who do, and makes it impossible for us not to notice, as Henry Mintzberg has observed, that "people at the so-called bottom in organizations have heads too, in fact often very good ones."

Thus what the hierarchy proscribed, the electronic network facilitates, and even *demands.* Indeed, nothing proves the obsolescence of hierarchical structures or underlines their essential inappropriateness for our era so profoundly as today's technology; nor is anything so responsible for their demise. Because information technology enables the cheap customizing and constant upgrading of products, it is destroying the very premise of economies of scale, which gave rise to large hierarchical enterprises producing standardized goods in the first place. The demise of standardized products spells the end of mass production, mass marketing, mass advertising, and mass sales. Anything conceived on the grand scale begins to look old-fashioned, grandiose, and lumbering, reminiscent of an almost Soviet-style, central planning approach. And so we all look on with a mixture of helplessness and awe as huge monolithic enterprises and undertakings—from major department stores to television networks, from the public school system to the U.S. Postal Service, from IBM's attempt to force Systems Network Architecture to Ford and GM's ill-fated plans to build a "world car"—lose ground to more specialized, targeted, and flexible competitors.

These rapid and profound changes put the burden on organizations to reconfigure themselves in ways that reflect *how people actually do their work.* Networked technology blurs the bounds between who devises tasks and who carries them out, and so by its very nature is profoundly antibureaucratic and democratizing. As a result, the very technology that as recently as the 1960s seemed about to betray us into a dehumanized future ("do not fold, spindle, or mutilate") is instead proving a powerful medium for people in organizations to achieve direct connections in disregard of rank or division, thus giving means and impetus to a more humanized workplace. In this context, it is understandable that we are beginning to speak of our organizations in a more humane language, to talk of cultures and values, relationships and inspiration, mentors and meaning, instead of using the old factory language of input and output, supervision and control. As Charles Handy notes in *The Age of Unreason,* "It is as if we had suddenly woken up to the fact that organizations were made up of people after all, not just 'hands' or 'role occupants.' "

In *Future Perfect,* Stanley Davis also observes that technology provides a kind of conceptual bridge that links how we shape our institutions and conceive of our economic life with our perceptions of science and our vision of how the universe operates. In recent years, those perceptions have been profoundly influenced by new conceptual models in both biology and physics. Rather than regarding individual organisms as separate and distinct entities, biologists now take a more holistic view, seeing all phenomena as inseparable elements of living systems. In living systems, the emphasis is always upon process and change; progress is not necessarily predictable and is often influenced by seemingly unrelated events; and short-term gains can easily mean disaster in the longer run. Nothing in a living system can be regarded separately from the eventual consequences it creates for the larger environment. As Erich Jantsch points out in *The Self-Organizing Universe,* "In life, the issue is not control but dynamic connectedness."

A similar emphasis obtains in the physical sciences, thanks to the quantum revolution. Instead of the universe being conceived of as a giant machine that functions in accord with fixed laws—Newton's vision—quantum science reveals a cosmos continually in flux, in which every bit of matter is continually redefined by its relation to the whole. The physicist Fritjof Capra has described this great invisible architecture as "an interconnected cosmic web, in which the threads of all forces and events form an inseparable net of endless, mutually conditioned relations." This way of conceptualizing our universe emphasizes the profound and inescapable interdependence of all things, and thus affirms the value and importance of every fragment of the greater whole—the "universal interwovenness," as Capra calls it.

Quantum physics insists that energy is simultaneously particle *and* wave, rather than just one or the other. Thus it demands that we start thinking in ways that move beyond dualities and instead emphasize balance, acknowledging a measure of ambiguity that lends itself more to intuition and sudden recognitions than to explanation or logical analysis. The web provides a perfect metaphor for how science now perceives our universe in operation: not as a precisely calibrated great machine in which each constituent part is locked into its own immutable slot, but rather as pulses of energy that continually evolve and assume shifting shapes as the various elements interact, and in which *identity is inseparable from relationship.* And because the web of inclusion serves and promotes the notion of relationship above all, it provides a useful model for helping us redesign the institutions that frame our lives.

The "dynamic connectedness" of the web means that web organizations reflect organic rather than mechanical principles; that is, *they work in the same way that life does.* This naturally makes them more congenial environments for human beings to exist in; more nourishing, more favorable to growth. This congeniality is important, for as we move away from the notion of the organization as a great machine —rational, static, compartmentalized, and closed—we also move away from perhaps *the* essential aspect of the estrangement of human beings from nature that took root in the Industrial Revolution: the belief that, to be efficient, organizations must mimic the design and workings of a machine.

Early critics of industrial development recognized that organizing human enterprise according to machine principles left people out of the equation—with the predictable result that they either became thoroughly wretched, or adapted and so lost their vitality and soul. Jonathan Swift in *Gulliver's Travels* mocked the absurdity of living beings trying to measure and quantify all their endeavors in accord with mathematical equations, in defiance of how the organic world of which they were a part actually worked. His "Projectors," with their elaborate charts and graphs and eagerness to measure everything, continually miss whatever point they are attempting to grasp, since their efforts are based on a paradigm divorced from the actual world of which they themselves are a part. Wordsworth and the Romantics take Swift's insights further, seeing in the organization of the great mills of the early Industrial Era an earthly image of Satan's enterprise in Hell.

The subordination of people's skills and imaginations to the rigid architecture of the machine cut them off from their original source, and so has thrown the human world out of balance. In the pre-industrial world, people understood that institutions can thrive and labor can be satisfying only when they are in harmony with the principles that govern nature. I had a vivid demonstration of this one afternoon some years ago, when I was studying the great medieval frescoes that portray local events in the ancient town hall of Siena. In the frescoes, the serene felicity and general prosperity enjoyed by the populace under a wise and beneficent ruler is contrasted with the strife, discord, and ruin brought on by misrule. Nature conspires with and reflects local political conditions in the frescoes, for with bad rulers come crop failures and drought, while under good rulers the wheat grows high and the wine is good. The underlying message is clear: violate the principles that animate and govern nature, and unremitting human misery will result.

Of course, the situations depicted are extreme, exaggerations. Yet with that almost childish directness that characterizes the medieval sensibility, the frescoes make clear the correspondence that must obtain between natural laws and the workings of structures that serve human needs. The same notion finds subtler expression, one more suited to modern tastes, in the timeless precepts of the Tao. The sage Lao-tzu emphasizes that, to succeed over time, an organization must act in accord with such principles of nature as nonresistance, flexibility and moderation. Its leaders must seek balance by reducing excess and building up that which is insufficient. They must achieve impartiality and perspective by developing intuition and cultivating an appreciation of timeless values.

The organization that seeks strength and longevity must aspire to these qualities. But what method of operating will assist in their development? Considering this, I am reminded of how Dan Wolf shaped his organization by asking the kind of questions that elicited from people ideas they had not even realized they had. The Socratic dialogue he used to build awareness in the course of give-and-take seems an ideal resource for any organization that seeks to serve human needs, since its passionate and open-ended dynamism reflects the evolutionary and responsive unfoldings of nature.

It is worth noting that Socrates made himself accessible by frequenting the *agora* or marketplace, which lay at the center and served as the heart of ancient Athens. Yet from this central position, he assumed a role more characteristic of the periphery—that of gadfly, persistent doubter of conventional wisdom. Thus by his actions he linked the center with the periphery, building tendrils of connection that established a true web of inclusion. The process was unscripted, unpredictable; it evolved as it went along. In the chapters that lie ahead, we will observe people in the ranks of a variety of organizations who have met extraordinary challenges by building structures that permit them to open real dialogues, asking questions to which they do not already know the answers in advance.

Two

What It Is,
How It Works,
How It Feels

The discovery by quantum physicists that matter is neither particle nor wave, but always simultaneously both, destroys the basis of the either/or approach that we have grown accustomed to using when we analyze something or define it. And so, in attempting to describe the workings of the web of inclusion, I will approach it both as a *pattern*, a model for coherently ordering people and their tasks; and as a *process*, a way of thinking and acting, of behaving and solving problems as they arise.

THE WEB AS PATTERN

The structure of the web of inclusion first presented itself to me when I tried to draw rough approximations of the organizations run by the women in *The Female Advantage.* What I came up with always bore a literal, architectural resemblance to a spider's web. That is, the structures were roughly circular in shape, with the leader at the central point, and lines radiating outward to various points. The points formed loose concentric circles, which were bound together by an irregular interweaving of axial and radial lines that crisscrossed the structure in a kind of filigree. This interweaving made the structures inextricably integrated and connected—patterns, really, of relationship. I added the term "inclusion" to the notion of the web because the women who led the organizations labored continually to bring everyone at every point closer to the center—to tighten ties, provide increased exposure, and encourage greater participation.

Also like a spider's web, the structures were continually being built up, stretched, altered, modified, and transformed. Since they did not exist as closed systems, they might appear slightly different on different days, as people at various points assumed new responsibilities, which in turn demanded that new lines of connection form. Titles were fluid, reflecting changing tasks. Axials or radials might shift and lead somewhere else, redirecting the flow of responsibility and information. At their outer edges, the webs were permeable, a bit loose, which left open the question of who was part of the organization and who was not. This permeability served to allow outsiders access, and gave insiders ways of connecting directly to the outside.

As I studied both the women's organizations and, later, the web-style structures that form the subject of this book, I began to notice that various aspects of the web tend to reinforce one another. This sets in motion a kind of centripetal force that gives the structure as a whole a coherence greater than the sum of its parts. Since web structures are circular rather than pyramidal, those who emerge in them as leaders tend to be people who feel comfortable being in the center of things rather than at the top, who prefer building consensus to issuing orders, and who place a low value on the kind of symbolic perks and marks of distinction that define success in the hierarchy. This preference on the part of web-style leaders infuses their organizations with a collegial atmosphere, which in turn enables people to focus upon *what* needs to be done rather than *who* has the authority to do it. In addition, titles and office space in web organizations are allotted in ways that deemphasize the importance of rank, which increases access across divisions and accentuates the multiplicity of communication channels.

Webs also allow for great flexibility. As one woman business leader I interviewed pointed out, "When you have a circular arrangement, you can shift people around with relative ease. Since they don't perceive themselves as moving up or down, they don't worry that a shift really means they're being demoted, or assume they're being promoted and demand a raise." This flexibility further accentuates the emphasis on the actual *tasks* that people perform, as opposed to their position, thus strengthening the egalitarian aspects of the culture.

As I contrasted the companies I was studying with organizations of which I had been a part, I realized that the characteristics that define traditional hierarchies also tend to reinforce one another. Since hierarchies are pyramidal, information must travel up and down a strictly defined vertical chain of command, which discourages direct communication across levels. The adherence to channels accentuates the importance of rank within the organization, keeping the focus on what position a person has attained rather than on what he or she actually *does*. This accent on position is further intensified by the strict codification of titles and perks, such as office size and location being determined by rank rather than how much physical space a given job demands.

The insistence on restricted access serves the purpose of exclusion: the focus is on who, by virtue of rank, will *not* be invited to this meeting, who has *no* right to that information, who may *not* communicate directly with whom. All these don'ts and can'ts further strengthen the power and dominance of the organization's top leaders, creating a kind of caste system that isolates people who are not in leadership positions rather than broadly involving them in the overall process. Those below the leadership level are given narrow information, just enough to enable them to perform their jobs, while information available to those at the top is very broad. The overriding emphasis on leadership sends a message to those at the bottom that they are relatively unimportant to the overall functioning of the organization, thus making them feel less personally autonomous, less valued, weaker.

The top-down emphasis on power and privilege tends to assure that the kind of people who emerge as leaders in traditional hierarchies are those who enjoy exercising power from a distance, and feel comfortable with the lack of collegiality that pervades their organizations. Aware that isolation is both the key and measure of their authority, such leaders also understand that, in order to remain secure, they must constantly accentuate the gulf between themselves and potential rivals by continuing to accumulate the perks that serve as visible symbols of power. Thus even if the leader of a top-down company *wanted* to communicate more freely across levels, he would be held back not only by the lack of channels, but also by his recognition that to do so would only serve to diminish his distance from others, and so inevitably dilute his power.

The mutually reinforcing characteristics of both webs and hierarchies have the effect of concentrating and distilling their very different attributes, causing both kinds of organizations to become *more like themselves* over time. Both have a deep structural integrity; in both, the architecture determines how people within them interact with one another, how they are motivated and rewarded, how they perform. This structural integrity is one reason that piecemeal efforts to reform or "flatten" pyramidal structures during the last decade have so often floundered, despite fine intentions, costly consultants, and elaborate plans. Hierarchies, after all, have flourished in Western culture precisely because all their constituent parts and presumptions work well together; they are an efficient means for accomplishing a specific range of tasks. If we are now beginning to recognize that companies built on this model are poorly suited to meet the needs of today's environment, then the challenge becomes not to tinker with the original structures, not to find ways to patch over their deficiencies and streamline their workings, but rather to search out different models to serve a profoundly different world.

. . .

The emphasis here is upon *models,* not upon a single model. The web of inclusion, because it is organic, configures differently for different organizations in order to reflect the strengths and talents of people at every level. Because it is defined as much by its process, by how it works, as by the patterns it suggests, the web may be best understood as a guiding set of principles and attitudes. It permits the organization to shift and adapt to changing circumstances, while remaining open at the parameters and constantly pulling people into the decision-making process. The management scientist Henry Mintzberg has recently proposed that we do away entirely with rigid organizational charts based on what positions people hold, and instead draw maps that depict how work in an organization actually gets done. Webs of inclusion, because they encourage and permit people in organizations to continually redefine their work, allow for this flexibility and responsiveness.

By its nature, the web of inclusion is continually evolving; this is absolutely what the present environment demands. Things have changed since the days when Henry Ford, designing his vertically integrated River Rouge production plant in accord with the principles of scientific management, could create *the* prototypical design for a major industrial enterprise, which would then be precisely copied by organizations around the globe. Indeed, the most obsolete aspect of the hierarchy may in fact be *its applicability to all situations,* which operates in disregard of the evolutionary principle of requisite variety. Requisite variety means that any given species—here, an organization—must exist in sufficient variety if that species is to flourish and survive; a failure to achieve this leads to extinction. Because the web of inclusion is flexible, in a continual state of adaptation, it accommodates itself to this most basic of evolutionary imperatives. And so the very structure of the web operates in accord with organic principles—the principles of life.

The Web as Process

Even more than a pattern, the web of inclusion can be defined as a process, a method, a way of thinking about tasks and accomplishing them in time. And because webs may be different in size and shape, and serve different purposes at different stages, they are perhaps best described in terms of the principles by which they operate. For it is the *means* by which webs achieve their ends that most distinguishes them from other organizational units; thus in their operation are webs best defined.

1. Webs operate by means of open communication across levels.

In every web-like structure, there is the equivalent of that bulletin board at the *Village Voice* that kept information flowing freely. But bulletin boards are easy enough to establish, especially in our electronic era; unless they are also used fearlessly, they are of little use. This means that an organization must be willing to share even sensitive information with its people, and do so without regard to position or right-to-know. If an organization limits the information it shares, or restricts it to people at specific levels, it will only spur cynicism among employees.

In my speechwriting days, I worked for a large company that, faced with plunging morale, launched what was billed as an open information offensive. The CEO and several senior VPs scheduled an interactive television show, a kind of bulletin board of the airwaves, in which employees were encouraged to call in with their most pressing concerns. But the questions were screened in advance so that anything sensitive or controversial—anything relating to future downsizing or changes in the pension plan—never made it into the "open" forum. Needless to say, morale did not improve.

A dramatic contrast is evident in the approach of Nancy Singer,

President and CEO of First of America Bank in Libertyville, Illinois. When Singer's organization merged with five smaller banks, she found herself facing a classic situation for organizational strife. Where there had formerly been five of everything—senior loan officers, for example—there would now be only one, which threw people into uncertainty, even panic. Yet Singer managed to keep fear under control by means of an assertively open policy based on the sharing of information.

First, she met personally with every person in every position in each of the five banks, and discussed with each where he or she might fit in the new organization. After these meetings, she immediately sent notes to everyone in every position, summarizing exactly what had been discussed. In this way, everyone knew everyone else's concerns, so that no one had to fear that he or she was being undercut behind the scenes. Everyone knew precisely what everyone else was thinking, saying, and doing, so there was no room for destructive speculation.

"These kinds of negotiations are almost always kept absolutely private," Singer notes. "And most people assume that they should be. But keeping everyone posted on all the discussions about reorganization and job shifts is the only way to defuse suspicion and get past gossip and innuendo. Fear and speculation tend to run wild in these kinds of situations, setting people against one another, often for no reason, and making it hard for people to function on a daily basis." The communication blitz, by contrast, "served to cut off the grapevine. It destroyed insecurity and uncertainty, those two greatest enemies of change." In the process of keeping all lines open to everyone, regardless of position, Singer, a woman who describes her organizational chart as "Jell-O pinned to the wall," made a crucial start in configuring her expanded organization as a web.

2. WEBS BLUR DISTINCTIONS
BETWEEN CONCEPTION AND EXECUTION.

When management in a top-down organization assembles a task force, the top executives typically define the objectives that the task force is expected to implement. This division of labor between thinking and doing reflects industrial notions of work, in which tasks are broken down into manageable components, and only top management is given enough information to make decisions. But dividing thinking and doing into rigid functions destroys the value, even the possibility, of feedback, for if a task force only executes, it cannot use what it learns to modify the original conception as it goes along. Thus the division of conception and execution is inappropriate for organizations trying to respond to fast-changing events; it is inflexible, almost by definition.

Also, today's technology renders the division of thinking and doing entirely obsolete, by giving those on the front lines access to the information and expertise they need to make strategic decisions. A clear example occurred during Operation Desert Storm. In that first post-modern war, technology became an instrument for radically diffusing hierarchical power in the very prototype of the chain-of-command hierarchical organization, the military unit. Sophisticated software programs capable of both identifying and hitting targets pushed power down to men and women on the front lines. Thus pilots and tank commanders in the Kuwaiti desert were forced by expert systems to make split-second decisions that their staff commanders would formerly have made. Their doing so blurred the line between reconnaissance and attack.

In Desert Storm, unlike in the Vietnam War, the subtle subversion of the military emphasis on chain of command that took place was not a result of ideology or morale, but *was built into the very technology available for war.* This aspect of Desert Storm exemplifies the point made by Stanley Davis in *Future Perfect* that, when expertise is transferred onto software, the software user becomes the expert, which immeasurably enhances his or her authority and power. Webs of inclusion provide an ideal structure for taking advantage of this aspect of technology, emphasizing the value of information taken in by those at the front ranks and so restoring to them decision-making power. Webs are also a particularly effective way of dealing with a fast-changing situation, enabling those who gather information to evaluate it in the process, and so modify and adapt their plans as they go along.

3. WEBS CREATE LASTING NETWORKS THAT REDISTRIBUTE POWER IN THE ORGANIZATION.

Traditional teams and task forces are usually disbanded once the mission they have been configured to accomplish is complete. People then return to their "regular" jobs and the organization continues to make use of them as in the past. By contrast, webs not only link people together in unorthodox ways, reaching across levels to do so, but also enable them to keep and expand those links once their task is finished. Maintaining these new links provides people with allies and contacts beyond those for which their job descriptions allow, and so encourages new centers of power to emerge within the organization. Such centers of power may not necessarily be reflected in an organization's management chart, but are indicative nonetheless of how work actually gets done.

IBM provides a cautionary example of what can happen when successful and flourishing webs are not permitted to create lasting networks that redistribute power. Throughout the 1970s, the company had ignored the growing strength of Apple Computer because its executives believed that the personal computer would appeal only to home hobbyists, and so would never make inroads into the business market, which was then dominated by IBM mainframes. One reason for their overconfidence was that the purchase of technology in most companies was controlled by Management Information Systems directors, who tended to buy what IBM marketing executives told them they needed. As long as IBM controlled the MIS people, the company believed, it would not have to worry about its business market.

The advent of the Apple II changed all that. Because it was priced at less than $3,000, mid-level managers at many organizations were able to get approval to buy the machines themselves, thus weakening the stranglehold on technology of the MIS directors. IBM was suddenly forced to recognize that it would have to offer a personal computer if it wanted to hold on to its business market—and that it would have to do so as quickly as possible. And so the company set up a twelve-person task force in Boca Raton, Florida, and charged it with doing whatever had to be done in order to bring a PC to market within a year.

The Boca Raton unit was configured as a web-like structure that explicitly mimicked the design of Apple in its early days, and operated free of IBM's rigid hierarchy. Engineers worked intensely on team projects, free from the demands and scrutiny of marketers, who in the past had always specified what kind of technology they wanted to sell. Indeed, IBM's marketing division, historically the company's engine and its power, was opposed to the very notion of developing a personal computer—on the grounds that no one in the company knew how to market it! One would be hard pressed to find a better example of inward focus.

Inverting the balance of power between engineer and marketer marked a radical departure for IBM, as did abandoning the usual top-down channels of command and control in order to encourage constant and open communication within the Boca Raton unit. Yet under this innovative structure and given imaginative leadership, IBM managed to develop and launch its first personal computer in only eighteen months. The IBM PC, introduced in August of 1981, immediately began ravaging Apple's share of the business market. Being able to purchase desktop technology from IBM enabled MIS departments (what Alvin Toffler has called "the data priesthood") to reassert control.

The popularity of the IBM PC would have many long-range effects upon the world, *yet it did virtually nothing to change the way IBM was run*. The web-style unit down in Boca, far from influencing the larger culture, became quickly subsumed within the established bureaucratic structure, with its rigidity, impermeability, and strict job definitions, and its inverted balance of power that favored managerial expertise. Once the threat to its dominance in the business market seemed to have been quelled, the company returned to doing business as usual, reabsorbing the web configured to develop the PC rather than using it as a model for widespread change.

Once again, engineers found themselves designing products to please marketing executives, rather than working with them on teams. Once again, skills were compartmentalized, multilayered reporting channels strictly enforced, the chain of command rationalized. The PC unit was transformed into a corporate division, as those who had tried to block the PC's development were sent to sell it. Very quickly, the IBM PC was being manufactured, marketed, upgraded, and refined just like any other IBM product. It would take nearly a decade more of bureaucratic inertia before IBM, humiliated and frightened by enormous losses, would begin the serious and painful business of looking back on the Boca Raton team, and trying to learn from it how the company might be restructured.

4. WEBS SERVE AS A VEHICLE FOR CONSTANT REORGANIZATION.

No organization can hope to be both flexible and specialized unless its own structure is able continually to evolve. Because the web of inclusion is always spawning new lines of connection, and connecting people in new ways, it can serve as an instrument for constant reorganization. The structure of the web thus makes it easier for organizations to practice what the Japanese call *kaizen,* the process of making continual improvements; at the same time, it enables them to constantly redefine the nature of their business. The chapter on Intel will demonstrate how web-like structures within an organization can serve the larger whole by helping it continually adapt to ever-changing situations.

Webs also help facilitate continual reorganization because they are so permeable around the edges. This enables suppliers and subcontractors to function as a part of the organization that they serve, broadening the base of innovations from which the larger organization may draw. The engineering firm of Asea Brown Boveri provides an example of the process. Run from a modest headquarters in Zurich, this vast international firm affords its regional divisions great autonomy of operation. In a recent reorganization, the company assigned thirty percent of its already lean headquarters staff to newly created companies designed to offer services to ABB on a competitive basis. These new companies were encouraged to innovate and then share those innovations with their former parent. Thus ABB's permeability enables it continually to redefine its nature by adapting to changes as they occur at a grassroots level.

5. WEBS EMBRACE THE WORLD OUTSIDE THE ORGANIZATION.

The *Utne Reader,* which has been described as a kind of *Reader's Digest* for younger and more highly educated readers, reprints articles from what it terms "the best of the alternative press," and packages them together with a small percentage of commissioned pieces. A bimonthly based in Minneapolis, it is known for having high-end demographics, accurate circulation figures (it offers no premiums or discounts), low overhead, and an intensely loyal national readership. Its subscribers tend to view the *Utne Reader* as an aspect of their identity, a statement about their own political and social values. This kind of identification is invaluable for magazines and radio stations seeking to build a reliable and faithful base.

The *Utne Reader* recently undertook an effort to strengthen this identification by broadening its subscribers' opportunity to be involved. A network of *Utne* "salons" has been set up to enable subscribers to get together with like-minded people in their own neighborhoods. The salons reflect the assumption that subscribing to the magazine demonstrates a shared set of values, which means that subscribers would enjoy meeting directly with one another. To provide the link, each issue of the *Utne Reader* now includes a card that the reader can mail in, affirming that he or she wants to join a neighborhood group. The magazine then sorts replies by zip code, and, for a yearly fee, sends the respondent the names and addresses of all the subscribers who live nearby. It's then up to the individual salon members to get in touch with one another, set times to get together, and devise individual agendas—some discuss specific topics, some form book clubs, others simply socialize.

The effort has been so successful, with several hundred groups forming in the first year, that the *Utne Reader* has begun publishing an entire newsletter for salon-goers. Articles are contributed by salon-goers themselves, and usually reflect what they are doing in their salons. The newsletter in effect makes *Utne Reader* subscribers into contributors, strengthening their sense of ownership and affiliation. By sharing a portion of its subscriber list with its readers, the *Utne Reader* is blurring the lines between who is on staff and who is not, who is a subscriber and who is a contributor. This inclusion of customers in its web expands the magazine's reach and scope, taking reader loyalty and identification to its limits.

6. WEBS EVOLVE THROUGH A PROCESS OF TRIAL AND ERROR.

Webs are often instituted in response to some specific organizational crisis, when there is little time to develop detailed blueprints or long-range strategic plans. This means that appropriate structures begin to evolve as people charged with specific tasks try one approach and then another, discovering what works and what doesn't as they go along. Often, such discoveries will be made under the extreme pressure of time or financial constraints; rarely will they take place all at once. And while support from top management is essential, such webs often evolve at the grass roots, among people who may be far from the power loop.

Thus the process of the web bears similarities to the concept of "guerilla marketing" that has emerged in recent years. Like guerilla warfare, guerilla marketing emphasizes and takes advantage of the reconnaissance potential of those on the front lines. By its very nature, guerilla marketing implies the need for front-line participation in decision-making, and for building strategy from tactics as tactics evolve. Trial and error is thus implicit in guerilla marketing, as is the integration of conception and execution: one learns and modifies as one goes along.

The front-line emphasis of guerilla marketing makes it difficult to practice in an organization that has adopted a top-down hierarchical structure modeled on the traditional military unit, where those on the front lines do not have the power to analyze or decide. For similar reasons, guerilla warfare is rarely fought with success by conventionally structured soldiering divisions—as the U.S. military found to its woe in Vietnam. Guerilla tactics rely on structures that permit information to be gathered and analyzed in the field, *at the same time that experimental tactics are being tried out.* Web-like structures, because they diffuse decision-making power toward the edges and encourage new routes of communication to form, make possible the kind of trial-and-error tactics characteristic of a vigorous and imaginative field command, which operates in the heat of and follows the flow of battle.

THE TEAM AND THE WEB

The flexibility of the web of inclusion permits it to work in a variety of ways. It can provide structure and give firm but malleable order to an entire organization. It can serve as a mechanism for building relationships among different organizations that share a common interest, helping them to expand their effectiveness and reach. Or a web can be configured as an internal unit within a larger organization, a pattern that provides a model for change in the organization as a whole. Most of the studies in this book will detail the evolution of these internal webs, which give scope for unprecedented influence and participation on the part of people in the ranks, enabling them to transform the very nature of their organizations.

But in order to achieve these ambitious ends, a web of inclusion must be more than just a team; although there is an overlap, the two are very different. A team addresses itself to the achievement of a specific task, and so is driven by ends rather than by means. When these ends have been achieved, the team either disbands or is absorbed into a regular unit or division within the larger organization. So long as the team is conceived of instrumentally, as a tool for achieving a goal, it has little chance for affecting the greater structure of which it is a part.

A web, though often configured to achieve a specific mission, plays a more important and lasting role. By emphasizing process as well as structure, by establishing new ways of approaching problems, of thinking, of connecting people, of giving them information and motivating them, a true web also *helps to transform the organization of which it is a part.* Thus a web cannot simply be reabsorbed into the larger hierarchical culture without losing its identity and undermining the purpose that it has served. A web serves as an organic, home-grown vehicle for carving paths that enable an organization to adapt to radically different, and constantly evolving, circumstances. The homegrown emphasis is important, for another feature of the web is its tendency to configure at the grass roots, in the ranks.

A web, then, may be defined as *a team that goes the distance.*

A true web affects every aspect of the organization of which it is a part, eventually altering the whole in its own image. Often, a team may have the potential to develop as a web but will never get the chance, because the organization as a whole proves too resistant, and top management too eager to preserve its powers. The history of large American companies over the last twenty years is full of examples of organizations that, like IBM, refused to learn from web-like units that configured within their midst. Instead, top management isolated them and diminished their influence, refusing to learn the lessons they had to teach. Indeed, much of the decline of American competitiveness over the last several decades can be traced to the refusal of hierarchies to learn from internal webs.

We can see this history played out clearly in the difference between how Ford and General Motors responded to the challenges that faced them in the 1970s. Both companies had flourished in the two decades following World War II, in part because fighting had devastated the national economies of potential rivals. Freed by a lack of competitors to run their businesses in whatever way they wished to, Ford and GM focused on diversifying their holdings throughout the sixties. In the process, they often neglected the products that had laid the original foundation for their success and grew accustomed to taking their customers for granted.

But by the 1970s, the environment was changing. Other nations had recovered enough to begin offering American manufacturers real competition, and the sophisticated and demanding members of the baby boom generation were proving less loyal to American labels than their parents. Eager to buy more fuel-efficient cars, these consumers were taking their business first to Volkswagen, then to Datsun, and finally to Toyota and Honda. Ford, driven nearly to bankruptcy by its precipitous losses, had little choice but to heed the evidence that its customers wanted a different kind of car than those the company had been manufacturing.

In order to develop such a model, the company allowed a group of insurgents within its advanced vehicle workshop to come up with a design for an automobile unlike any ever manufactured in Detroit; the group assumed the name of Team Taurus. From the start, Team Taurus was configured as an integrated web, an open and pliable structure that emphasized communication across both vertical and horizontal lines. It was the only unit within Ford—indeed, within all of Detroit—in which product planners, designers, specifications engineers, manufacturers, and marketers worked together. It was also the only unit with a mandate to continually test its product, instead of waiting until it was ready to be shipped. As such, the Taurus effort introduced Ford to a different process and structure, one that was entirely opposed to the rigidly hierarchical "chimney" structure that had always defined Detroit's culture—a system in which functional divisions worked entirely alone, focused on internal challenges, and so had no opportunity to learn from one another as they went along.

The car that Team Taurus developed of course became a smash success, the key in restoring the company's fortunes. But more important than the success of the Taurus as a product was the fact that Ford *as a whole* was open to learning from the process by which the car had come to market. After a series of bruising internal wars, in which the heads of various fiefs fought to retain the power of their position, the Taurus became the model for redesigning Ford's entire organizational structure. The chimneys were dismantled, the various divisions integrated according to product, and inspections built into the process of making cars. Assembly line workers were reorganized into work teams, instead of being strung out along straight lines to do repetitive tasks—the Industrial Era configuration that had been the great workplace innovation of the first Henry Ford.

General Motors, responding to the same crisis, also permitted an integrated web to configure within its midst, in the form of a joint venture with Toyota. The New United Motor Manufacturing Inc., or NUMMI, based at an old plant in Fremont, California, was intended to provide the means by which GM could learn the Japanese system of building quality into the manufacturing process, as opposed to tacking it on as the cars rolled out the door. In order to meet this goal, GM had to integrate its manufacturing processes at the plant and also permit the kind of grassroots involvement in decision-making on the factory floor that characterized and defined the Toyota Production System.

Despite vast gains in productivity and high quality ratings for the Chevy Novas manufactured at the plant, however, the larger company failed to learn any lessons from the success of NUMMI, because these lessons conflicted with its own hierarchical culture. Ingrained in the GM culture was the belief that workers were adversaries, not partners, and that technology, rather than people and training, would ultimately save the company. James Womack and his several co-authors have extensively documented the unremitting hostility with which the NUMMI project was viewed by GM managers in *The Machine That Changed the World*. Chairman Roger Smith dismissed it as a mere "educational experiment"—interesting, perhaps, but nothing that the company as a whole might learn from; nothing that might change the way it built cars. Other executives sought virtually to sabotage NUMMI's success because it threatened their cultural beliefs.

A major problem was GM's deep pockets: the situation at the company was simply not as dire as that at Ford. Its insulated executives were thus free to imagine that they could afford *not* to learn any lessons that might cause them to question their company's conventional wisdom and rigidly top-down structure. GM's refusal to learn from the web-like NUMMI "experiment" would persist into the early 1990s, by which time the organization lay nearly in ruins. Only in the manufacture of the Saturn were the lessons first obvious from NUMMI permitted to seep in, although it remains to be seen whether GM will also reabsorb that spectacularly successful effort.

THE WEB AND THE ART OF IMPROVISATION

In *A Pattern Language,* a fascinating study that proposes a decentralized and intuitive approach to architecture, building, and the planning of cities, the authors make the point that the most successful and fully integrated designs almost always evolve piecemeal, rather than resulting from some grand scheme conceived and instituted all at once. Strategy develops in the course of making small decisions that solve immediate problems and fill specific needs. This approach permits those constructing a given structure—a building, a street, or a town— to discover small mistakes and correct them before they become so big that they threaten the entire project.

The authors of *A Pattern Language* also make clear that there is such a thing as appropriate size: to be successful, architectural entities must find the right scale. Towns and buildings that are too small end up restricting the expansive spirit of modern civilization, while those that are too large self-destruct by reason of their inability to live in ecological harmony with the resources that sustain them. Appropriate size is an aspect of building and development that cannot be determined well in advance: It becomes clear only in the course of a project's being used.

The notions of taking a piecemeal approach to design and finding appropriate size are also valuable for organizations, which after all are simply less physically tangible architectural forms. Both notions are well served by the structure of the web of inclusion. Organizations that permit individual webs to configure within their ranks and operate with relative autonomy are free to try out major changes before committing vast resources, and to learn what works and what does not before procedures become so established that the information is rendered without practical value. An organization that encourages webs can also experiment with variously sized internal structures, learning to make and implement decisions with different levels of resources.

Because they evolve through trial and error, webs rely upon improvisation, which is open-ended and takes place at the front lines. An emphasis upon improvisation can help organizations to overcome the challenge of accommodating individual expression *while also building strong allegiance among the group.* Only by balancing these two often conflicting values can both creativity and cohesion flourish. But achieving this balance can be especially challenging for American organizations, since there exists a strain in American life and thought that exalts individual effort at the expense of group values. The attitude is a legacy of our frontier heritage, which has mythologized the rugged loner who strikes out on his own, claims new territory, and shapes it in his own image. The wildcat oil strike and the cattle drive, those prototypical forms of American enterprise, have always operated according to the Western adage that "you get while the gettin's good, and then move on." Which means that others will be left to clean up the mess.

Given today's profoundly interrelated world—Fritjof Capra's "inextricably woven net"—this bias toward untrammeled individualism becomes an indicator of disfunction. We are faced with finding a way to resolve the need for autonomy with the need we have to exist together on the planet. In an effort to correct the imbalance in favor of individualism, many organizations over the last decade have looked for models to Japanese companies, which have had greater success in promoting values of relationship, and thus greater success in promoting teams. Yet just as our own unique history has shaped the particular challenge that we as Americans face in confronting a more interdependent world, so is that history also rich with cultural traditions that can help us meet the challenge with confidence and skill.

Our national talent for improvisation is perhaps chief among these traditions; it has been remarked upon as a defining aspect of American ingenuity by observers since De Tocqueville. Improvising, making do with whatever materials that come to hand, suiting new methods to new circumstances—these are as much a part of our frontier legacy as exalted individualism, and have provided strategies for adapting to frontier conditions and opportunities as far back as Cortés. Certainly, it is no coincidence that improvisation is *the* essential and defining feature of our nation's only indigenous art form, jazz. Or that the jazz band pioneered for the world the form of improvised ensemble playing, in which spontaneous exchange provides the context for soloists to create within a communal unit, *thus reconciling individual expression with group endeavor.* As the critic Stanley Crouch has observed: "The demands on and respect for the individual in the jazz band puts democracy into aesthetic action. The improvising jazz musician must work in the heat and pressure of the moment, giving form and order in a mobile environment, in which choices must be constantly assessed and reacted to in one way or another."

There's a saying among jazz musicians: "don't make it up if it doesn't help." In other words, express yourself only when it contributes to the larger effort. The very existence of the improvising ensemble suggests that individual and community needs should not be viewed as an either/or proposition, but rather as two tendencies along a continuum of creation. The improvising jazz band is an open system, a dissipative structure, both richly coherent and in constant flux. Thus it is capable of endless transformation. As a network that resolves issues of autonomy and relationship, it is capable of being both intimate and expansive, of reconciling individual expression with the cohesion of the group.

Achieving such a reconciliation is paramount for organizations today—as well as for democratic society as a whole. Obviously, hierarchies cannot be of much help. Their emphasis upon rank and division promotes the interests of the individual over those of the group, while permitting little room for individual expression except among those at the very top. The web of inclusion, by virtue of form and function, structure and process, creates a context for improvisation, thus bridging apparently conflicting claims. The web also, by establishing a stabilizing core, provides space for the central fire that gives improvisation its context, its heat and spark.

HIGH RELIABILITY AND THE WEB

In the day-to-day life of organizations, how can effective webs be instituted? What kinds of situations create circumstances that enable a web of inclusion to form? What kinds of organizations help webs to flourish? And why are some organizations open to learning from the webs that configure in its midst, while others view such webs as a threat?

Some clues about what makes webs work can be found in observing "high-reliability" organizations, those in which even minor mistakes have the potential to escalate into catastrophe because of the dangers inherent in the organization's enterprise. Dealing with emergency on a routine basis, such organizations must achieve unusually low rates of failure in order merely to survive. Thus they must operate by means of mechanisms that help them to avoid mistakes almost entirely, while also preventing those that do occur from escalating beyond control.

Although the challenges that high-reliability organizations confront are specific to the nature of their business, successful efforts at resolution are nevertheless increasingly useful as models for other kinds of enterprise. For they reflect in an extreme way the interconnectedness that characterizes today's world, in which individuals, organizations, and nations are more dependent upon one another than ever in the past. The combination of increasingly dense populations living together in close proximity, linked ever more closely by powerful technologies, has pushed us all into a profound state of interdependence. We now share by default in one another's successes and failures, all of which prove more beneficial—or more costly—as they affect ever greater numbers of people. This means that we all have a stake in encouraging organizations to find ways to respond speedily and proactively to mistakes. The very nature of our world is high reliability.

A research project undertaken by a group of industrial psychologists at the University of California, Berkeley, examines how high-reliability organizations build structures that help them to keep even minor errors at a minimum, while catching those that do occur very early. Although they don't describe it as such, the researchers emphasize one common characteristic of high-reliability organizations: *they have the built-in ability to reconfigure as webs whenever danger arises.* This adaptability, this power to do quickly away with the chain of command, appears to be the secret advantage of organizations that experience life at the limits.

The subjects of the study included a U.S. Navy nuclear aircraft carrier, the *Enterprise;* the Oakland Air Route Traffic Control Center, which is responsible for most air traffic control north of Los Angeles; and the Power Control Center at Pacific Gas and Electric's San Francisco headquarters. The researchers found that the official management charts of these organizations conformed outwardly to the traditional hierarchical pattern, with its strict divisions between those who make decisions and those who carry them out and its clearly defined reporting channels. The researchers categorized the people in these organizations in conventional ways. There were the Big Wheels—the decision-makers or "taskers"; the Cogs—those who carry out decisions, or "operators"; and the Specialists, such as engineers or accountants. But the researchers also noted that these categories reflected only one aspect of a structure that was in fact a hybrid, for all these people assumed different roles depending on the situation.

A facade of top-down authority existed, in which orders were barked out, and subordinates responded as spit-and-polish yes-men. Yet this almost ritualized hierarchical structure dissolved whenever tensions ran high, exposing the operation to possible crisis. When this occurred, everyone worked together on an equal footing, as specialists among specialists in a collegial atmosphere. Rather than issuing orders, superiors were inclined to listen and consult. Furthermore, whenever real physical danger threatened, the top-down system collapsed entirely. Cogs then assumed full authority to operate as Big Wheels, taking the initiative in issuing commands, directing operations, or even bringing work to a sudden halt. Thus the usual division between making decisions and carrying out orders unceremoniously broke down, with the roles of taskers and operators becoming, in the heat of crisis, indistinguishable.

The researchers noted that the chain of command was able to dissolve so quickly during crisis because, even under normal circumstances, everyone in the high-reliability organization took equal part in essential tasks relating to the safety of the enterprise. For example, on the *Enterprise,* keeping the deck free of debris during an aircraft landing is a matter of life or death—not just during a crisis, but every day. As a result, the daily "walkdowns," in which the deck is inspected and cleared, include both enlisted men and officers of the highest rank, who walk shoulder-to-shoulder scouring the deck for litter. Competition to find debris takes place with a total lack of deference to hierarchical rank or division.

This exercise gives Cogs the regular experience of working directly with Big Wheels, rather than in subordination to them. Thus it prepares them for the experience of performing as equals in a crisis. It also gives Wheels a chance to participate directly with their subordinates, in a situation where they are not permitted to pull rank. Because tasks such as walkdowns are both nonhierarchical and absolutely crucial, they drive home the message that "we're all in this thing together." With teamwork a daily reality, Cogs and Wheels have a chance to share equally in responsibilities and rewards.

In addition to safety rituals that imply an egalitarian underpinning to the more immediately apparent hierarchical structure, the intensive and unremitting training of those who hold operating, as opposed to tasking, positions give even Cogs in relatively menial positions the expertise they need to assume command when the situation warrants it. Indeed, it seems as if repetitive and ongoing training, often in simulated hazardous situations, is the key to achieving flexibility in the midst of crisis. Given the extraordinary technological complexity of high-reliability organizations—the mammoth power grids at PG&E, for example—combined with a predictable level of unpredictable events—everything from snowstorms to lightning to a drunk crashing into a pole—training must be both continuous and very broad. No one can hope to take command of a developing catastrophe unless he or she understands what is at stake in the broadest sense. For the system to work, everyone who is a part of it must understand its basic process.

The Berkeley researchers identified another characteristic that enabled high-reliability organizations to reconfigure as webs in emergencies. Noting the complexity of the tasks confronting these organizations, the researchers recognized that the people at the top of the chain of command could not possibly know everything about their operation. There was simply too much to learn, and not enough time in which to learn it; indeed, this became more true the higher they rose in their organization. As a result, the Big Wheels were dependent on the Cogs not only to execute tasks, as in an industrial enterprise, but also to master areas of knowledge that they did not have time to master themselves.

Thus the very complexity of the high-reliability organizations gives rise to a kind of mutual interdependence between taskers and operators. The leaders must feel comfortable learning from and trusting their subordinates, since those subordinates often possess vital knowledge beyond the scope of their superiors. This implicit role reversal further prepares the organization when confronted by crisis to abandon its hierarchical configuration for that of the web.

The Berkeley study concluded that an ability to dissolve top-down structures would become more vital as our population continues to grow and technology becomes more complex. The cost of error will force every variety of organization to develop more high-reliability characteristics so that it can respond appropriately to stress. Webs of inclusion, evolving as a grassroots means of addressing specific problems, provide a way for organizations to shift into high-reliability gear by permitting individuals to assert competence without regard to formal job description. At the same time, webs acknowledge and build upon that sense of mutual need that increasingly characterizes our interwoven world.

PART II

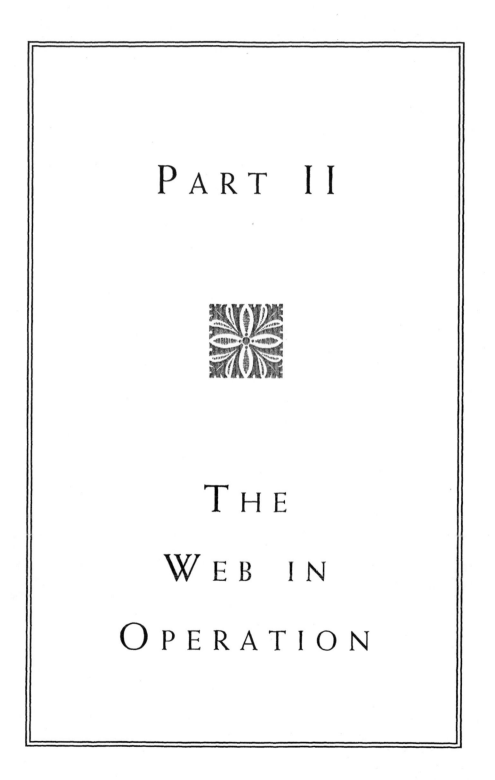

THE

WEB IN

OPERATION

Introduction
to the Studies

"*What we need now is a new breed of company that combines the entrepreneurial spirit of America with the humanistic approach characteristic of many Asian firms.*"

—Joel Kotkin and Yoriko Kishimoto
The Third Century: America's Resurgence in the Asian Era

Clearly, the web of inclusion provides an architecture for helping organizations to restructure in ways more reflective of how we now perceive our world in operation. But in practical, concrete terms—the terms of everyday application—how do webs actually perform their work? How do they enable organizations to draw ideas and talent from a broader base? How do they encourage new lines of communication to flourish? And perhaps most important, *how do webs help organizations to face the specific and extraordinary challenges that will inevitably confront them in the next century?*

The challenges are multifold, yet each involves the breaking down of barriers between divisions and departments in order to integrate the tasks and functions that people within the organization perform. The crucial areas in which organizations are being challenged to break down barriers include:

■ MARKETING. In today's world of wildly proliferating services and products, each organization must find a way to become entirely market-driven in order to carve out a special niche for itself. This means that everyone in the company must not only develop marketing skills, but must begin to *think* like a marketer, constantly conceptualizing how a product or service might suit a need or solve a problem. This will only occur when marketing is no longer isolated as a special function or division that comes into play when a product is ready to hit the market.

■ DIVERSITY. The unrivaled ability of the United States to assimilate people of different cultures will emerge as our great advantage as the global economy becomes more interlinked, and as a more diverse labor force comes to characterize enterprise in general. Diversity really means being able to draw from a wider base of talent; a base diminished in nations where a strong class structure locks most people out from power, or where strictures against a particular group—for example, women—inhibit its members' full participation. Recognized as such, the effort to broaden the base becomes too important to be restricted to a "diversity department," a practice that marginalizes its importance and contributes to the kind of Balkanization that is the very antithesis of true progress.

■ EMPOWERING THE FRONT LINES. During the 1980s, American companies spent hundreds of billions on technology—and often had little to show for it. Rigid and top-heavy corporate structures were simply not suited to take advantage of information technology's essential capability, which is to diffuse information down and out to the front lines. As a result, today's organizations are being challenged to reengineer *the very nature of their work* in order to reflect and adapt to what their technology enables. They are having to acknowledge that every increase in the speed and power of software and every decrease in that software's price further strengthens this balance of power in favor of the individual at the grassroots level, who has the ability to link up to ever more valuable networks.

■MAKING TRAINING PART OF THE PROCESS. As products and services proliferate at increasing speed, and as technology gives people in the ranks more power, the nature of what we have come to know as training will radically change. It will become an ongoing, rather than a one-time, event, and as a result will have to be integrated into the process of daily work. This spells an end to training departments as isolated divisions—and an end to people who "do training" but don't also know how to do the work. Training will be reconfigured as education, a continual process in which everyone participates, sharing knowledge and skills, as in the pre-industrial master-apprentice model.

■BUILDING STRATEGIC ALLIANCES. More powerful technologies enable organizations to get smaller. At the same time, what John Naisbitt calls *The Global Paradox*—the notion that the bigger the world econ omy, the more powerful its smallest players—is clearly at work. In order to stay small and lean, organizations must find ways to develop partnerships with those who can supply what they cannot. This will force them to redefine the nature of their borders, which will become more permeable, more about opening gates than defining who's in and who's out.

Addressing these challenges by breaking down internal and external barriers will not only enable organizations to become more agile in responding to changing markets and customer demands, but will also render work more satisfying in human terms. For only by dismantling the structures that isolate people's tasks and functions can we move beyond an industrial heritage that, defining tasks too narrowly and exalting the role of supervision, has deprived most people's daily work of dignity and meaning. Only by reintegrating doing and decision-making, design and execution, can we restore context and autonomy to the labor that frames most people's days, and thus motivate them to deliver their best, and most imaginative, effort.

Such an integration enables people at every level truly to participate in the broad scope of work, freeing productive and creative energies formerly restricted by arbitrary divisions and barriers. This alone can foster the attitude of ownership that is essential if all the tasks that comprise daily work are to have real meaning to those who perform them. Webs of inclusion provide a powerful means by which individuals can participate broadly in the lives and futures of their organizations. Part II of this book will provide a close look at how five very different companies are using webs of inclusion not only to meet the particular and pressing challenges of the day, but also to return autonomy and self-expression, and thus joy, to the work being done by those in the ranks.

THREE

Marketing Is Everything: Intel Corporation

"Just as the demands on companies have shifted from controlling costs to competing on products to serving customers, so the center of gravity in the company has shifted from finance to engineering to marketing."

—REGIS MCKENNA

Focusing on the customer, becoming market-driven: these are the stated goals of most organizations today. We hear them exalted in executive speeches, reiterated during seminars devoted to management topics, exhorted upon in business journals. Referring to the customer has become a kind of mantra, a way for managers to indicate they are in step with the latest thinking.

But what do the familiar phrases really mean? How can an organization hope to keep in constant touch with a market that is constantly changing, or to serve customers who are often paralyzed by sheer variety and choice? Perhaps even more important, how can an organization caught up in the escalating tides of modern product cycles even be sure who its customers really are, or how those customers might best use their products? And how can it find those customers in the first place?

Marketing must provide the bridge, the key, must serve as the instrument and means for bringing a producer of goods or services together with potential buyers. But given the proliferation of products and services that has resulted from increasingly programmable and fine-tuned technology, the very nature of what marketing is and what it can achieve has changed almost beyond recognition in recent years. Gone are the days when marketing could be conceived of as a separate function, not all that distinct from advertising, concerned primarily with honing and protecting the corporate image. As Regis McKenna, marketing guru for scores of Silicon Valley companies, the man who helped put Intel on the map and launched Apple's MacIntosh, has observed, marketing today is not about *luring* the customer with promises, but rather about *matching* what customers need with what the company can supply.

McKenna defines the role for today's marketer as that of the "integrator." The integrator works *inside* the company to represent the needs of the marketplace to the technicians who develop the products; he or she must therefore be knowledgeable about the manufacturing process. But the integrator also works *outside* the company, attempting to discern what the customers' concerns might be, so that those needs will be met by what the company supplies. McKenna is very clear that companies in the future will be successful to the extent that a full integration of inside and outside interests is achieved.

These interests can truly coincide only if organizations begin to regard their customers *as full participants in the development and adaptation of goods and services*—a strong step in the direction toward mass customization, collaboration, and virtual co-creation. The shift, McKenna points out, is from manipulation to involvement, from selling and persuading to sharing information and knowledge. Marketers were the old "hidden persuaders" that Vance Packard warned about in the sixties; but given today's technology, the line between producer and consumer begins to dissolve. Marketing fills the gap. Thus McKenna's famous dictum: *"Marketing is everything."*

Given the quick evolution of products, marketers can no longer limit the definition of the customer—because the customer is always changing. But the process of expanding or refocusing on who the customer is also changes a company's conception of why it is in business, whom it serves, what its ultimate purpose is. Once this process begins, the very nature of its enterprise is set free to evolve. Since the process is fluid, it incorporates a constant element of risk: continually evolving means continually entering and leaving behind whole new kinds of business. The risk implicit in constantly redefining the customer means that forays into new markets must be small and specific, aimed as much at providing information as finding customers. Research, the traditional job of marketers, gets integrated at the front lines with operations—necessitating the breakdown of barriers.

Because of their decentralized structure, permeability, and emphasis on creating new links and channels, webs of inclusion are particularly useful for organizations seeking to rethink who its customers might be, and then reaching out to them in imaginative ways. And because webs are fluid, and can expand and contract to meet specific needs, they provide a ready means for integrating reconnaissance and operations, for working on the tightened scale that keeps costs down.

At Intel Corporation in Santa Clara, California, a small and innovative web of inclusion began configuring in early 1991 that enabled the company to redefine who its customers were—and eventually, the nature of Intel's business. The Intel web seemed to grow naturally out of a series of previous web-like structures, all aimed at identifying specific problems with Intel's customer base. In the process of interacting with the company's larger culture—one already characterized by openness and flexibility—these webs began to coalesce in a way that came to reshape the company's overall strategy. As such, Intel provides us with a kind of laboratory in which we can observe, trace, and study the process of web-style transformation as it has been occurring in one of the most successful and brilliant companies in America today.

THE VALLEY CULTURE

Intel is the world's pre-eminent and most profitable maker of integrated circuits, those silicon chips that power everything electronic. The company employs twenty-five thousand people and had revenues in 1993 of $8.78 billion, along with one of the highest earnings per employee ratio in the world. The heart of its value lies in its research and development projects, which were expected to reach $3.5 billion in 1994. Andrew Grove, the President of Intel, is fond of proclaiming that his people routinely "bet the company" on huge research projects. In wilder moments, he expands this to declare that they "bet millions on science fiction."

Intel today functions in some ways almost like the old Bell Laboratories—a private company whose commitment to research qualifies it as a national resource. But Intel seems nothing like the old Bell Labs when you pay a visit, for the place is saturated with Silicon Valley style—informal, fast-moving, nonbureaucratic, wildly diverse. There is little similarity to the traditional military ethic and strict hierarchical structure that prevailed at, and indeed epitomized, pre-divestiture AT&T.

When you drive up to Intel's headquarters, a sprawling five-story building of sky-blue glass that looms over the suburban strip of Route 101 running through Santa Clara north from San Jose, the first thing you notice is that there are no reserved parking places in the vast lots: it's first come, first served, no matter who you are. Inside, too, the nonhierarchical Valley ethic prevails, for everyone, from the Chairman to support staff, sits in cubicles, which are available only in several sizes. The outer rim of walls is not blocked off by enclosed offices as in most buildings; it rises above the cubicles, enabling natural light to fill every floor for an open, spacious feeling. Intel's fluid and egalitarian use of space, which will be discussed more fully in Chapter 8, is worthy of note, for it reflects much about how the company is structured.

The organizational chart is very flat, with only six layers for thirty-five thousand people—down from thirteen layers in the early eighties. Virtually no positions are solely supervisory. Lines of command are multiple and diffuse, with much overlapping of departments, and everyone reporting to multiple bosses, performing multiple jobs, and sitting on multiple councils. This overlapping enables the company to run as leanly as possible, for people are constantly being shifted to where they are needed, which saves having to overhire in times of expansion. Reorganization is continual and evolving, a way of life; there is no such thing as a static job. Carlene Ellis, presently Vice President for Information Technology, points out: "I've been here twelve years, and in that time I've had seven different jobs. Fourteen, really, since each job was reorged once, which completely changed how it was done and who for."

One aspect of Intel's culture that made its practice of constant reorganizations work is its emphasis on nonpositional power. The role of nonpositional power in the formation of webs was pointed out by Ted Jenkins, an engineer with a philosophical bent who has been with Intel since its founding. "Intel's great strength," he declares, "lies in the way the company allows resources to flow to wherever there's a problem. I've thought a lot about why, in so many other companies, this just doesn't happen, and I think it's because in most organizations resources tend to accumulate—they get stuck wherever someone is in a position of great power. So what you end up with in most companies is a few powerful people who have more resources than they actually need, while everybody else has to try to make do with less. It's static, irrational, and inefficient."

Jenkins attributes this situation to the fact that traditional hierarchical organizations are structured specifically to validate and exalt positional power. "In most organizations, it's easy to figure out who's powerful: you just look at where someone stands on the org chart. The only kind of power that really matters is the power of position. That makes it very difficult for other kinds of power to develop. The people at the top hold on tight, so no one else can establish any kind of alternate power base. And it's this absence of other power bases that permits resources to get stuck." Position, however, is a relatively crude way of measuring power, as Jenkins points out. It cannot begin to reflect the subtleties of alignment in a company such as Intel. "Here, there's no single way of being powerful. The power of position is just one aspect. And I wouldn't say it's the most important aspect at all."

Enumerating alternate sources of power, Jenkins names first *the power of expertise,* of knowing and possessing crucial skills. "A company like Intel very naturally emphasizes the power of expertise because eighty percent of the people we hire are engineers." As in a partnership of professionals—accountants or attorneys—people are chosen because they exhibit specific skills, rather than because they have potential as all-purpose managers. And since skill is so highly regarded, anyone who exhibits an unusual level of skill tends to accumulate power. "We place a very high value on the power of expertise, and the way the company is run tends to increase it," says Jenkins. "We have this intense level of training that never stops, which of course broadens and deepens expertise. Also, because we are continually undergoing reorgs, people move around in the company quite a bit, which also tends to increase the scope of people's expertise."

Moving people around a lot also helps develop another alternate source of power: *the power of personal relationships or connections.* "Because people are always being shifted, they develop a lot of connections in the company as they go along. They know a lot of people, because they've had a chance to work with so many of them—they have personal friendships, and they also have a pretty good idea of what the people they know might be capable of doing. This makes for a very networked organization, with lots of informal lines of communication, lots of links that would never appear on any organizational chart. This is absolutely invaluable when you're trying to put together a team, because people know all kinds of unexpected places to look for various kinds of skills. You can put together a very creative team that gives people a chance to develop new talents—which of course then also increases their expertise."

Ted Jenkins also mentions the importance of *the power of personal authority* as crucial in developing alternate centers of power. In any organization, he points out, you have people who, by virtue of their personalities, their natural leadership skills, and the trust that they inspire, wield a power greater than their official position would indicate. Yet in traditional hierarchies, such people are often viewed as a threat, disruptive links in the functioning of the chain of command. "In a company like Intel, such people really thrive," notes Jenkins. "They make a big difference in terms of where resources flow. And again, the power of personal authority is really emphasized as people get shifted around, because their experience is broadened and more people come into their orbit."

Jenkins believes the primary reasons Intel has been able to encourage alternate centers of power are its penchant for constant reorganizations and the unusually low turnover rate among people who work for the company. "In this organization, people don't leave. They're paid fairly, they have a great profit-sharing plan, and they get a lot of opportunity to move around—it's always something different. In companies where people are constantly leaving, it's hard for alternate power centers to develop.

"It's especially hard to develop the power of personal connections if you're not in an organization for very long, and without personal connections, it's hard to put strong teams together. Everyone knows that companies have two organizational charts—the formal one, listing everyone's position, from the president on down; and the informal one that shows the actual routes of connection that allow things to really get *done*. It's the informal power structure that always determines how effective an organization will be. And stability is essential in order to build a strong informal structure. Also, reorgs don't do much but disrupt a company if people are always coming and going. I think your emphasis is always going to be on positional power if people don't stay with the organization."

In the Heart of the Valley

It seems fitting that Intel should provide an opportunity for watching how webs form and function, for the organization lies at the very epicenter of the ever evolving web of enterprise that is Silicon Valley. Intel was born in 1968, one of the first companies spun off from Fairchild Semiconductor, which was itself the original prototype of a Valley start-up. Fairchild came into being when all the engineers who worked for William Shockley walked out one day to protest Shockley's management style. Shockley had been the head of the Bell Labs team that invented the transistor, but in the early sixties, he had returned to his hometown of Palo Alto to found the world's most advanced semiconductor company. Much later, he would gain notoriety as a proponent of racist evolutionary theories.

The eight engineers who abandoned him to found Fairchild were thus imbued from the very start with a notion of business as a collegial enterprise, one in which expertise should be valued over positional power, and the independence and individual talent of people throughout the ranks should be honored and recognized for what it was: the true strength, the reserve power, of an organization. The Fairchild founders went on to spin off scores of other ventures in the years ahead, thus seeding the Valley for decades to come with talent that was stamped with an antiauthoritarian and egalitarian ethic, while also driven by an entrepreneurial spirit.

Intel was co-founded by the legendary Robert Noyce, a former Shockley protégé and himself a member of the original Fairchild group. Noyce was the co-inventor of the original integrated circuit; it was he who figured out that transistors could be lithographically etched onto silicon chips, then miniaturized many times over, thus permitting dozens of transistors and resistors to exist on a single chip. This invention made possible the drastic shrinking in size of computers, laying the foundation for the personal computer industry. At his death in 1990, Noyce was Chairman of Sematech, a consortium seeking to build American competitiveness in high technology by pooling research on costly ventures such as supercolliders and super-conductive ceramics. The collaborative and integrated nature of this effort was reflective of the legacy Noyce left behind at Intel.

Intel's other cofounder—and still its Chairman—was Gordon Moore. While at Fairchild, he had formulated what would become known in high-tech circles as "Moore's Law," which holds that the number of transistors on a chip will double every eighteen months, which has the effect of continually reducing prices. As a chip loses value, it in consequence drives down the price of any product of which it is a component, spelling financial disaster for even a success-ful product if it is not upgraded or replaced regularly over time. This quirk means that high-tech value is always defined in terms of how *new* a product is, rather than by how much it costs to produce. Moore's Law was the first formal recognition of a phenomenon that has had tremendous implications for high-tech development, for it made clear that economies of scale would no longer apply in the post-industrial world.

This reversal of a basic premise of industrial economics has oc-curred because, whereas high-tech development costs are high, pro-duction costs continually become cheaper, while the cost of the natu-ral resources that comprise the products is essentially negligible. A corollary to Moore's Law therefore holds that, if values can no longer be wrung out of mass production, they must be created by continually upgrading, improving, and modifying an existing product. The impact of this truth cannot be overestimated. It means that high-tech organi-zations, in order to survive, must incorporate continual change as part of their daily process: they barely have a month to sit back and bask in success. For no high-technology product can be considered success-ful in and of itself; *each must be understood as part of the learning curve for what will be produced next.*

Under the leadership of Noyce and Moore, Intel patented the first microprocessor, which mimics the mainframe's central process-ing unit by integrating logic, memory, and communication chips. The microprocessor made it possible for small computers to handle business functions, which enabled desktop machines to move beyond the hobbyist phase. All subsequent advances beyond the mainframe have been based upon this invention, the microprocessor being nothing less than the computer's brain. Having patented this essential device in the early years of its existence, Intel moved quickly to capitalize on its production, its greatest coup being its agreement to produce chips for the IBM PC.

By the mid-late eighties, Intel had established the standard with its 286 microprocessor, known throughout the industry as "the 286." It comprised the guts not only of the IBM PC and all its clones, but those of scores of other computers—more than 100 million machines around the globe. The success of the 286 provided Intel with the huge reserves of cash it needed to fund the costly research that enabled the continual upgrading and improvement of its whole range of products. For given the ruthless exigencies of Moore's Law, which decrees that any high-tech innovation loses value the moment it hits the market, the company had no choice but to make enormous investments in technology, continually developing new products, new versions, new upgrades, and putting them out on the market.

THE THREAT OF DISASTER

By late 1988, the time had arrived for the company to introduce the next generation of microprocessor, the successor chip to the 286. The atmosphere at Intel as it prepared for the release is recalled by people in the company as euphoric: after years of work, the 386 was finally ready to hit the market. Everyone was sure that Intel had come up with another winner, for the 386 microprocessor was far from being a mere upgrade.

This represented a major step forward into the future, a revolution in what desktop computers could do. The new chip had 32-bit capacity instead of the standard 16-bit—a tremendous increase in terms of speed, capacity, and power. Developing it had been a great technical success, in the tradition pioneered by Robert Noyce. Everyone at Intel—the engineers, the marketing department, and the great international sales force—was convinced that once the 386 got out there, it would sweep the field.

Instead, a few months after its introduction, the chip was threatening the company with the specter of almost total failure. The problem had nothing to do with the quality or attributes of the 386. Intel's customers, it seemed, were attached to the 286, which was viewed as the workhorse of the personal computer industry. The 386 was regarded as being useful only if you needed tremendous power; it was also considered very costly. The resistance from the market was of course potentially disastrous for a high-tech company like Intel, and pointed up with particular poignancy the paradox inherent at the heart of Moore's Law. This is that failure can result from any *too* successful product, since its very success will discourage its buyers from wanting to replace it.

When a new product meets market resistance, the producer will very often try to find a way to cut its price, and this is what Intel at first sought to do. The company's executive committee sent the engineers back to the drawing board to develop a scaled-down model of the 386, a version that would have most of its power and could perform most of its functions, but could be priced not much higher than the old 286. An engineer named Dennis Carter, then in his late thirties, was put in charge of the effort; he had been working as Andrew Grove's Special Assistant for Technical Affairs.

"We came up with a chip we called the 386SX," he says. "For what we were trying to do, it was absolutely the perfect product—scaled down, but still a 32-bit chip. The idea was just to introduce people to 32-bitness, get them hooked on that, make 16-bit obsolete forever. We were so excited and proud that we'd got it right. So we put the new chip out there, and then all stood back like good little engineers and waited for it to sell. But we *still* couldn't move it! No one wanted the thing—*no one.*"

Dennis Carter felt that it was incumbent upon him to figure out a solution—or at least to get an inkling where the problem might lie. Intel simply had too much invested in 32-bit technology to accept the possibility of its defeat. The company's position was particularly precarious because it had just emerged from a major recession that had devastated the computer industry in the mid-1980s. Considering the problem from a variety of angles, Carter tried to imagine just where the hitch might lie. The *market* had rejected an excellent product: so might not the problem lie in who constituted the market, in just who Intel defined as its customer base?

Intel had always defined its primary customers as computer manufacturers, companies like IBM and Dell and Compaq that bought microprocessors for use in the assembly of their products. These "original equipment manufacturers," or OEMs as they're called in Silicon Valley, have traditionally comprised the major market for microprocessor chips. Intel had other, secondary customers as well: manufacturers who sold circuitboards to OEMs, and distributing agents who acted as microprocessor brokers for both circuitboard makers and computer manufacturers. But the OEMs had always been Intel's main customers, and it was in order to serve them that the company deployed and trained its huge sales force.

Certainly, Intel had never considered the people who *bought* computers to be its customers. Nor did it envision itself as selling to MIS professionals, those technology buyers who since the advent of the IBM PC had purchased desktop units for large companies. The consumer market—"end users" in Valley jargon—were viewed simply as customers of Intel's customers, encountered necessarily at one remove. After all, Intel was a technology company, not a maker of consumer products. Since their invention, microprocessors had always been sold as components, internal parts used in the assembly of a larger product. It was considered inconceivable to think in terms of selling them to the public, comparable to the manufacturer of automobile steering columns trying to sell its products directly to drivers instead of to GM or Honda.

And yet, as Dennis Carter considered it, the steering column analogy was not really accurate, for the microprocessor chip is hardly just another component in a complex product. It is, rather, *the* essential element, the piece that powers the product of which it is a component; the rest is just plastic shell, and an operating system that inter-prets the chip's commands. Thus the microprocessor is what the customer *is really buying* when he or she purchases a computer—even if it had never been considered in that way. And so it began to occur to Dennis Carter that perhaps Intel was being stymied in its efforts to sell the 386 because the company misperceived who the customers for it actually were.

"What we began to realize was that 32-bit architecture was great for the computer *user;* since you can run a lot of very powerful and useful programs off it. But the computer *manufacturers* were doing just fine selling products based upon the 286—which not incidentally was also becoming cheaper for them to buy. They were doing very well on it, so they didn't feel any incentive to spend a lot of extra money just to make their products more useful to the buyer. When we considered that, we began to wonder if we weren't making a funda-mental mistake, counting on the OEMs always to represent our inter-ests in the market. Here was an obvious case of their interests not necessarily coinciding with ours. But since we'd always regarded them as our real customers, that took a while to see."

Still, Intel *had* to start selling its 386 chips. Moore's Law decreed that the company must move the technology on to the next stage, or be stuck selling a product that was losing profitability with each pass-ing day. Adding to the sense of urgency was the fact that Intel's engi-neers believed that the PC manufacturers who were their customers would themselves become obsolete, unless they made the step beyond the 16-bit chip in a timely fashion. If they did not, the market would simply move to other kinds of technology. "It began to dawn on us," says Dennis Carter, "that our only real hope was to appeal directly to PC buyers. If we could convince them of the benefits of 32-bit strength, they might start to demand boxes that ran on the chip. And if *that* happened, the buyers could in essence pull the market for us, forcing manufacturers to start using the 386."

The notion of reaching out to end users was revolutionary for a manufacturer of computer components, and would entail a complete realignment of how Intel positioned itself in the market. As it was, the company had no links to computer buyers and no routes of contact for reaching out to them, since its sales staff was entirely focused on manufacturers. Intel had no relationships it could leverage, no credibility with the general public, no history as a consumer products company; it didn't even have an advertising agency at the time. Nor did Dennis Carter, as the President's Special Assistant for Technical Affairs, have the authority to undertake marketing microprocessors to the general public.

Going directly to the public would entail the kind of total reorientation that most large companies would be unable even to conceive of putting into practice. One thinks of the Detroit auto makers' initial response when the market began to reject its cars: they tried to cut costs so that they could reduce their prices, but for a long time continued making and marketing cars in the same old way. Reconceptualizing to whom a company sells means re-envisioning why the organization is in business, which calls into question its very reason for existence. Doing so in turn undermines the prestige of the chain of command, unsettles established turf, and exposes an organization to incalculable risk. However, the very crisis that Intel had passed through during the mid-1980s recession made possible the kind of radical repositioning that Dennis Carter had begun to believe might be the only way to save the 386SX. By radically opening up the company and creating a flexible structure that let resources flow toward problems, Intel had set the stage for webs to form at the company's roots.

Stop Doing What's Stupid

The problem facing most companies, according to Carlene Ellis, Intel's Vice President for Organization and a member of the sixteen-person Executive Staff, can be summed up fairly simply: *"You just have to find a way to stop doing what's stupid."* That is, you must constantly question the utility of what is driving the organization—not only in terms of the present, but also in regard to what lies ahead.

Most people in organizations are far too concerned with maintaining the status quo to be able to do this—in particular, the people at the top. People become *invested* in doing what's been done, in defending its need to be done, because it justifies what they have been doing. This prevents them from questioning the basic underlying assumptions that lie at the root of their enterprise. They don't ask, should it be done at all?

That Intel persistently asks questions is due to an earlier baptism by fire. "You have to go back to 1985 if you want to understand why we were able to handle the problems around the 386," Carlene Ellis points out. "Intel had always been this growing, successful company. We were known for having a growing, stable employee base—we were a place where people stayed. And believe me, we benefited enormously from having such a low turnover, because only when people really know their way around can they figure out how to get stuff *done* here. So most of us assumed this was just the nature of our company. We took our stability for granted, without really having earned it."

Then, in early 1985, the whole industry "suddenly just went through the floor. Everyone got caught with a massive overstock of microprocessors, including us. It was a terrible crisis, we just couldn't sell our stuff, and to deal with it we had to let thousands of employees go. The company was just torn apart—great people thrown out on the street, very bitter. Those left behind were as scared as those who left. They couldn't concentrate on their work. The motivation was just gone. Fear was up as people waited for the next hit. Here everyone had all worked so hard to build up trust over the years, and now we were watching it be destroyed overnight. Seeing what happened scared us to death."

As head of CIS at the time, Carlene Ellis was in a particular position to feel the pain. She was sensitive to it because of what she had witnessed growing up in a small town in the South. "I remember like yesterday how NASA suddenly cut thousands of people from the space program. Huntsville, Alabama, just fell apart—the town, people's families. You'd see all these incredibly talented engineers walking around doing nothing. I remember it gave me a feeling of terrible waste." At Intel in the mid-eighties, Carlene Ellis feared reliving that experience, and became convinced that "we were watching something that we could never let happen again."

Of course, layoffs had always been considered part of organizational life, a given; inevitable because the nature of business cycles is to expand and contract. "But what we realized in about 1985," says Carlene Ellis, "was that while that might have been all right for industrial factories—though I doubt it—it's *not* acceptable for a company like Intel. Whenever you have highly trained people, you're just shooting yourself in the foot when you have to fire them. *They* comprise the value of your company, so it makes no sense. Also, if you're going to ask people to be creative, you have to provide an environment that inspires them. People *have* to be motivated if you want them to think, and constant fear destroys motivation."

The lesson of the late eighties for Carlene Ellis, then, was that "layoffs are a last resort. They destroy your foundation and it's tough to rebuild. Once you make the commitment to try never to let people go, however, you have taken the first step toward reconceptualizing how your organization works." With support from the Executive Staff, Carlene Ellis's Human Resources department began in 1990 to formulate a plan so that "ideally, we would *never* have to go through layoffs again, no matter what the external situation. The fact that the economy was cyclical could not be used as an excuse." In order to achieve the goal, however, "We had to completely change the way we were thinking. We had to start looking at everything from the standpoint of where we were going to be in the future. We had to know what kind of skills we were going to need. Not just for the next year or so, but way down the road as well."

The goal became never to hire permanent people whose skills would become obsolete, or who would not be needed if and when the industry hit a downturn. "Once you decide to start thinking of it like that, you have to really start listening to people—your administrators, analysts, planners, designers. You have to find out exactly what *they* need, in terms of skills and support. You have to challenge them to think about what their work will be like in the future, which of course gets them thinking about the company, and the industry, as a whole." This in turn drastically alters the role played by Human Resources, which is no longer in the position of simply trying to find good people and then hiring and training them in an all-purpose way. Human Resources becomes instead more the partner of the business units, prodding them to think in an integrated and large-scale way about what they will be needing over the long term.

Once people are hired, they must then be trained in a broader sense of skills, so they can perform a lot of functions and be shifted around with relative ease. "You can't afford to hire someone who can only function as a process engineer, for example. You have to train that person in design engineering as well. That means moving him around a lot, which therefore means he has to get his training while he's on the job. The whole trick to avoiding layoffs is that you have to be both lean *and* broadbased, having lots of utility people. When I think back to what I saw at NASA, I'm sure one of the problems was that everyone was trained very narrowly, for just one specialty."

Carlene Ellis makes clear that Intel's culture of constant reorganizations and broadbased training is not only a strategy for ensuring a work force that is flexible and lean, but also a way of building in a bias for the pragmatic and tactically-based approach. With jobs assumed on a provisional basis, and training conceived of as ongoing, people get used to trying things out and learning from whatever works. Such an approach, she points out, facilitates innovation by encouraging people to take responsibility for projects as a whole, rather than focusing only upon the part that they have to play. The emphasis on strategy built from tactics thus encourages large-scale thinking among people throughout the organization, by spreading responsibility and the opportunity to improvise around.

As a former school athlete, Carlene Ellis is fond of observing that Intel "plays by sandlot rules"—the stress is on working together, on learning and improvising within the context of play. "When I played basketball in college," she recalls, "I always hated the zone defense. You just stood there guarding, no matter where the ball was. Lots of companies play that way today: the market moves or disappears entirely, but they're still standing there, guarding this empty spot. They do it because that's what they've been taught to do, and no one has thought to give them permission to stop doing something because it's stupid. But when you move beyond the zone, and start moving the ball, all you've got is this core of people, with everyone accountable and responsible, all over the ball. And *that's* where the technology has moved us. We don't have time to play the zones. It's all one-on-one out there today."

WEAVING THE WEB

Intel's restructuring in the wake of the 1985 recession made it easier for internal webs to form by accentuating those aspects of the company that permit and encourage alternate centers of power to develop. But the recession also paved the way for what was to follow by forcing Intel to reorient itself, to question the bedrock assumptions of its enterprise. The depth and level of questioning about such basic issues as layoffs prepared the way for Dennis Carter to question just who Intel's customers really were, and in the process of doing so, to reinvent the market.

In early 1989, Dennis Carter went before the Executive Committee and told them he thought it was time to see if the 386SX could be marketed to end users. Because the company had a tradition of funding unorthodox experiments if they were tried out on a small scale, the Committee gave him $5 million to see what he could do—"five million dollars to change people's buying behavior across the U.S.," as he later said. His first and most obvious problem was that he had no staff, for the effort was not assigned to any department: it existed as an independent team, one of those one-on-one core units of which Carlene Ellis approves.

Dennis Carter's first step in weaving the web that would enable Intel to reach out directly to computer buyers was to draw on people from throughout the company, borrowing them from their various divisions so he could cobble together the beginnings of a team. Creating impromptu teams for quick action is not as difficult at Intel as it might be somewhere else, because of the tradition of people working for multiple bosses. This kind of matrixing gets people used to flexible structures, and accustoms them to being moved around.

To work full-time in the new effort, Dennis brought in Sally Fundakowski, a former market researcher, since the first step would obviously be to figure out the market. "I had left Intel a few years before," says Sally. "I'd been bitten by the start-up bug and went off to start my own business, but the times were very tough. Then one afternoon, I was sitting in this pie restaurant in Palo Alto, just a week away from having my second child, when Dennis walked in with his kids. He started talking to me about his new project. He just got very excited about it, so I got excited just listening to him. Right on the spot I made the quick decision to go back to Intel and work for him."

As an entrepreneurial kind of person, Sally Fundakowski liked the idea of "doing something just unheard of, something that would completely redefine the market. Intel had always had this audience of a few thousand engineers, and now suddenly Dennis was thinking about ways that we could widen that to millions of people. There was this huge element of risk: we stood to really alienate the manufacturers and distributors we'd always sold to. We were going to be messing with people who'd always been *their* customers! All these elements came together and made the project so intriguing. It was absolutely a renegade kind of deal."

Sally's early market research was full of surprises. "Naturally, we had to find out what our customers thought about us, the end users we were going to try to reach. Well, the first thing we discovered was, they had no idea who on earth we were! We could hardly believe it—here we were so successful, but even MIS people in big companies didn't know us. Only fifty percent of *them* had even heard of the 286. So you can imagine how things stood with the general public."

Market education was obviously going to have to be drastic. "We realized right away we needed to do something very dramatic in order to change people's buying habits," recalls Dennis Carter. "But whenever you do something dramatic, there's the chance you'll make some mistake and undermine yourself. Sally and I needed more experience before we could forge ahead, and to me you get experience by trying things out on a small scale, so you can learn from your mistakes without it costing too much money." Although Intel prides itself on taking risks, Dennis Carter also notes that "there's this other side of us that's very methodical. Don't forget, we're a bunch of engineers! So *when* we do something risky, we always proceed in small steps, gathering information and trying to measure everything as we go along. We don't just pick some strategy and then go ahead because we sound good when we talk about it to ourselves." Strategy must derive from tactics, in other words: tactics implemented at the grassroots level.

The team decided to test an appeal to the end user market in Denver. In preparation, Dennis Carter enlarged the web, enlisting Ann Lewnes, then on the staff of Intel's internal magazine. "If we were going to try to persuade people, we obviously needed someone who could write." Together with Sally Fundakowski, they flew to Denver. Dennis Carter recalls: "When we got to town, we had no network to buyers, very little name recognition. We had to start out by walking cold into retail stores. We just went in and struck up conversations with people who made a living selling PCs. Mostly, we asked questions: we were trying to get an idea of what their customers looked for, what the dealers themselves thought their customers wanted."

The retailers seemed intrigued that people from Intel would take an interest in their business. As the dealers began to ask questions, the Intel team began to coordinate a response. They developed programs to train the dealers in what 386 technology was all about. "This effort required us all to do a little of everything," says Dennis Carter. "We came up with point-of-sale displays and wrote backup material. We started focus groups of PC buyers, and listened to what they had to say. We interviewed people who planned to buy PCs, and asked them what they thought was important. Everything we did was about getting feedback, creating a loop, an interface so we could listen to the market."

Next, they hit the local media. They got themselves booked onto Denver radio shows, and even put up a billboard advertising the 386SX. Most important, they monitored everything, so that every effort, even if it failed, would supply information and so function as research. Following up on PC buyers after the information blitz, the team discovered that people were beginning to alter their purchasing plans in response to what they were learning about how 32-bit technology could be of use to them. "People in Denver were starting to tell dealers they wanted 386 capacity in their new computers," recalls Dennis Carter. They wanted to be able to run the programs they might need in the future."

Judging the Denver effort to be a success, the team decided to expand the approach, trying it out in twelve major metropolitan markets, but formulating a slightly different approach in each, so that they might learn as much as possible from their efforts. To cover so many markets, of course, more than the core of three people would be needed, so Dennis Carter turned for help to Intel's sales force. This huge international organization had been designed precisely in order to sell Intel's technology to manufacturers and distributors. That's where the sales managers' relationships and thus their loyalties lay. Quite predictably, it was at this moment of expansion that the team encountered its first resistance within the company, for their effort to borrow sales people for their project stirred a lot of flak.

Dennis Carter recalls: "Some of the area sales managers couldn't believe it—'you want to take *my* people for *your* little program?' They were particularly worried that, by going directly to computer buyers, we were going to alienate the original equipment manufacturers, who had of course always regarded the buyers as *their* customers. But finally, we were able to persuade them. We convinced them that, if their sales people got into contact with actual PC buyers, they would learn a lot of stuff that they could then turn around and share with the OEMs. We pointed out that what we wanted to do would actually *improve* the sales force, instead of just distracting them from their jobs, by expanding their reach and building up their networks."

But was persuading the area sales managers of the advantages of his project the only reason the team succeeded in its task? Wasn't the power that Dennis Carter held as Andrew Grove's special assistant also useful in persuading field sales managers to agree to lend him their people? "I have to say that, while it may have helped a little, it was not a primary reason," he maintains. "Leveraging power that way doesn't work very well around here. It spurs resentment, makes people resist you, and then you have problems when you have to deal with those people down the line, which in a networked company like this you always do. Plus I can honestly say that being in a high position at Intel doesn't mean as much as in other organizations." Dennis Carter adds, echoing Ted Jenkins: "Positional power at Intel means as close to nothing as you can get."

WIDENING THE WEB

In the process of expanding its effort to reach computer buyers in twelve major metropolitan markets, Dennis Carter's team had to vastly expand its scope, yet the core of people at its center remained very small. The evolving web also remained mutable and flexible, for the nature of the work kept changing as new tasks needed to be done. For example, Ann Lewnes, who had been brought in because of her writing skills, came up with the idea of starting an advisory board of Fortune 500 MIS directors. Intel would share information about what it was doing with these people under nondisclosure agreements, while they in turn would help Intel get a better idea of exactly what business users were going to want from their technology in the years ahead.

Ann Lewnes's effort, undertaken on her own initiative, proved valuable not only because of the information it developed, but because it provided a mechanism for developing ongoing relationships where none had existed. Learning from the success of this improvisation, Ann Lewnes then expanded her efforts, setting up first an advisory board of PC dealers, and then a network of people who were involved in various PC user groups. As her work with the advisory groups grew more demanding, she dropped other aspects of her tasks, evolving in the process a whole new job for herself.

Ric Giardina, an Intel lawyer who would later join Dennis Carter's team, points out that this sort of improvising has a long tradition at Intel. "You might find yourself on a multidisciplinary team that's doing something really new, something completely different from your regular divisional work. As you get more into it, the new work starts to feel more important, and you realize that your regular divisional job is interfering with what you're trying to do. So you go in and tell your divisional head you don't really have time to do your regular work anymore—he or she will listen, and more than likely let you go. At other companies, this would set off a big turf war, with your boss and the team leader both fighting for your time. What makes Intel different is that people actually care about what's best for the company as a whole. Plus most people here have worked in lots of different jobs inside the company, so it's hard to get stuck in the turf mentality."

As swat teams of sales people were assigned the task of developing specific markets for end users, the original core of people in Dennis Carter's web found themselves doing less execution and more training. At this point, Charlene Hama was drawn onto the team to coordinate the training. "We got Charlene involved," says Sally Fundakowski, "because she knew all the key people in field sales, this huge organization spread out all over the world. She's one of those people at Intel who's been around the place so long that she always knows who you need to bring in when you want some help." Charlene Hama says: "My expertise was with the field sales groups, and also with our major customers—I'd been in a group that worked directly with the OEMs. Plus, I had production experience, so I knew the people in the factories and the warehouses." In Ted Jenkins's definition, Charlene was someone whose strong relationships helped to counterbalance the effects of positional power within the organization.

* * *

The first national declaration that Intel intended to reach out to computer buyers came when the company ran a series of advertisements that became known as the Red X campaign. Dennis Carter's team worked with a small agency in Utah to develop an ad for general interest and business magazines. These were considered an unlikely venue for Intel, but the best way to build fast recognition for 386 technology among computer users outside the major markets where the swat teams were at work.

The Red X campaign announced in no uncertain terms that the days of the 286 microprocessor were over. The era of the 386, of "32-bitness" and massive upgradability, had arrived. The ad was clean, simple, and dramatic.   Premiering in *Business Week*, the two-page declaration created an immediate sensation. "People were horrified," recalls Dennis Carter. "They thought we were insane to announce that our own most successful product was obsolete. But we *had* to do something strong to get attention. And we certainly succeeded in that —there were editorials all over the place. *USA Today* actually ran one on the front page, denouncing what we had done as stupid."

What *USA Today* and the other editorialists were overlooking, of course, was that Intel was being driven to redefine its market by the relentless logic implicit in Moore's Law. For if the economics of high technology require that any given product must begin losing profitability as soon as it hits the market, then manufacturers must do the unthinkable and help hasten the demise of their own products *in proportion to how successful those products prove in the market.* Still, Intel was taking a gamble. Would the public feel manipulated by the company's open declaration that the technology it had been selling was out-of-date? Or would people be so persuaded of the advantages of the 32-bit microprocessor that they would overlook the manipulation?

Because the swat teams had established new lines of communication with PC buyers and dealers in major markets across the country, Intel was able to start getting feedback on the campaign with virtually no delay. "We had built up this great intelligence network," says Sally Fundakowski. "Within just a couple of weeks, we knew the ad campaign was having an enormous impact. People all over the country were beginning to change the way they bought PCs. They were becoming more sophisticated and demanding, thinking in terms of their future, as opposed to just their present, needs." The change was in some ways comparable to what happened in the 1960s when consumers began thinking of their audio systems in terms of upgradable components. That spelled an end to people walking into stores and simply asking for a "stereo," and then settling for a name brand because it was familiar, even though they had no idea of the quality or what its speakers could or could not do.

Both the swat teams and the Red X campaign proved successful in drawing attention to the new 32-bit technology, and computer users were soon pulling the market in its direction. In addition, the fact that Intel manufactured integrated circuits was becoming known to the general public, a recognition which would prove indispensable in the years ahead. Still, the very success of the end user marketing project was inadvertently sowing the seeds of a potential long-term disaster. For without quite being aware of the danger, Intel was building awareness for the value of the 386 microprocessor rather than for the company itself.

THE MEANING OF CLONES

By the summer of 1990, Dennis Carter's initial web had succceded in its objective: making the 386 chip as successful as the 286 had been in its day. "The whole world was 386," as people at Intel had begun to say. But by the late fall, a couple of smaller Silicon Valley ventures—Advanced Micro Devices, Cyrix, Chips & Technologies—had figured out how to approximate the workings, though not the design, of the 386. Within months, they were selling these "imitators," as they are called, at far below what Intel was able to charge, considering that the company had to recover the costs of developing the chip in the first place. As a result, over the course of the next year, Intel would lose nearly *half* the business it was doing on the chip that it had managed, after a large investment and the brilliant repositioning of its entire marketing strategy, to make the mainstay of its enterprise.

The imitators in no way tried to disguise that their products were modeled on Intel's; on the contrary, they announced it by incorporating the number 386 as part of their names. After all, Intel had poured the full range of its tremendous resources into making the number recognizable among computer users: why shouldn't the imitators try to benefit from that? And so it was that Intel, the market leader, found itself in a situation similar to that of IBM in the early eighties, when, after investing hundreds of millions in the development of a personal computer, it had to stand by and watch its market being taken away by IBM clones. As IBM had, Intel took its competitors to court, feeling it had an even stronger case, for the use by the clonemakers of the actual 386 number seemed a particularly clear infringement upon Intel's trademark.

Clones, or imitators, as Intel prefers to call them, are a phenomenon unique to the post-industrial world, which is why the word clone was never used until recent years. Knockoffs have always existed, of course, but in fact they are not clones, for a knockoff mimics only the outward *appearance* of an original, and usually does not do that with much sophistication. Because a substantial proportion of an industrial product's price is determined by the cost of raw materials and labor, a low-cost imitation is easily discerned. A Jaguar knockoff that uses a mass-produced engine with plastic parts instead of one assembled by hand from tempered steel is not a clone; nor is a laminate veneer cabinet that follows the lines and design of one fashioned from solid walnut. Any low-priced imitation of an industrial product must rely on low-priced component parts and shortcut labor, and thus is always compromised in obvious ways.

By contrast, a clone works in a way that mimics almost exactly the workings of the original product. As such, it can exist *only* when development costs are high but production costs are low. In microelectronics, the true cost of a product lies not in the raw materials that comprise it; sand, the substance of silicon chips, is always cheap. Nor is manufacturing costly, since computer-aided processes do most of the work. The real value of high-tech merchandise lies almost entirely in the cost of the knowledge that has gone into the fashioning of something that has never before existed in the world. The price for this knowledge is all paid up front, during the research and development phase, which is why high-tech products are expensive to invent but cheap to reproduce. It is this anomaly in pricing, in fact, that accounts for Moore's Law; because costs are low downstream, profits evaporate.

The challenge for the would-be imitator of a chip lies in discerning how the original is made; this is usually achieved by a process of reverse engineering. Starting with the close observation of how the original works, the imitator then *reasons backward* to discover what set of instructions might achieve the same results. The copyist can then approximate the encoded message that transmits the information on the original chip; the message need not be exact, so long as it *does* the same thing. Once an engraving has been made, a nearly exact copy of the original can be devised using the same inexpensive materials. And just as long as the operation rather than the code is imitated, the cloner is not necessarily in violation of the original producer's patents or copyrights.

Though unforeseen at the time it was formulated, the development of the clone lay implicit in the reverse economics of Moore's Law. And it is because of these reverse economics that high-tech companies like IBM and Intel are so swiftly punished for an inward focus that neglects the customer. IBM was brought low by its inability to define its customer precisely, and its unwillingness to learn from the webs that configured within its midst—in particular, the web that developed the PC and was then promptly reintegrated into the larger bureaucracy. Intel, unhindered by the bureaucratic legacy of the Industrial Era, appears to stand a greater chance of surviving the challenge posed by the imitators, for it has begun to incorporate the way of working that Dennis Carter's team improvised into the larger strategy of the organization. What Sally Fundakowski calls "the webster skills" that the group developed are now enabling the company to respond to the potential disaster that resulted from the triumph of the 386 marketing campaign.

The loss of nearly half of its market for the 386 microprocessor in 1990, though shocking, was only the start of Intel's problem with imitators. By the following spring, word was out that the copyists were only a year away from being able to imitate the 486 chip—a product that Intel would not even be introducing until that fall. It had taken the clonemakers nearly four years to figure out how to copy the 386; now, with that time on the verge of being drastically cut, the cost of producing the imitator chips would rapidly decline. As the chips grew cheaper, the incentive for original equipment manufacturers— Intel's old customers—to buy them would grow more intense.

Intel *had* to respond; the question was how. The manufacturer of products that are being cloned does not have many options. Since the company must recoup its research and development costs, it can never compete with the imitator on the basis of price. One of the few tactics open to the originator is to speed up product cycles, continually spawning new products at a rapid and unrelenting pace. This draws clonemakers into a perpetual game of catch-up: by the time their clones are ready for market, the products upon which they are based are about to become obsolete. In this way, the original manufacturer can hang on to its markets, but the cost is enormous, since its spending on research must proportionately increase.

Despite the dangers, in the early winter of 1991, Andrew Grove, declaring that "speed is all we have," announced a drastic program to shorten product cycles. Instead of waiting until one generation of chips was ready to bring to market before starting work on the next, Intel would develop successive generations almost simultaneously. Entirely new families of chips would be introduced every two years, some with as many as thirty variations, as a way of keeping the clonemakers at a perpetual disadvantage. In order to achieve this level of efficiency, the company would have to accentuate those aspects of its operations that emphasized coordination and cooperation. And so the web of inclusion that had configured in its midst would serve as a model.

THE WEB EVOLVES

Taking clonemakers to court, speeding up product cycles, and cutting prices were all defensive moves, and Intel took them. But the company had also to thrust decisively forward. This meant finding a way to convince customers that there were concrete advantages to buying Intel products, in terms of quality, reliability, and service—and doing so within the framework of the company's new definition of its customers. As had been true for 286 technology, computer manufacturers had no strong incentive to buy the premium-priced Intel chips unless computer buyers demanded that they do so.

Thus it soon became apparent that the web configured to reach out to end users had only begun its work. As Sally Fundakowski noted, Intel not only needed to create an identity for specific products; it also had to begin to do so for *itself*. In effect, this meant finding a way to represent itself to the general public as a premier manufacturer of what were essentially consumer products. Casting about for any kind of precedent in such a marketing attempt, Dennis Carter could find only one instance in which Intel had achieved anything like this kind of recognition. It occurred in Japan, where the subsidiary Intel Japan KK had launched a kind of corporate identity campaign.

In the Japanese market, curious and informed technology customers are eager to know precisely what components comprise the products that they buy. In order to inform them, Intel's Japanese subsidiary had encouraged the computer manufacturers who used its integrated circuits in that country to publicize the fact in their advertising. And so the rather awkward slogan "Intel In It" was affixed to ads for Japanese computers, English slogans having great cachet among Japanese consumers. In traveling to Japan, Dennis Carter found that even in the country's public transport system, colorful banners boasted of Intel's name. By piggybacking onto manufacturer's advertising, the company had become widely known without a great expenditure of money.

That this could be done rather easily in Japan reveals how essential aspects of that country's attitudes toward antitrust laws encourage cooperative ventures in a way that remains impossible in the United States. U.S. statutes make it difficult for companies that source or supply one another to achieve any communality of interests, to share advertising or promote one another's products. In Japan, similar laws exist, but are rarely enforced, because they conflict with the nation's deeper culture of encouraging and promoting long-term relationships. Intel Japan KK could permit some Japanese manufacturers to use its name without fear that other manufacturers would sue it for showing favor, because companies in Japan consider it disgraceful to take suppliers—or partners, as they prefer to call them—to court.

Still, Dennis Carter felt convinced that persuading U.S. manufacturers who used Intel components to advertise the fact would be the best way to establish the company in the public imagination. And so in February of 1991, he proposed to the Executive Staff that Intel offer a cooperative advertising deal in order to persuade the OEMs to make use of Intel's name. "I had no idea what they'd think," he says. "It was taking the end user marketing idea to the extreme, actually using the manufacturers to sell Intel to the general public. It was revolutionary and risky, but Andy Grove just looked at the plan and said, 'So, let's get started on this tomorrow!' "

By this time, End User Marketing had evolved into a whole department, with Sally Fundakowski at its head. In configuring the new web, Dennis Carter relied upon her and her staff, but gave the team a new shape to fit its mission. Once again, he had to borrow people from throughout the company, people who had flexibility in regard to their time. His first recruit was Pat Perry, who had previously been involved in training field sales engineers to work with OEMs. She had good contacts among the OEMs' marketing forces, and was also available for an assignment; her old job had just been reorged, and she was preparing to take a long sabbatical in the spring.

"I was at loose ends when Dennis called," Pat Perry recalls. "He was all excited about trying to do co-op advertising with our OEMs, which meant that they would put our name in their ads. The whole thing sounded strange to me—I figured, what was in it for the OEMs? Why should they use their ad dollars to promote an integrated circuit? But Dennis kept saying, *we're* the most important ingredient in a computer. When someone buys Dell, they're also buying Intel. And if they know we're the best, that can only help Dell."

Cindy Tsuyemura soon joined the group. "I came from marketing and communications," she explains, "but over the years I had developed this specialty of knowing about trademarks. I'm not sure how it happened—I had just hung around the legal department a lot, picking up bits of knowledge. Because I knew something about the subject, I saw early on that there had been problems in how we'd handled the 386. While we got recognition for the product, we didn't get any for Intel—we weren't *branded* as a company, as trademark people say. We did a good job of reaching out to the end user, but we hadn't realized all that was involved in marketing to the public. We were still in the learning stages. That was the basic thing about the group, we learned from our work as we did it."

Just as the new team members were starting to test how the OEMs felt about the co-op advertising idea, Intel's trademark suit against Advanced Micro Devices was rejected by the U.S. District Court in California. "Losing the trademark made it seem as if our campaign to develop awareness for 386 technology had been an absolute disaster," Sally Fundakowski says. "AMD and Cyrix were going to be the ones to benefit. So suddenly, the work our new team was doing seemed ten times more important than it had the week before. We had to start getting people to think of *us*, not our specific products—even though we'd just spent five million dollars getting them to think in terms of the 386!"

When the trademark was lost, Ric Giardina was pulled into the web. Ric had joined Intel only the year before, but had already determined that he wanted to change the way the legal department operated. "When it came to legal, the company was still too compartmentalized. There was no integration into the overall business process.

The business people made decisions, and then sent things down to us lawyers to check. We were the gatekeepers, the people who said no, which of course made everyone in the rest of the company resent us. It was like old-fashioned manufacturing, where you wait until the very end of the process to check for flaws."

Ric Giardina was already looking for ways to change the process in his own department. He had no mandate to do so, and, being new, not much positional power; still, he was determined to make a difference. That was why he had come to work at Intel in the first place; he had seen it as "the kind of place where you could create something on your own, be imaginative, really leave your mark." Now, joining Dennis Carter's group, he was being given a mandate to integrate legal and business processes within the context of a concrete situation, rather than first figuring out a strategy and then testing it. "We had this excruciating time element," Ric remembers. "We'd been hit by the clonemaker crisis, and we had failed to keep our trademark. That forced us to improvise, to learn as we went along." Ric now believes that the true utility of flexible web-like structures lies in their ability to integrate functions, and do so in a way that enables people to learn new skills in the process of expanding their jobs. Inevitably, because webs form around innovative projects, both the learning and doing are done under fierce constraints of time.

INTEL INSIDE

The newly configured web agreed that the phrase "Intel In It" sounded awkward in English, and decided instead to offer the slogan "Intel Inside" to computer manufacturers willing to participate in the new co-op advertising program. The arrangement would be similar to that pioneered by NutraSweet and Coca-Cola, under which Nutra-Sweet pays a portion of Coke's advertising costs and Coke features NutraSweet's name in its ads and on the Coke bottle itself, effectively making the soda an advertising vehicle for the sweetener.

The advantages of such a scheme would cut two ways for Intel and the computer manufacturers who participated. The computer makers would cut their ad budgets by getting Intel to subsidize a portion of their costs, and would also benefit from the implicit message that its internal components were of such high quality that they were worth advertising in themselves; no company was about to advertise that it was building computers based on clones. Intel in turn would garner vast recognition from the mass publicizing of its name, and would also establish its components as *the* quality product. As with NutraSweet, Intel microprocessors would become identified in the public mind as the premium article, the original, "the real thing."

The Intel Inside slogan would be represented as . Ric Giardina notes that "All of the specifications had to be exact, the size of the letters, everything, in order to maintain the integrity of the trademark." Once the symbol had been agreed on, the team had to go out and sell it to the computer manufacturers, a task made far easier by the lines of communication established by the earlier web. Sally Fundakowski recalls how the people at IBM immediately loved the Intel Inside slogan when it was proposed to them at a meeting in early 1991. "They asked us to get the program together in time for the spring campaign for their new personal computer, which was set to debut with a full-page ad in *The Wall Street Journal*. Of course, that sounded fabulous, but it was already the end of February, and the ad was set to run on April 22!"

The problem lay in complying with U.S. antitrust legislation. In order to offer the co-op advertising program to IBM, Intel had to make precisely the same offer to all its customers before the deadline for *The Wall Street Journal* ad. Says Sally Fundakowski, "Here we had just under nine weeks in which to develop the program, write the guidelines, do all this meticulous legal work, and then notify everyone in the world of what we were doing! And when I say everyone, I mean all the computer manufacturers who bought our chips, plus all the distributors of their products, plus all the circuitboard makers who sold to either. Some of these companies were very small, maybe two employees working in one outlet somewhere in a suburban mall. We barely knew who they were, or how to find them. But we had to track them all down and then make them all the same offer, or else let the IBM thing go."

Ric Giardina recalls: "Our team had to do everything at once. There was no time to devise any particular structure. We organized ourselves at weekly GYATs—that's the Intel name for unstructured meetings—it's short for 'get your act together,' and it implies *right away*. For the Intel Inside program, our GYATs would usually last three or four hours. We'd come together, decide what had to be done, and people would volunteer to take care of this or that. Then we'd go off in our own directions and work like crazy on our assignments, and come back and make a report at the GYAT the next week. It was all improvised, and we managed the process ourselves as we went along."

In management-by-GYAT, any semblance of specific job descriptions broke down. Everyone in the web assumed a wide variety of tasks. "It didn't matter whether someone came from marketing, communications, finance, training, or sales," says Ric Giardina. "Everyone did a little of everything. I was writing scripts for Andy Grove to do video presentations for the OEMs. I was selling ideas to the sales force, I was managing the business end—most of the time, you'd never know I was a lawyer." Sally Fundakowski adds, "We had no time to treat training as a separate part of what we were doing, because what we were doing was completely new. We had to train as we were learning, which meant that we all became trainers, teachers really. As we made up the process, we tried to impart what we learned."

Dennis Carter had formulated the strategy and championed it with the Executive Staff. But as the emphasis shifted to implementation, his active involvement diminished. Says Cindy Tsuyemura. "Once we started, I seldom even saw Dennis. He was the big-picture man. He knew how to impart an idea and then leave people alone. We had no time for formal reviews—if we needed something from Dennis, we just grabbed him in the hallway or the cafeteria and told him about it." Sally Fundakowski concurs. "Dennis was more a mentor than a boss. He didn't involve himself in the everyday workings of the group, or supervise us in any sense. Mainly, he set the parameters for what we were trying to do and offered guidance on specific problems. He was also our advocate, our godfather in the company. He got the Executive Staff so excited about our project that it became the key to the company's whole marketing strategy. That helped us commandeer the resources we needed."

Commandeering resources was crucial. For one thing, co-op advertising involves huge amounts of money—Intel was splitting the costs on an enormous campaign. Also, the web, in order to function around a small core of people, had to make large demands—on the legal staff, the marketing department, and the sales force. Commandeering resources also meant commandeering time, drawing people from throughout the company as they were needed. One major characteristic of the Intel Inside web was its flexibility—it expanded and contracted to suit specific needs. The core of four—Ric, Sally, Pat Perry, and Cindy—grew to eight or even twelve, and then contracted again, depending upon what needed to be done. Some of the core members still retained other responsibilities. Says Ric Giardina: "I was still supposed to be supporting the software organization with legal work—that was my divisional job. But I was spending all my time with Carter's team. So after a while, I told my division head that I didn't have time for my regular job, and he let me go."

As customers were located and backup materials developed, Dennis Carter stepped back in; together with Pat Perry, he made the presentations on Intel Inside to the company's major customers. Recalls Pat Perry: "Our goal was to get maximum feedback from our biggest customers as soon as we could, before going full-bore ahead." Based on reactions from customers like NCR and Dell, Pat then began training the sales force to make more presentations. Legally, Intel was obligated to offer the co-op ad program worldwide, in Europe and Asia-Pacific. "I was key there," says Pat Perry, "because I had great worldwide contacts. That came from my being in corporate sales and marketing for seven years." As Ted Jenkins noted, the stability of Intel's workforce and the fact that most people have held a variety of positions were useful in widening the web's pool of contacts.

As the deadline for *The Wall Street Journal* ad approached, Janice Wilkins, a controller and administrator, joined the Intel Inside web as Program Manager. "I came in at the height of activity," she recalls. "We were learning very rapidly, everyone doing a little of everything, but none of us realized the potential scope of the program. We thought we had about five hundred customers, and we had somewhere in the three thousand range! We also didn't realize how eager people would be to participate—acceptance was quick and eager, which made things even more chaotic. My role was to structure that chaos, to try to set up orderly procedures, and to make sure our assets were protected."

A number of times, Janice Wilkins pushed to bring in an outside consultant to give the web a reality check. "But the team vetoed it. They felt it went against Intel's culture—it's the *norm* here to trust your gut and take your chances, and they didn't think an outsider would understand that. I had confidence in them, so I backed off." Janice Wilkins admits that, as Program Manager and someone who was used to looking after the company's money, she was less comfortable with improvising than the others on the team. "But that was part of my role. If the effort was really going to be successful, we were going to have to get beyond the improvising stage. For one thing, there was so much money involved!"

The Intel Inside web managed to notify all the company's customers in time to permit Intel to participate in IBM's *Wall Street Journal* ad. After it appeared, other computer manufacturers began expressing strong interest in joining Intel's co-op program. According to Janice Wilkins, "Seeing our logo in print really made other customers want to sign up for the program. That was much more persuasive than getting a letter from us. So very quickly, Intel Inside began to take off. It was something people wanted to be part of."

By the end of the summer of 1992, the company's cash was flowing into co-op ads that appeared in mainstream newspapers and business magazines; within months, "Intel Inside" had become a mark of quality recognized by computer buyers. In the spring of

1993, the campaign was extended to television, and soon the company was moving ahead with a co-op program to affix Intel Inside labels on the boxes in which its customers' computers were sold. Thus had Intel developed an entirely new approach to marketing that had transformed it into a high-tech consumer products company with a strong identity among and direct ties to the general public.

In the process of effecting this transformation, the Intel Inside web had created a continuum of links that fulfilled Regis McKenna's definition of "evolutionary" marketing as "marketing that integrates a company's customers, sourcers, and suppliers into a single system, a coherent process." Only by achieving this level of integration, which truly recognizes a commonality of interests, can an organization hope to "own its market," McKenna points out. Owning the market means defining it, setting the standards for its operation, and expanding or narrowing it in order to suit the organization's evolving needs. Only by owning its market can a company hope to achieve the kind of substantial earnings that enable it also to take the leadership role in research and development.

As McKenna also points out, Japanese companies over the last two decades have been particularly successful in achieving ownership of their markets through use of *keiretsu,* those clusters of affiliated companies that band together for mutual advantage. The acceptance of interrelatedness implicit in the *keiretsu* structure has given many Japanese companies their edge in pricing, flexible supply, and service, the accent on relationships being the key to survival in today's complex and interrelated world. The individualistic heritage of many American organizations—a heritage reinforced by our outmoded anti-trust laws—has tended to work against such cooperation, leaving U.S. companies to find other strategies for transcendence. The evolving web that grew out of Dennis Carter's early efforts to reach out directly to computer users helped the company achieve this kind of transcendence, strengthening its market ownership in the face of imitators. In effect, the web created an inclusive feedback loop among

Intel and its customers and suppliers that replicated the essentials of the *keiretsu* structure.

"THE PROCESS OF CHANGE IS NOT LIKE AN INK STAIN"

Once the co-op advertising venture had been established, the Intel Inside web began its inevitable evolution into a full-fledged program, administered and structured along more conventional lines. The days of four-hour GYATs were over, and those who had formed the very core of the web began to assume other roles, though their work had transformed not only the company's notion of why it was in business, but the nature of the team members' jobs as well.

Ric Giardina, having given up his divisional job, set to work on a multidivisional team whose mission was to assure that naming and branding was integrated into the product development process, instead of being tacked on at the end. The work he did in the web transformed him into a lawyer with an acknowledged specialty in trademarks and copyrights. Cindy Tsuyemura, who now reports to Sally Fundakowski, spends the majority of her time with Ric, having also developed her expertise. Pat Perry took over the network of corporate MIS directors that Ann Lewnes had originally set up. Under Pat, the informal effort has become a worldwide program with ten full-time employees that works with technology experts at all the Fortune 500 companies. The unit serves both as a resource for research and development, and as a means of contact between Intel and major technology customers. Charlene Hama put her connections at the factories to use, overseeing the effort to put Intel Inside stickers on computer boxes. And Dennis Carter moved from being Andrew Grove's special assistant to the newly created position of Vice President of Corporate Marketing, from which he guides Intel's effort to reconceptualize itself as a presence in the consumer market rather than a maker of high-tech components.

"The process of change is not like an ink stain," Ric Giardina reflects. "It's not something that starts in one place and then spreads all around. It's more like a lot of little splatters that keep getting bigger and bigger, and then some of them come together and co-alesce." He views the Intel Inside effort, the Red X campaign, and the early attempt to reach out to end users as such splatters: the way they came together changed Intel's very notion of why it is in business. He points out that Intel has always had a tradition of task-oriented teams, but believes that the inclusive and permeable structure of the more recent webs has taken that propensity much further, encouraging a level of integration that has made the company more web-like, more inclusive and permeable as a whole.

The blurring of job descriptions, the nonhierarchical way of assigning tasks, the total dedication of the team: all these aspects of the Intel Inside effort made it comparable to what occurs in high-reliability organizations when they are confronted with stress. Although such organizations tend to be profoundly hierarchical in ordinary circumstances, the chain of command dissolves when tensions run high and physical danger becomes a factor; then everyone works together as specialists on an equal footing in an intensely collegial atmosphere. One of the challenges for business organizations is to find ways to sustain this process when mortal, physical danger is not a threat. The Intel Inside web managed to achieve this because the larger organization is geared toward giving people an extraordinary measure of flexibility and independence in normal times.

Cindy Tsuyemura captures the essence of what it is about Intel's culture that enables rapid and flexible response. "Certain things were very important to our team's success. To begin with, all of us, while we are very much individuals, also share certain qualities in common. We are not just experts in one area, but are knowledgeable about Intel as a whole. We've been around, worked for lots of people, so we know who to go to to get what we need, in terms of resources, champions, trainers, information, technology. Plus, we're all the kind of people who don't have preconceived ideas about what we'll do and what we won't: we'll stuff binders, draft a document, drive a customer to a factory. Our attitude is always, just get the job done. We don't worry about who does what, or who gets the credit, because we aren't always looking over our shoulder, wondering if we're pleasing our boss."

Cindy believes that total team efforts work better at Intel than at most companies—"certainly better than anywhere I've ever worked" —because the company makes an effort to hire people who are strong, assertive, and opinionated. "Most organizations *say* they want strong people, but they don't know what to do with them. What they're really looking for is people who'll go along. They think go-along types will be better at teamwork, but this isn't true, because people who don't have strong beliefs don't have that much to contribute. They lack a sense of urgency, of commitment. Here at Intel, there's a mystique around individualists, people who are very vocal and verbal, people with strong opinions about how to get things done. These are the only kind of people who'll fight for a project, do whatever's necessary to get it through. Intel looks for that kind of person in the first place. Then also, they know how to keep them. They understand that strong individuals need to be left *alone,* need to work the way they want to, instead of always being questioned or forced to give an accounting. When you're free, you can move quickly, which is a great incentive to assertive people. In my experience, assertive people won't stick around if they don't feel free to *move.*"

As success transformed the "renegade effort" that so attracted Sally Fundakowski into a full-scale co-op marketing program, the creativity that had characterized its evolution had its effect on the company as a whole. But what about the program itself? Would it remain flexible and creative now that its responsibilities and purposes had been spelled out? Certainly, that fluidity was tested in December 1994, when the Pentium Processor crisis hit and waves of customers began demanding replacements because of a flaw that turned up in an obscure algorithm. Intel was unprepared for the intense publicity that discovery of the flaw occasioned, which resulted directly from its focus on marketing to consumers. Ric Giardina and other "websters," as Sally called them, were pulled together on a multilevel team that met twice daily for six weeks. Their decision to replace the processors on demand seemed to satisfy the press and the public, though ironically doing so will probably only strengthen Intel, since its imitators will hardly have the budget to offer to replace minor flaws in the future.

The real question for Intel Inside remains, what will happen as the crisis recedes and the program becomes institutionalized. Carlene Ellis, from her position as Vice President of Organization, worries about it. "I've been on projects," says Carlene, "that were done very much on the wing—flexible, innovative, everyone working together with tremendous focus. But then they grew and grew, and suddenly you couldn't see the outer limits: you couldn't get your vision wrapped around all that was going on. In a way, the whole issue with teams comes down to a question of peripheral vision: how can you grow a project in such a way that you can still see its outer limits—or beyond? Because when a project gets too big, your vision starts to scatter at the outer edges. And people don't really feel like a part of something if they can't see it whole."

This problem of growth is exacerbated when the way a unit works changes in response to its size, Carlene has observed. "The real disjunction arises when what has been a step function goes linear. A web operates by steps, by jumps—there's no fixed process yet. You're developing your process as you go along, which means you're on a learning curve all the time. But what if the web needs to double or increase to three times its size? That's not a natural act." Carlene reverts to her basketball metaphor. "It all comes down to, how do you change from basketball to football? When you're in the web, you're playing NBA rules, improvising. Then all of a sudden you've got to expand, so you have to put in processes and controls. You get a quarterback, and suddenly everyone's role is defined—who can carry the ball, who runs interference. Those sort of definitions break the web apart: the cohesion of the small group is gone. You're back to bureaucracy, which is about definition. You move from learning to training."

Carlene thinks that "the answer may lie in how the web is spun, by which I mean integrated into the larger whole." If the organization of which the web is a part is itself fluid, the web can send out new radials and axes as it grows, retaining flexibility and subdividing into manageable size. "The key is to keep change a constant throughout the larger organization, so process is always being improvised. And I see that starting to happen in organizations now. The technology is pushing us in that direction. The speed of the technology demands you constantly innovate, and that in turn pushes you to improvise. So the old quarterback-style division of labor becomes obsolete: the rules of football don't allow for much improvisation!

"I sense this profound change coming in how people are going to be doing their work. It has to do with building innovation into everyone's daily process. I see it happening at high-tech companies here in the Valley, although it doesn't have strictly to do with high tech. It's more the fact that the technology is forcing us to perform all our actions in real time. People have real-time information to respond to —it's right there on the screen—which means they have to react to situations as those situations are taking place. We all saw it happening with Desert Storm: real time drove it, you could watch it unfold, and everyone in the field had to react, to improvise their responses. I do think this is why the metaphors we're starting to use now—the web, and I also like the amoeba—are all organic images. Real time forces you to organize structures that are more reflective of how life actually works. And once we start reflecting life, we have to let go of all those false barriers that were built in when work reflected the machine. Real time means that nothing can happen behind closed doors, because everyone has access to information. In our organizations, we're moving toward the essence of participatory democracy."

FOUR

Dealing with Diversity: the Miami Herald

Diversity programs have become a kind of growth industry in American companies over the past decade. Changes in the makeup of our society, and in the nature of work itself, have made the assimilation of people from wildly various backgrounds into a common culture a major concern for many organizations. Assimilation was once a task left to the public schools; today, it increasingly occurs in the workplace. And yet to speak in terms of assimilation is no longer really correct.

The past few decades in America have been characterized as "the age of redefinition," in which we have continually broadened our definition of who counts in society, who can and should make decisions, who is part of our democracy, even who deserves respect. This reevaluation, which began in the 1960s with the civil rights movement, has emboldened people who were formerly considered outsiders—blacks, women, immigrants, sexual minorities—to press for the recognition that their outsider heritage possesses a value that, expressed and preserved, can help the organizations of which they themselves are a part to thrive. The desire to conform to a single model—implicit in earlier assimilation efforts—no longer exists; in a society as complex as ours, there can be no single model. A global workforce and a global marketplace, increasingly comprised of people born outside the United States, have rendered the concept obsolete.

The changes wrought by this social evolution are reinforced by the changes in the kind of work that most people do, which increasingly requires them to interact with complex technology. People who do so cannot simply show up, punch in, and fulfill a specific number of tasks in order to do an acceptable day's work; as Henry Mintzberg has observed, this approach is fine if your task is to carry pig iron, but not if you do work that requires a brain. In order to think effectively and well, people must feel involved and committed to what they are doing. Persuading those who have in the past felt as if they were outsiders to take this attitude of involvement is difficult but essential; it is in fact *the* fundamental goal of diversity programs at their best.

Those who feel ownership in their work tend to take a broad view of the potential and problems of their organization, rather than viewing everything from the perspective of their own department or division. Thus breaking down barriers between different groups within an organization also provides an opportunity to break down barriers within the organization itself, restructuring it to be less rigid and hierarchical. Those who formerly saw their interests as unrelated or marred by destructive rivalries can discover common links, find points of connection as they broaden their concerns. Thus diversity in its broadest sense implies not only an alteration in who gets to be part of the structure, *but in the shape and workings of the structure itself.*

This merely points up the absurdity of efforts intended to make an organization more inclusive that are either compartmentalized within a single department, such as Human Resources, or based upon a series of exercises devised by an outside consultant. Because an appreciation for diversity is inseparable from inclusiveness, an effective program must be organic, specific to the culture, reflective of the purposes for which the enterprise exists, and integrated into the overall process of work. The effort must be structured in such a way that it provides new and significant points of connection that bring former outsiders into the decision-making loop, widens the scope of their access, and increases their control over the direction, purpose, and rhythm of their work. If diversity does not transform the way an organization works as a whole, it quickly degenerates into a numbers game ("we need one woman and one Hispanic to fill those slots"), and becomes a focus both for resentment and company-wide jokes.

Because of their decentralized form, their permeability, and their ability to create links across divisions, webs of inclusion provide precisely the kind of grassroots structure that can make diversity programs work. Such webs may develop within a department or division, but given the disregard in which the issue of diversity is often held by those who fear they may lose power, or who view it as a "soft" or do-gooder concern, these webs need strong and patient support from the top. It is in a profound paradox that determined and authoritative leadership is required for an effort that, at its best, will decisively dilute centralized and top-down power, thus making an organization more reflective both of how today's technology functions and how Americans live and work today.

CRISIS AT THE MIAMI HERALD

At the Miami Herald, a series of webs of inclusion have evolved over the past two years that have enabled the paper to achieve greater diversity within its ranks and its leadership. This has enabled the paper to speak with greater credibility for a community of readers and advertisers so diverse that it looks now the way America will look in a decade. By creating links and alliances between those who formerly had little contact with one another, these webs have also permitted the paper to respond to major and threatening crises in ways that parallel those of a high-reliability organization. This ability has proved crucial during the last two years as the company has been hit with a series of events so potentially crippling that many an organization would have folded under the pressure.

The crises included a depression in the newspaper business in which advertising revenue fell by an average of twenty percent; anger among certain elements of the local Cuban exile community so severe that they culminated in death threats and vandalism; and the catastrophe of Hurricane Andrew. There could indeed be no better example of the role crisis plays in spurring meaningful change than the *Miami Herald* in recent years. Nor could there be a better example of how a strong diversity effort, by breaking down internal barriers, can unleash the kind of strong and concerted action needed to deal with unexpected events. "If the hurricane had occurred before we started to change how we did things, we could never have responded like we did," says Joe Natoli, the *Herald*'s Director of Production. Adds Chris Mobley, the Associate Publisher for the Broward County edition: "The storm put us to this huge test. Were we going to be a bunch of competing fiefdoms like we'd always been in the past, or were we really going to get together and make things work?"

The *Miami Herald* is the flagship paper of the Knight-Ridder group of twenty-nine newspapers across the United States. The *Herald* shares its headquarters with its corporate parent at One Herald Plaza, a wide, low building of early sixties vintage set on the waterfront just off Biscayne Boulevard, adjoining the MacArthur causeway as it leads out to South Beach. Having begun publishing in 1910, the *Herald* has long been considered one of the nation's best newspapers, as well as the best newspaper in the South. Its coverage of both local and international events has garnered it fourteen Pulitzers and countless other prizes.

The paper serves not only Miami, but the whole South Florida metropolitan area, encompassing Dade, Broward, and Palm Beach counties, as well as Monroe, which threads south to include the Keys. The *Herald* maintains major bureaus throughout Central and South America and in the Caribbean, and specializes in coverage of the region. It also publishes a Spanish-language edition, *El Nuevo Herald*, which covers community and international events of particular interest to Hispanic readers, and features separate opinion pages and columnists. Altogether, the *Herald* employs 2,500 people and has a circulation of more than 400,000 daily and 500,000 on Sundays.

Inclusiveness is a word you hear a lot these days if you roam the halls of One Herald Plaza, particularly since the hurricane, which hurled its fury upon South Florida in August of 1992. And yet inclusiveness has always been a particularly difficult value to instill at a large metropolitan daily, where factionalism is institutionalized, seemingly built into the process. The news side and the financial side of newspaper operations tend to reflect opposing cultures, the first built upon the pursuit of truth, the other upon the pursuit of profit. When the situation is at its worst, newsroom people tend to view those on the business side as lowly money-grubbers who threaten the independence of the paper with unseemly considerations of what advertisers might think, while those on the business side view newsroom denizens as hopeless prima donnas, living in an unreal world that allows them to overlook the fact that their paychecks come from advertising dollars.

These cultural differences are exacerbated by the way in which most newspapers operate. For with the exception of a few insiders being trained for top positions, few people at a paper have the opportunity to gain both editorial and business experience. Indeed, the editorial and business divisions usually occupy different floors in the building, and the people who work in the two divisions rarely even see one another, except at office holiday parties. Not only do they seem to have little in common to begin with, but institutional loyalties and structures drive them further apart.

The conflict does serve a specific purpose, however, for it works as a tool to ensure the independence of the news operation. Vic Bubnow, a key *Herald* executive, views the traditional antagonism as understandable and even useful, but also notes that a severe financial crunch can exacerbate its negative aspects. "The divisiveness between business and editorial is in many ways formal and intentional, and in normal times, I guess that's fine," he says. "It used to be, we'd work out the budget here in finance, figure out how much the news operation needed to spend, and then raise advertising rates to accommodate what was needed."

In the late eighties, however, the recession put an end to this mode of operation. "You could no longer just pass cost increases along. Advertisers got more demanding, and you had to keep rates down if you wanted to stay competitive. Balancing the budget began to mean finding ways to trim costs, which left everyone to fight over a smaller and smaller piece of the pie. When that happened, the old divisiveness degenerated into real hostility—people had no feeling for one another's problems because they didn't know how to talk to one another. There were no channels in the paper for communication across divisions, so any sense of common interest just disappeared."

Thus by the end of the eighties, interdepartmental antagonisms had reached the breaking point at the *Herald*. "It was a bad environment," Vic recalls. "You couldn't work well. And beyond that, it was no way to *live*." The only solution was to break down the divisiveness, "to somehow get everyone thinking and acting as a team." But achieving this seemed almost impossible, for the company was divided into functionally independent units that were just as rigid as the old "chimney" system had been in Detroit and were reinforced by an even longer tradition.

Added to the structural problem was the increasing Balkanization of employees so characteristic of late eighties corporate life. Women at the paper were furious that, with a single exception, no woman had ever held a top leadership position; homosexuals were demanding the right to insurance for their partners. The people at *El Nuevo* felt that Hispanics were treated as second-class citizens; their main newsroom wasn't even in the One Herald Plaza building, but out in a semi-remote Hispanic neighborhood. Nor was the Hispanic community itself united, but undergoing rapid change; no longer solely Cuban, it was increasingly Colombian, Venezuelan, Nicaraguan, Salvadoran. All these groups were demanding a greater share in the action; as the pie shrank, bickering over portions grew more bitter. Roberto Suarez, who had arrived from Knight-Ridder's *Charlotte Observer* at the founding of *El Nuevo Herald* in 1987, recalls that the *Herald* upon his arrival was "like an armed camp—just tremendous antagonisms."

And so two things came together at the *Miami Herald* in the late eighties to make life there difficult: the tradition of divisiveness that characterizes newspapers in general had become unworkable because of the ongoing financial crisis; at the same time, the divisiveness was being exacerbated by the growing impatience of those who had long been outsiders to break open the power structure that they believed controlled the paper. The lack of communication between groups and factions, the absence of structures that could link or bring them together, were putting strains on people at every level.

Chris Mobley, the Broward Associate Publisher, sums up the atmosphere. "I came up through the newsroom. By the late eighties, I'd finally reached the inner circle, which is where I had always wanted to be. But the feelings among people at the paper were so hostile that I just looked around and thought—I've worked long, hard hours to get to *this?*" What most disturbed Chris was "the environment of good-old-boyism—that kind of backslapping culture that's supposed to grease the wheels but in fact just keeps the wheels stuck. Its only real purpose is to keep people on the outside feeling as outside of things as possible, so the insiders can all feel good about themselves."

"It's up to Me to Insist on Change"

Into this contentious atmosphere walked David Lawrence, who assumed the publisher's job at the *Herald* in 1989. Dave Lawrence is a big man with a Southern accent, who was born and raised on a farm as one of nine children. Youthful though white-haired at fifty-two, handsome yet rumpled and a bit forgetful, he exhibits the distracted yet passionate air of a visionary: he's a great talker, but also clearly a sensitive listener. It pleased him greatly to return to Florida to take leadership of the *Herald* after a career in journalism that had taken him all over the United States.

Dave Lawrence's previous job had been Publisher of the *Detroit Free Press,* which is also a Knight-Ridder paper. His tenure coincided with the *Free Press*'s petitioning the Supreme Court to permit it to consolidate its advertising and circulation departments with those of the Gannett chain's *Detroit News,* so that both papers could remain in business despite the city's shrinking economic and population base. During that difficult three-year tenure, when the entire staff of two thousand had to live with the daily uncertainty of whether the paper would survive, Dave Lawrence got his education in how to deal with people in a divisive situation. "The big thing I learned during that time was that, if a company is in crisis, it is essential that you be completely open with your staff. That's the only way you can keep the place from being overwhelmed by rumors. You cannot be secretive *at all* about issues that affect their lives because they immediately perceive that as unfair, and it disturbs them to the point that they can't do their work."

When Dave Lawrence arrived at the *Herald,* he had already established a national reputation not only as a strong editor and leader, but as an industry firebrand on the subject of diversity. He had given blistering speeches around the country about how poorly newspapers were doing in this regard, and would continue to do so in his position as President of the American Society of Newspaper Editors. He viewed diversity as inseparable from "simple fairness." And from experience he understood that fairness—its institution and perception— was the most effective way to deal with divisiveness in an organization. Fairness would thus become his primary means for dealing with the negative atmosphere that had been evolving at the *Herald,* as people fought over a shrinking share of what had once been an expanding pie.

Dave Lawrence is careful to make it clear, however, that for him diversity does not mean quotas. "You will never hear me say, the next person for a particular job will be of this ethnic group or that gender. I believe doing that would be immoral, insulting to anyone—minority or otherwise—with talent, and it would certainly undermine overall morale. Besides, I'm not a social engineer." Still, he says he feels a strong responsibility to get people who have been outsiders into positions where they can assume leadership in the organization—not only by hiring them, but by creating opportunities that enable them to broaden their reach, scope, and experience and thus advance. "And when I say leadership, I mean decision-making, I don't mean funny-farm titles or pointless positions that have been devised to give the impression that you're moving ahead in this area. You see that sort of thing done all the time, but it's always false and dishonest, and everyone in the company knows it and disrespects it."

As the leader, he believes, "it's up to me to insist on change. And I have to insist strongly if it's ever going to happen. This is not going to be a painless effort, you can't kid yourself on that—pluralism *does* mean we'll see fewer white guys when we look around. That upsets people—you hear it in our pressroom, where Joe Natoli promoted a young woman to be Assistant Manager. He did it because she had talent and he wanted to give her a chance, and she could bring new ideas to an area that needed innovation. She's the only woman in that kind of position, but that threatens some people, who see that some kind of barrier has been breached. You'll hear guys saying, 'I guess I have to wear a skirt to get a promotion around here.' That's going to happen, certain men *are* going to feel they're losing out."

For Dave Lawrence, encouraging diversity is inseparable from developing a less hierarchical structure for the organization; again, he has no illusions that achieving this will be simple. "Anyone who's tried it will tell you, it's *easier* to run an organization in a top-down hierarchical style—it's quicker, cleaner, and much more efficient. That's why people continue to cling to it, especially when things get rough. With the top-down approach, you don't have to get buy-in from people in order to do something. If people *don't* buy in, you just tell them to do it anyway." Still, he believes that, in the long run, this kind of efficiency is ultimately self-defeating. "If people don't feel they're participating in the decisions that affect them, they'll never really give you their best effort. Also, you just plain miss too much information when you as leader are focused on telling people what to do instead of asking them what they think."

In any case, Dave Lawrence believes that the most important point is that the old top-down style *just plain does not work anymore.* "People are different now—they'll leave if they don't like how they're treated, and this is especially true of younger people. They're not in awe of authority like they used to be, they're not afraid of the boss— they tend to trust their own instincts and be more independent. There's also a huge change in the workplace because more women are in it. It means that *everyone*—not just women, but men as well—is more conscious of how his or her work will affect their home life. They won't stand for certain things, like too much stress, terrible hours. They're concerned about its effect on their families. This is a big shift in priorities, a real revolution in values, and people in leader- ship positions are going to have to deal with it."

Because of this revolution, Dave Lawrence has come to believe that he can run a better newspaper only by including people at every level of the organization in the decisions that directly affect how they do their work. This means cutting across the boundaries that divide people according to function or rank, and creating alternate structures that ensure everyone direct access to those they need to reach. This process, which Dave Lawrence describes as "fragile and alien to how most companies work," enables people at the grass roots to acquire unaccustomed allies at the top, and to gain concrete experience in confronting major organizational problems. It also provides grass- roots contacts for those in high positions who might have been iso- lated and so cut off from important information. These alternate structures that cut across divisions parallel the alternate power centers that Ted Jenkins noted had a long history at Intel. But at the *Herald,* the very nature of the culture and history worked against them.

AN EMOTIONAL, SOULFUL EXPERIENCE

At the *Miami Herald,* the webs configured specifically in order to help the paper achieve greater diversity also played *the* vital role in forging common interests across divisions that had formerly eyed one another with suspicion. Chief among these was the web formed in the fall of 1991 to examine the issue of how people in the company were treated with regard to fairness. The idea for the effort had originated at the grass roots, when a staffer in the training department, Julia Mast, had sent a dense three-page memo to Dave Lawrence outlining steps for "Project Diversity."

Julia Mast was convinced that the key to achieving pluralism was for management to listen to and learn from employees; she believed if "diversity experts" were brought in from outside, this would never happen. Management first needed to find out "what it's like to work here" for most people in the organization, and then address employee concerns based on that. She also emphasized that meaningful change would not take place as a result of training programs or committees, but would require real growth on the part of people throughout the company. The issue of diversity, she wrote, "brings forth profound issues of loss, personal values and belief systems, acceptance, self-esteem, anger, fear, uncertainty, power and control. You know full well the gut-wrenching pain around all this."

Julia Mast later left the company, but her memo provided the impetus and the blueprint for major change, inspiring Dave Lawrence to ask two staffers to lead a Task Force on Fairness in the Workplace. Although commissioned from the top, this task force came to qualify as a true web of inclusion because of the freedom with which its members pursued their mission, the openness with which they confronted painful and controversial issues, and the channels they created in the process of bringing these issues to everyone's attention. By broadening the range of people making decisions, while giving them more control over defining their work, the task force developed into an alternate center of power, redefining how issues would be addressed at the *Miami Herald.*

Sue Reisinger, Managing Editor of the *Herald*'s Broward edition and co-chair of the group, recalls: "Our original purpose was to address problems faced by women, who were disgusted by the lack of women in senior management. But very quickly, others in the group—there were twenty-three of us altogether—began bringing up other issues that they thought deserved attention. Some involved other subgroups—gays or older people, who felt underrepresented, undervalued, even threatened. And some were specific issues that might seem trivial on their own, but had great symbolic importance in terms of fairness."

The group set their task as "finding out just how people felt they were treated at the paper, what they resented, and what would make them feel more valued in the organization." Members began the effort by canvassing the entire staff, asking everyone to fill out detailed and confidential questionnaires on issues related to fairness—in pay and promotion, job satisfaction, the distribution of perks, harassment. "We tried to be very specific in our questions," says Sue, "so that people could be blunt about what needed to change. And we told them to bring up anything—nothing was off-limits.

"For example, we found tremendous resentment over the issue of who got reserved parking spaces. These had always gone to senior management, but now people had begun to question why that was. You had all these guys parking in the building, while pregnant women had to trudge across open lots—people didn't like what it implied." This is the kind of trivial yet emotionally fraught issue that organizations usually will not address; top managers will say, "The issue is diversity, what does that have to do with parking?" But the *Herald* had framed the diversity issue in terms of simple fairness, and permitted grassroots concerns to set the agenda. Since parking rules came up as an issue, the organization had to address them.

Once the task force had identified issues of concern to people, they published the raw data from the surveys, posting it all over the building. This was done to show that the process was absolutely open;

there would be no weeding out of controversial or uncomfortable material in order to make the study more palatable to senior management. The fact that everything was published, Sue Reisinger notes, "made people in the company really believe we were serious about hearing what they didn't like."

Sue's strong initial misgivings about the project reflected not only her doubts about whether the paper could deal honestly with the issue of fairness, but also the divisiveness that had characterized the *Herald* in its armed camp phase. As a managing editor and journalist, Sue was fiercely loyal to the news side of the organization, and Dave Lawrence had asked Vic Bubnow, Vice President for Finance, to co-chair the task force with Sue. This disturbed her: "I just didn't see how we could work well together, or share any philosophy or values in common. In my mind, Vic's chief role was to keep an eye on the bucks, and that made him my antagonist. I didn't know him. I hadn't worked with him, and didn't really know people who had. I didn't see any basis for me to trust him at all."

At first, the task force seemed too large and unwieldy. Says Sue: "There were too many issues, everyone with their own pet project. At the beginning, Dave Lawrence had said, just get back to me with five doable things, but I quickly saw that was not going to work. There were too many areas that needed attention, which made things seem chaotic, unfocused. At first, we had these huge, unstructured weekly meetings, with everyone holding forth on their favorite topic. I wondered how we'd ever get anything done, especially since people came from all over the company, were very different, often barely knew one another, and had no experience working in this unstructured way."

The group decided to break up into subgroups that would deal with specific issues—parking, older employees, women, homosexuals, promotion policies. Each subgroup would work on its own, and then report its progress at the weekly meeting of the task force as a whole. The minutes from these meetings would then be posted in the halls, so that people could see the work as it went along. "Because it was so open," says Sue, "you didn't have the usual surprises. Everyone knew exactly what was going on." Most obvious was that the project was expanding its scope and improvising its methods as it went along, exercising autonomy in its interpretation of its mission.

Over time—and it took lots of time, with task force members meeting weekly for more than six months—extraordinary transformations began to take place. "First of all," says Sue Reisinger, "I think what made things start to happen was that the subcommittees did all this tremendous and very professional research. They didn't just make statements—they went out and dug up facts people had never known about the paper, or at least had never quantified." Findings were very specific—for instance, the fact that with one exception, women who held management positions at the paper were all single and childless or had husbands who worked at home.

The research began to range more widely, as members of the subgroups took it upon themselves to study what people in other companies were doing to address particular concerns. "People took their work so *seriously*. They would call other newspapers to find out what they were doing—all on their own initiative. Someone heard about how these open staff meetings were run at Montefiore Medical Center in the Bronx, and interviewed the people involved to get more data. We, *all* of us, began to find ourselves in these intense conversations with all kinds of people, about where they worked, how their workplace functioned, and how they felt about it. We started thinking in very big, very imaginative ways." The research, carried out on a grassroots level, was of a quality that companies pay hundreds of thousands of dollars to commission from outside consultants. "But it was *our* information, *we* got it. And people around here were very proud of the fact."

Another reason the task force began to work, according both to Sue and Vic Bubnow, was that a number of members were very strong in their views; they were the rabble-rousers at the paper. "It was the kind of thing," says Vic, "where you had the loudest voices for whatever cause heading up the committees, so that everyone in the company knew that the effort was real, and nothing was going to get swept under the rug. Frankly, I didn't think it was going to work. I thought having that level of intensity would be too divisive—I couldn't see how all these people with all these hot buttons could even begin to work out consensus opinions. It seemed like an intimidating and uncomfortable process. And, believe me, it was!"

Yet Vic believes this very uncomfortableness was crucial to the task force's success, because it forced everyone to confront the issues on a personal level. "Like me, for instance. I thought I understood a lot about why women got discouraged, or how gays felt discriminated against. But I didn't understand these things at all, I'd just read about them in some management books. Remember, *I'm from finance,* so I didn't have a high comfort level dealing with this stuff—it seemed alien, not a real part of business. But I had these incredible experiences, listening to people, hearing what they had to go through, and looking inside myself. Soon, I began to feel more relaxed in the discussions. And now I'm actually comfortable talking about this stuff. I know how to listen."

Looking back, Vic believes that participating on the task force was "the most meaningful thing I've ever done in my work life. It just simply changed how I approach people. The reason it worked was that it wasn't just this dry intellectual experience. It was this soulful, emotional process that took place at the level of your guts. It changed me—I'm now a different sort of person."

The process also worked, Vic believes, because it involved a real element of risk. "As a valued executive in this company, I knew I was taking a chance by being direct, by expressing my thoughts and feelings as they came up. But you *had* to be direct in that process, or people would have seen you were holding back, and that meant you had to trust the other people. We all had to, and it was frightening, but our trust was rewarded, and once that happened, the barriers really started to fall. We could start to think about things in terms of what was good for the paper, instead of for our particular group or department. So besides changing specific things, we also modeled a process by which divisive issues could be addressed in the future."

BEYOND FRAGMENTATION

Essential in this wrenching effort was Dave Lawrence's total and very visible support. "People knew," says Vic Bubnow, "that nothing was going to get suppressed once their information and recommendations got to the top. They also knew that nobody was going to be punished for being extremely outspoken or taking a strong stand, or pushing aggressively to make a point. Plus in everything he did, Dave was careful to let people know that he considered the task force to be of major-league importance. He wanted to be constantly updated on our meetings, and then he'd ask us individually what we thought. If anyone on the task force was unhappy about something, they could go into his office and talk it out. It wasn't one of those typical corporate efforts, where a task force is assigned, a big speech is made, and then everything goes on like before."

Just as the findings from the internal survey were published, so was the research done by the subgroups—even when it was raw and controversial. Ellie Brecher headed the women's committee; she's a reporter who prides herself on being "a big pain around this place," one of the gadflies who, Vic believes, gave the task force credibility. She says, "I had done this little survey of my own. I looked at *Bayview,* the newsroom newsletter, and compared the number of stories that showered praise on men with the number that praised women. Well, it was just shocking, how unbalanced it was when you looked at it in terms of numbers, of space given to stories about men and women. I figured people would say, 'Well, maybe women haven't done much that's worth writing about,' so I went around and found all these instances of things women had done that hadn't gotten any recognition, when identical things done by men were singled out."

Ellie believed her research was important. "It could look like a little thing. But when people feel their efforts are ignored, it undermines morale. People don't say anything, but they start to feel isolated, in a vacuum, like all their efforts will be unappreciated because of who they are. I decided I wanted to publish my findings in *Bayview* itself, in order to make as strong a point as possible. Plus *I* wanted to write it, so it wouldn't get watered down in the process, synthesized and tidied up for consumption. I never thought management would let me do it, but I got the story through. *That's* when I started thinking they might be serious."

Sue Reisinger's wariness about her co-chair on the task force also fell casualty to "all those wild, heated discussions that led to real bonding." Vic Bubnow, the "finance guy" with whom she couldn't imagine sharing any philosophy or common ground, turned out to be "just wonderful, great, someone I'd trust with my life." Working with him on a daily basis had a big effect on Sue. "It wasn't just getting to like him as a person, it was coming to appreciate his *office,* the value of the work he does, the responsibility the financial people have at the paper. I think for newsroom people to work with those on 'the other side' can be an incredible eye-opener. Once you know what they're dealing with, you can take a wider view."

It was not simply the detente between the financial and news sides that led to a changed atmosphere. According to Sue, "The process of working together on such heated issues changed how we look at things. When the task force started, everyone came in wanting something—benefits, insurance for gay partners, more promotions for women, a day-care center, whatever. Having to work it all out together forced us to be very realistic. We had to think in terms of trade-offs, of what could and could not be negotiated, of what financial realities the paper was facing as a whole. Instead of those decisions being made for us, *we* suddenly had to make them—and when you're responsible, you view things more broadly. Also, most people had only been used to talking to people in their own divisions, people who thought like they did, which tended to reinforce their original opinions. In the task force, we were thrown together with people we would otherwise hardly have known. And that gave us the exposure to look at the paper as a whole."

Vic Bubnow agrees. "Everybody used to take a fragmented approach to their work. The marketing people thought about marketing, the reporters did their thing. You didn't think in terms of an overlap. But going through this process of seeing things from other people's point of view has changed that, so we're not fragmented like we used to be. Now people really do ask themselves, how does this work for the paper? How does it serve the needs of this or that market? It's a much more polished approach! Certainly, it's changed the way I view things. It's no longer, how dare *they* ask for this in the budget? It's more like, how can I help them get the resources they need to do their job?"

Listening to those who worked on the task force speak about their experiences, one begins to see an additional role played by the formation of this particular web. The demands, depth, and length of the project helped it serve Dave Lawrence's stated objective to find ways to develop and identify qualities of wisdom and compassion among people in the organization. The "emotional, soulful process" described by Vic Bubnow made demands on its participants that broadened their human reach and deepened their sympathy and scope. And it is precisely this kind of maturing that needs to occur if a more inclusive style of leadership is to become part of the fabric of a place. For true inclusion draws on leadership skills from throughout the organization, while at the same time providing opportunities for people to develop those skills.

EXTENDING THE WEB

Following up on the work of the web is essential if it is to have any lasting influence upon how the larger organization is run. And it is precisely here where so many companies fail, here where they draw back from the opportunity to take advantage of their own profoundly useful internal mechanisms for change. Particularly when grassroots task forces have been convened to examine controversial issues, there is a tendency for management subtly to file their work away. The group's findings are termed "interesting," its members are profusely thanked, a promise is made to take all its suggestions under serious consideration. Then, once the task force is abandoned, the issues it dealt with are ignored in the interests of keeping the peace.

Yet even when management's intentions are more honorable, there exists a lack of mechanisms that organizations can use in order to incorporate grassroots suggestions for change. In keeping with the improvisational nature of webs, there is rarely any method set in advance for responding to the work undertaken within them—a strength that can also prove a weakness. Certainly, management at the *Miami Herald* improvised its responses to the Fairness Task Force, but on the whole their responses were both creative and appropriate. Perhaps this was so because the openness that characterized the project meant that there were few surprises by the time the work had been done; everyone in the company knew what was happening, so the task force's recommendations and conclusions would have been impossible to ignore. And it was in the directness of its response to the task force's findings, even at their most challenging and controversial, that management was able to achieve the buy-in that Dave Lawrence had deemed essential in the push for change.

Sue Reisinger recalls: "We put the conclusions reached by the subgroups together and then condensed them into a single document, which was circulated through the company as a whole. Working from that, we came up with nineteen key recommendations—a lot more than the five Dave had asked us for! We set time frames for when we expected these to be met, and suggested specific steps to implement them. Vic and I made a presentation to the officers, and got everyone's comments. Then—it was amazing!—Dave got back to us with the news that he had accepted every one of our recommendations—*all nineteen!* The only thing he asked for was some adjustment on a few of the deadlines, which he didn't think were realistic."

Dave Lawrence and Roberto Suarez, publisher of *El Nuevo Herald*, then sent a detailed memo to the entire staff, outlining the recommendations and pledging specific actions by specific dates. The pledges ranged from the major to the trivial: clear guidelines on how to deal with harassment, the institution of a new newsroom pay system that would be monitored for fairness, greatly increased privileges for part-time employees, broadened use of mentoring programs, a backup emergency child care system—and yes, a change in parking privileges. To provide oversight and to monitor progress on implementation of the new policies, the task force was merged with another group and reconstituted as a permanent Committee on Fairness and Diversity.

Tamara Simpkins, a young black woman who managed advertising accounts, and Doug Clifton, the newsroom executive editor, were chosen as co-chairs for the new committee. Dave Lawrence says, "Appointing someone at senior level like Doug was intended as a signal that we valued this committee, and wanted to give it the muscle it deserved." Tamara Simpkins and Doug Clifton had previously been paired together in a cross-divisional mentoring program that was intended to create alliances between senior managers and those at earlier stages in their careers. This alliance had added to Tamara Simpkins's visibility within the company—a visibility that only helped because she was widely perceived as being superior at her job and having potential for senior management in the future.

Doug Clifton recalls, "The mentoring program was done on a very human scale, so there's a strong bonding process that occurs. You and the person you're mentoring really get to know each other well, and you wind up having a stake in one another's careers. The exposure—perhaps especially for the person who's the mentor—broadens your point of view, because you talk to people you might otherwise not get a chance to." In addition, he points out that mentoring serves as another aid in the process of breaking down formerly rigid barriers between departments.

For example, after they had gotten to know one another, Tamara Simpkins approached Doug with the notion of giving a portion of page 2 of the paper over to advertising. She argued that it was premium space that could provide needed revenue; at the time, it contained a news summary and a section on people and the weather. Such a suggestion would usually occasion a turf fight, since the newsroom would regard any expansion of advertising as an encroachment. "But because Tamara and I really *knew* one another, she understood how to present the idea to me. I was more open to dealing with it than I might otherwise have been because we'd established this implicit layer of trust, which made it a lot easier to work things out. In the end, I revamped the section, created a stronger summary on page 2, then got extra space in the Metro section for the weather. The whole deal turned out to be a net plus—more revenue was generated, and editorial gained three extra columns of space."

Along with helping to break down barriers, the mentoring program also helped change attitudes by placing abstract goals in a human context. "I have really come to believe that a diverse newsroom is very important," says Doug Clifton. "I admit I didn't buy into the idea in the past, but now I've seen concrete evidence of how it works. I've also learned very specifically that the benefits of collegiality and inclusion lie in working things through to the point where you come up with a more creative solution than you ever could if you as department head just decided things for yourself. But it's very hard—and *so* time-consuming! Sometimes my impulse is to shout, *do it my way because I'm the boss.* But this new way of working where you have to reach consensus has tremendous value. Involving more people really does enhance your decisions because you have more to work with."

Perhaps the most significant symbolic recommendation made by the task force was to change the nature of the weekly officers' meeting, to make it more reflective of the paper's diverse staff. Says Ellie Brecher, the reporter who headed the women's subcommittee, "Basically, we heard all this talk about diversity and how important it was and how the paper was working toward it. But then you'd go into the officers' meeting, where the real decisions got made, and it would be business as usual: the same old white men just sitting around!"

Implicit in the promise to open the meeting was the pledge that more women, blacks, and Hispanics would be elevated to the kind of decision-making positions that would entitle them to take part in it; no "funny-farming of titles" had been part of Dave Lawrence's promise. He also had agreed to a timetable for achieving this goal, which would involve some substantial promotions at a time when advertising revenues were still slack. Until that target could be achieved, the meeting itself was simply broadened to include more people, some at a less senior level than those who had previously attended. Members of the diversity committee were rotated in on a monthly basis.

Two Kinds of Power

Whether this opening up of the meeting was more than a cosmetic effort has been a matter of vigorous debate at the *Miami Herald* since the task force finished its work in the late spring of 1992. Dave Lawrence admits a sense of urgency for more promotions, but calls opening up the meeting a good faith step. Others are less convinced. One night at dinner in a downtown Miami hotel, a group of women drawn from throughout the paper expressed their skepticism.

"What you have now," said Roymi Membiela, Advertising Manager for *El Nuevo Herald,* "is this big unwieldy meeting. Twenty-two people, where there used to be eight or ten. And the thing you notice right away is, the original core group all sits at the big table in the center, while everyone else huddles along the side of the room on couches! And the people on the sidelines, they almost never say anything. It's so blatant they don't feel they belong there!"

"But it's *their* fault if they don't say anything," objected Jeri Levine, the Director of Business Information Systems. "They need to just get in there and act like they belong."

Ellie Brecher said proudly, *"I* sat at the big table when I was rotated in. And you can believe I said exactly what I thought."

Everyone laughed, then a discussion ensued about whether attending a meeting had any meaning if one did not have the positional power that entitled one to a place there. Listening to the talk, I was reminded again of Ted Jenkins's point about the subtle yet driving importance of nonpositional power in organizations. Ted pointed out that positional power is always balanced by other kinds of power; in particular, the power of personal relationships or connections. He noted how an emphasis on relationships and connections was especially characteristic of a networked organization, where informal lines of communication exist and consequent alliances spring up far beyond those revealed on any management chart. Such alliances reveal the true heart of the organization, and hold the key to the actual distribution of power.

I thought also of the informal line of connection between Doug Clifton and Tamara Simpkins. It bolstered her nonpositional power within the company and so added strongly to her ability to get things done. It also enlarged her view of the challenges that Doug, as a senior manager, faced, giving her an understanding of the demands on leadership that extended beyond the limits of the job she presently held. Indeed, when some of the women at the table began arguing about whether Doug was "just absolutely hopeless," it was Tamara who always came to his defense. Teased about it, she responded, "I just think I have a clear view of all he has to deal with."

Still remembering Ted Jenkins's words, I enlarged my thoughts to include all the various relationships that had evolved from the Fairness Task Force, such as that between Sue Reisinger and Vic Bubnow. It became vividly apparent that, by uniting people on issues that cut across usual boundaries of division and rank, the task force web had helped transform the nature of the *Herald*. It had done this not least by creating rich reservoirs of nonpositional power among a wide diversity of people—people at every level in the organization. It was power that could be exercised in the cause of further change until positions opened up that defined that power and made it tangible. It was a step: it brought maturity and understanding to people in the organization. Yet it would be meaningless if positional power continued to be withheld from those who now had even more reason to claim it.

In this context, the opening up of the officers' meeting took on more than a symbolic meaning, for it had the potential to create connections between people at different levels that they might otherwise not have had the opportunity to develop. Obviously, in order to take advantage of this, the newcomers could not, as Roymi Membiela had noticed, sit on the sidelines, conscious of their second-class status. And indeed, at the officers' meeting I attended, when Dave Lawrence went around the room asking everyone to introduce themselves and say what was on their mind, the woman who had rotated in from the standing Committee on Fairness mumbled her name softly, then added, "I'm just here from Diversity."

In that "just" lay a profound acknowledgment that she did not conceive of herself as having much to contribute; that she did not belong, indeed believed that she had little to gain. Yet as Jeri Levine pointed out, it was up to her to take the step toward participation that would enable her to use this meeting to broaden the net of her connections, if nothing else. Doing so would serve her in the future, for attendance at such a meeting is a resource for bolstering nonpositional power that could prepare her to assume the positional power that had been pledged.

WEAVING THE FABRIC

The Fairness Task Force provided a prototype for the process of transforming the *Miami Herald,* for it had given a diverse group of people at a variety of levels responsibility for recommending major policy shifts. As Vic Bubnow observed, "What we did was model a process that the organization could use to deal with controversial issues in the future." What remained was to assure that the web's structure and method would be used continually, until they became part of the institutional fabric, part of "the way we work around here," as Dave Lawrence describes it.

A step was made in this direction when the company chose a similarly composed internal web to deal with the explosive issue of restructuring—in many organizations, a polite term for downsizing staff. The Futures Project, as it was called, was convened as a task force to address the issue of a $25 million revenue shortfall. Yet its stated mission was not primarily to look at how the paper might cut costs in order to make up the loss, but rather to discover how it might use the crisis, wrought by an industry-wide depression in advertising rates, to position itself more skillfully for the decade ahead.

Joe Natoli, the head of production, was asked to head the task force. Joe is an eager, talkative, and open-faced man who took a lot of heat for appointing a young woman, Kim Foster, to supervise the mostly male pressroom. He says, "The usual approach to addressing a budget crisis is for management to go to all the heads of divisions and say, we've got to cut back by such-and-such amount. Then all the heads are asked to submit ideas for cutting back in their area."

There's a lot of politics in this process, Joe Natoli points out. "All the department heads are trying to preserve as much as they can for their departments. Their natural interest is of course in keeping their portion of the budget as high as possible, since how much they get to spend is the measure of their power. Once their ideas have been submitted, management comes up with all kinds of permutations until they hit the magic number that enables them to balance their budget in the year ahead. But Dave told us we should *not* be thinking about restructuring in terms of cost cutting; that's not creative, not an integrated approach. Instead, we were supposed to look at the whole process of how work gets done around here, and figure out what was not essential." In the words of Carlene Ellis at Intel, Natoli's team had to discover "how to stop doing what doesn't need to be done."

Joe Natoli gathered seventeen people who held various degrees of nonpositional power from all over the paper. "The idea was to represent a wide range, to have a group that would be very diverse. We wanted some people who were very experienced, some who were less experienced. The group then broke into subcommittees—on advertising, circulation, newsroom, production, and human resources. Each had representatives from both within and outside those divisions, in order to provide both objectivity and inside knowledge." No department heads served on the committees examining their own operations. The structure was based on the desire to avoid a destructive turf war that might destroy the *Herald*'s hard-won increase in harmony between divisions.

The first order of business for the task force was to gather information. "We needed to know a lot more about how we worked. How much time everyone spent on specific tasks, how much of their work was purely supervisory, how their specific tasks related to the value of the paper as a whole." He recalls the work as "just grueling. We had to amass all this information, sort through it, and try to figure out what it meant. We were looking for overall trends. We also needed to figure out the things we could just walk away from."

For example, the early edition. A big paper is *supposed* to have one—"it's a kind of unquestioned tradition," says Joe Natoli. "Ours was unprofitable, but we had never really questioned if it was worth the effort. Now we had to give that hard thought. The same with our Sunday magazine—it was losing money, and advertising wanted to cut it. If we'd just gone to the head of advertising, we probably would have. But we had to balance that against the evidence that including the magazine was important for circulation. We wouldn't have had the perspective we did if we hadn't done so much research; on that particular issue, there would have been a battle between advertising and circulation. The whole thing really was a balancing act, and sometimes it all just seemed *too* hard. I was ready to say, let's just cut the budget and be done with it. But Dave felt that would be admitting that the *process* couldn't work, so we kept at it."

Joe says the committee decided it should try to complete its work in three months. "We could have taken a year, but we were eager to get the work done as fast as possible. People at the paper were so worried about whether they were going to lose their jobs that it was affecting morale. There were all these rumors, right up until the day we released our report." On that very day, in fact, a local television station reported that the *Miami Herald* was about to announce it was laying off four hundred people. "A real panic erupted. If we'd taken more time, I don't know what would have happened."

In fact, there were no layoffs. The company shrank its ranks by 152 positions by offering a variety of incentives. In retrospect, Joe Natoli has come strongly to believe that the fact that the group was diverse and operated inclusively enabled changes to be made without layoffs. "It became obvious that we were going to have to trim staff by just under two hundred people—not a lot for an organization of more than twenty-five hundred people, but we knew how traumatic layoffs could be. So we began to look at offering buyouts, wondering if they could possibly be justified in terms of cost. We studied what other papers had done, other kinds of businesses too. And we began to see that the real problem with buyouts lies in the way they are usually handled. Either too many are offered and not enough are accepted, so you have to end up laying people off anyway. Or else, too many are accepted, and you are stuck with this enormous cost. And then you have to go out and hire more staff and train them to do the very same jobs that you've just paid well-trained people not to do!"

That's where the grassroots, inclusive, web-like approach made all the difference. "Because of the way our group was constituted, drawing from all over the place and being so totally diverse, we had all this very specific information. We knew who people were and exactly what they did, we knew what stage they were at in their careers, if someone else in their family worked, what their concerns were about their health, if they had other things they wanted to do in life. So when we made our buyout offers, we were able to target them very specifically, with a good idea in advance of what people's response would be. So in almost every case where we offered a buyout, it was accepted, and we didn't have to offer too many. The process was *far* less costly than if we'd cast a wider net. And as a result of our accuracy—this was the real payoff—the paper was able to avoid letting a single person go!"

Another facet of the reorganization was the creation of more positions in the company that had broad responsibility but little line authority. Chris Mobley, the Associate Publisher for the Broward County edition, who holds one of these positions, thinks of it as being "horizontal, cutting across the old vertical channels that kept us divided." Mobley points out proudly that he has "no direct reports! All I have is a secretary and an assistant and a community relations person. I'm the Associate Publisher, but no one in the newsroom or advertising reports to me. If you look at where I stand on the management chart, you'll see I'm technically powerless. I've got no authority, just credibility. Whatever I do is what I define and what I create. And since no one works for me, I have to persuade people to go along with my ideas. But I do believe that horizontal positions like this are what weaves the fabric of this company together. You can't have a strong fabric if all the threads are going one way!"

"THE BIG ONE"

Hurricane Andrew began to batter south Dade County in the late afternoon on Sunday, August 23, 1992. By early evening, 90-mile-an-hour winds made buildings sway. By midnight, police and fire-fighters had been ordered off the streets. By 3 A.M., residents woke to find the houses that sheltered them from the storm flying apart. By 7 A.M. on Monday, people were wandering the streets, trying to discern what in the wreckage had once belonged to them. Approximately 123,000 people in Dade County were left homeless.

Mary Jean Connors, the Vice President of Human Resources for Knight-Ridder, the *Herald*'s corporate parent, boarded up her house in the Keys on Saturday and then left it behind; along with other islands off the mainland, the Keys were being evacuated. On Sunday afternoon, she drove to One Herald Plaza. "I pretty much guessed that if I didn't get to the office on Sunday, I might not be able to on Monday. Streets would be closed, everything blocked." She was not the only one with the thought. By the time the winds began roaring in on Sunday night, about three hundred people had moved into the building—*Herald* employees, their spouses, a lot of children. The building, though it abutted the bay, was deemed relatively safe because of its structure. But that was not the primary attraction. Says Mary Jean Connors, "We all knew that this is where we had to be."

Assuming the worst—it turned out to be a good assumption—people began improvising how they might respond to a disaster the scope of which they were only beginning to imagine. "We called people at other Knight-Ridder papers where they'd had disasters," recalls Mary Jean. "The *San Jose Mercury News*, where they'd had the earthquake, and of course the *Charlotte Observer,* where they'd been through Hugo two years before." As they gathered information, people at the *Herald* began to recognize the dimensions of the task that lay before them. "They told us in San Jose that we would become people's only real link to anything, the only proof that civilization still existed. They said people were going to be very isolated, with no clue as to the amount of the devastation. Our job would be to reassure them that the ties that bound them to the community still remained. We would be more important to people than they had ever imagined a newspaper could be."

About forty people gathered in Dave Lawrence's office for a series of meetings that were held through the night. "Our first decision," he says, "was that we were going to keep publishing no matter what, and we were going to distribute the paper by whatever means." The meetings provided a way to address the thousands of logistical problems that resulted not only from this decision, but from the burden of having three hundred people living in the office. Informal work groups configured to deal with dilemmas that ranged from where to get water to run the presses—the paper finally bought some from a local racetrack—or gasoline for delivery trucks, to how to feed the people living in the building. As employees worked around the clock, many did not know if their neighborhoods were still standing. There was no information. There were only impassable roads and phone lines down throughout the county.

As Chris Mobley describes the round of meetings that continued every few hours for the entire week, his terms echo those of the high-reliability organization. "Dave and Roberto co-chaired the meetings. Of course, there was no structure. Someone would stand up with an anecdote about something that had happened, we'd figure there must be lots of instances of the same thing, and then everyone would volunteer ideas about what we could do. Over the week, we compiled this six-page list of things that needed attention. It could be anything: sending a workman out to restore the phones at an employee's house; finding shelter for a staffer who'd lost her home; getting volunteers to drive around and give out the paper to people who had no other way to know what was going on. The whole time, I never heard anyone say we couldn't do something. The attitude was, we've got the talent, we can do it, we're responsible. The whole community was looking to us to help them—we were their only source for information."

In fact, many *Herald* people had lost their homes, so the work of caring for them would continue for months. Hurricane Andrew thus became a dramatic opportunity for the paper's management to exhibit the paper's concern for its employees. The informal work groups that came together in Dave Lawrence's office during the first few days evolved into a series of hurricane emergency programs that provided loans, outright grants, and services to employees in crisis. A version of the mentoring program duplicated itself: staffers who had been relatively unaffected paired up with those who'd been left in the worst shape. Knight-Ridder brought in people from its papers across the country to help with circulation, advertising, and news.

People at the *Miami Herald* seem to agree that if the 1992 hurricane had occurred in the days when the paper was characterized by rigid divisions, it could never have responded with the speed, grace, and total involvement that it exhibited. But by changing the fundamental nature of its enterprise to be far more inclusive, the paper had acquired a reservoir of goodwill among its staff. People were accustomed to being in things together, to thinking in terms of the long run. This saw the paper through events that surely would have destroyed a company beset by internal strife.

THE PARADOX OF INCLUSIVE LEADERSHIP

During the time I visited the *Herald,* almost everyone spoke of the crucial role that Dave Lawrence had played in fostering change. "Dave gets the credit for turning things around," said Chris Mobley. "Without him, I don't see how it could have happened." Carole Phipps, the Director of Training, said, "Just so long as nothing happens to Dave, God forbid, I see the situation and morale around here improving." Ellie Brecher added, "What makes things work in this place is that if you run into a brick wall, you can always go to Dave and he'll straighten things out."

But this kind of dependence on the leader can also produce real weakness, for the system is liable to collapse if the leader leaves. In addition, the leader's very accessibility can have the effect of setting up an alternate management structure, which encourages people to use him or her as the arbiter of first, rather than last, resort. This can stir up resentment from those who see their authority undercut, thus politicizing the process of decision-making and creating confusion in the ranks. It can also waste a lot of time. Dave Lawrence is aware of this. "It's a question of balance, and I certainly don't have all the answers. What we're trying to do here is very different, so you just have to feel your way."

He does, he admits, spend what might seem an undue amount of time following up on minor complaints that have the potential for undermining morale. "For example, I had a case last week, in our Broward County edition. A fellow there couldn't get authorization for money to send his clients Christmas cards. He was told that Dave Lawrence wouldn't approve it. Obviously, his boss thought it was easier to blame me than to deal directly with the issue. It's a small thing, but it was important to the guy who wanted to send the cards, because he thought it would be a nice gesture to people he'd worked with. Also, it was important because people around here need to know that the changes we're trying to make won't work if they resort to the old game of blame-the-boss."

So Dave Lawrence got involved. "By the end of the day, I'd talked to five people, just trying to get this thing straightened out. But I have to wonder, was it worth it for me, as publisher of this paper, to spend so much time on this relatively trivial issue? It's the kind of question I'm always torturing myself with, but there are no guidelines for the kind of organization we're trying to create. I'm left with my instinct, and I have to go case by case. But I *do* know that if I can make a point about this matter, and let people in the company know *why* I got involved, then I won't have to get involved next time. Or in any case, I shouldn't have to."

The dependence of the staff upon Dave Lawrence's interventions points up an essential paradox in the management style that, for better or worse, has come to be identified as "empowering." For operating in an inclusive, grassroots way requires a strong and committed leader, who may have to be downright autocratic in his insistence upon change. Recognizing the paradox, Dave Lawrence nevertheless believes that such insistence is the necessary first step. But the next step, he adds, is even more crucial. That is, "to arrive at an atmosphere where the move toward change and diversity cannot be reversed." That will happen, he believes, only when the move has become part of the fabric of the institution, the "way we do things," a process that people have adapted for themselves.

The webs of inclusion that configured at the *Miami Herald,* by bringing scores of people into the diversity effort, have taken some of the pressure off Dave Lawrence as the fulcrum and *sine qua non* of change. Thus they have enabled him to begin to create a process that will no longer depend solely upon him for its success, that could survive a change in leadership were that to occur. Having a leader who "insists" on diversity might be a necessary first step toward achieving it, but it must then be institutionalized at the grassroots if it is to have lasting effect. By developing tendrils of connection between people who formerly had none, and by giving concrete leadership experience to people whose positional power does not necessarily reflect it, the *Miami Herald* has taken a deeply instructive first step.

FIVE

Power to the Front Lines: Boston's Beth Israel Hospital

"In the new information-based organizations that are presently evolving, knowledge and expertise will be primarily distributed at the bottom, held by those who have the most direct contact with the customer."

—PETER DRUCKER

"Just as owners became dependent on managers for knowledge in the Industrial Era, so now managers are becoming dependent on their employees for knowledge."

—ALVIN TOFFLER

The need to get as close to the customer as possible is inspiring a variety of organizations to take a fresh look at those who comprise the front lines. For it is the front-line people who represent the company in the customer's eyes, who listen to the customer's suggestions and complaints, who know from direct and concrete experience which products or services are of value to the customer and which are not. The front-line people form the point of intersection between the organization and the wider world it seeks to reach; they are the permeable border through which new information flows. An organization's flexibility and quickness to adapt can in large measure be determined by how permeable this border is: how easily new information moves from the outer perimeter to the inner core, how much authority and freedom those at the perimeter have to make decisions.

Redefining the role of those on the front lines, transferring authority to the perimeter—this is the real meaning of that ubiquitous buzzword "empowerment." Executives talk enthusiastically about empowerment, but in fact pushing decision-making down into the ranks is often a very painful business. For it involves nothing less than the dismantling of the long-standing barrier between those who think, plan, and conceive and those who execute and do. This barrier has defined the very nature of Industrial Era enterprise, and it still governs most aspects of how organizations are run. This barrier is also *the* fundamental source of managerial and executive power, and thus supplies the underlying rationale for enormous gaps in pay between those at the top and those at the bottom. Little wonder that it is difficult for most executives wholeheartedly to support the empowerment of those who comprise their company's front lines.

The division between those who make decisions and those who execute them has a long precedent. It informs the essential structure of the two prototypical models of hierarchy in the Western world, the Catholic Church and the military. Consider first the Church. As Christianity became the official faith of third-century Rome, its leaders established an elaborate structure in which priests with varying degrees of authority (bishops, archbishops—the ascending ranks were modeled upon the ranks of angels) were meant to serve as a buffer between God and His largely illiterate people. Indeed, the very word "hierarchy" means "the rule of priests." Under the system, Church hierarchs alone had the authority to interpret God's will, divine His will for His people, and make all decisions regarding faith and morals. The faithful were in turn expected to do as the hierarchs instructed: the favored metaphor was that of obedient sheep under the protective care of wise shepherds. Thus in matters of spirit, decision-making was left to the hierarchy from the earliest days in the civilization we now know as Western.

A similar hierarchy has prevailed in the military services, which in early Europe adapted their structure from that of the Church. The system has only recently begun to change in progressive countries with advanced technology like the United States. Under the traditional system, the top brass were invested with the authority to make strategic decisions, while mid-ranking officers have been charged with figuring out the tactics that would best advance these aims. Soldiers in the ranks were expected to execute the orders as they were handed down.

Henry Ford transferred this military structure to industrial manufacture with the invention of the assembly line. By breaking down tasks so minutely that virtually any able-bodied person could perform them, he saved his company the expense of hiring skilled workers. Since assembly line laborers had no skills, high turnover presented little threat; this enabled managers to set wages at what the market would bear. A reform of sorts came about when unions formed to provide assembly line workers with a counterhierarchy of their own, thus ensuring higher wages and a measure of job security. But the divorce between decision-making and execution was never breached: indeed, many industrial unions fought to preserve the mindlessness of their members' work, so determined were they not to "collaborate" with management. There is, after all, a kind of comfort in having merely to follow orders—as both obedient soldiers and those who have unquestioningly followed Church hierarchs have always recognized.

In the name of efficiency, the factory model spread to white-collar jobs and to service companies in this century's early years. Routine work was de-skilled, standardized, dumbed down. Decision-making was reserved for executives and managers, who had to be reasonably well trained, while those on the front lines and in the back offices had only to carry out simple orders. Because their work was made fairly mindless, these people did not require much training or preparation, so individual workers could easily be expended. As happened in manufacturing, this led quickly to the formation of unions, which protected front-line people from a measure of exploitation, but institutionalized their lack of decision-making power as well.

Strangely, the inevitable alienation of the front lines that resulted from this system has rarely been viewed by managers with alarm, despite the fact that, in service companies, these are the people who represent the company among those it seeks to serve. The problem becomes vividly apparent in many large retail stores, where executives devote huge budgets to continually expanding the range and selection of merchandise and redecorating whole new departments that are nevertheless hopelessly understaffed, or served by surly clerks who have little stake in customer satisfaction. It rarely seems to occur to store managers that their customers are being driven away by poor service rather than insufficient amounts of merchandise, which tends to be so profuse as to be confusing. And when the managers *do* get the message, they blame the clerks on the floor instead of a system that builds alienation in at the root.

But flexible and speedy technology is making this old industrial dichotomy between thinking and doing obsolete. It is indeed technology, along with the need to nurture customer relationships in a fiercely competitive era, that makes empowering the front lines a major imperative for organizations today. As Alvin Toffler observes, "Whenever we see radical new technology alongside an old work system, it is likely that the technology is being misapplied and its real advantages wasted." Information technology demands that operators have the power to make decisions if they are to take advantage of its speed; waiting for approvals to make their way down the chain of command cancels out the advantages of installing high-speed workstations, and so turns them from an investment into an expense. But the "old work system" that Toffler speaks of—characterized by the division between thinking and doing—continues to waste costly investments in technology, even as it squanders the ideas, talents, and resourcefulness of people.

The web of inclusion, with its decentralized structure, multiple lines of communication, and emphasis upon the value of those who have not achieved top rank, provides an extraordinary means by which an organization can redefine the role of those on its front lines, and so begin to coax forth the best from them. The inclusive nature of the web redistributes power throughout the organization, not least by broadening the range of connections and blurring the line between those who decide and those who *do*.

Because web-style structures institute change tactically, at the grassroots level, they bring grassroots experience to bear on every challenge. Thus they provide a means for accustoming front-line people to the exercise of authority in the very process by which they come to assume it. For it is not only true that managers have *taken* power away from those whom they manage; the people who work for them have also *given* it away. Thus not only managerial intransigence, but also deep and long-standing habits of cynicism and passivity among those who are managed, must be countered if front-line people are to play a constructive role in the forefront of the organization.

THE STRANGE CASE OF MEDICINE

Among the first service industries to divide the tasks of labor according to the factory model were those in the business of providing health care. In the early part of the century, as efficiency experts and industrial scientists turned their attention to medicine, hospitals were transformed into factories dispensing care to the sick. In the name of efficiency, tasks were broken down into standardized procedures, specialties were developed, and a chain of command was set rigidly in place. As the front-line workers who interacted directly with patients and provided them with continual care, nurses were cast into roles that paralleled those of assembly line laborers in manufacturing firms. They were expected to execute orders handed down through numerous hierarchical levels, and to forfeit decision-making to those higher up the chain.

Nursing expertise was devalued as an expertise of *care*, while an expertise of *cure* was exercised by doctors. Doctors assumed the heroic role of diagnosticians, surgeons, and prescribers of medications, while nurses were limited to administering procedures in accord with doctors' orders. As on the assembly line, nursing tasks were divided into the smallest possible units and distributed accordingly: one nurse would take patients' temperatures, another would distribute drugs. Under no circumstances were nurses permitted to make decisions about what a patient might need—although they were often the only ones around when that need became urgent. A rigid separation between the tasks of medicine and the tasks of nursing prevailed, the result of a series of early-twentieth-century "reforms" aimed at making medicine more lucrative for doctors by restricting its practice to "young men from the better classes," who alone could afford to attend schools equipped with the costly research laboratories mandated with clear deliberation by the reforms.

The imbalance of power reflected in the division of tasks has been made more extreme in medicine by the fact that nurses are usually women, while doctors have almost always been men (most schools that would admit women were closed early in this century as a result of the above-mentioned reforms). This imbalance has been further exacerbated by the profound difference in the amount of money that nurses and doctors have traditionally been able to earn, and more recently by the fact that doctors are paid directly by patients or reimbursed by their insurance companies, while nurses are paid either by the hospital or by a doctor, since insurance firms do not reimburse independent nurses. Professional courtesies and custom have also emphasized the gap: until very recently, a nurse was taught to stand whenever a doctor entered the room, to bow slightly and then offer him her chair. Nursing schools also instructed students in such arts as preparing and pouring a doctor's coffee, and addressing him in a soft voice with modestly averted eyes. Teaching such "skills" helped define the nurse's place in the health care hierarchy, reinforcing a physician-nurse relationship that was essentially that of master and servant.

Things began to change in the early 1970s, when a shortage of nurses threw the hospital system into the first of what would prove to be a series of recurrent crises. The advent of greater opportunities for women in a variety of professions resulted in a decreasing interest in the possibilities of nursing as a career. At the same time, a quickly expanding system needed more nurses than ever in the past. The result was a substantial increase in nursing salaries. As the field became more lucrative, nursing education began to expand into the universities, and hospital-based schools, with their vocational overtones and tradition of using unpaid students for clinical practice, closed their doors. As nurses became more highly educated and their practice more professional, they began to develop specialties and enroll for advanced degrees. The days of pouring coffee for doctors were over.

Hospital hierarchies remained firmly in place, but nurses began to chafe in their role as front-line workers in an outmoded system incapable of making full use of their advanced education and high level of expertise. In addition, nurses, being in the most direct contact with patients, were becoming increasingly dissatisfied with the way in which most hospitals provided patient care. As technology made medicine more industrialized, patients were increasingly viewed as objects, whose disparate symptoms were treated in isolation from one another by a variety of specialists who rarely communicated among themselves. As the structure of hospitals adapted to serve the needs of the specialist, it became ever more difficult to treat patients as human beings with complex and interrelated illnesses.

But just as technology had industrialized medicine, so as it continued to evolve did it also provide the means for hospitals to become more humane in their practice. By providing access to quantities of information about patients that had long been reserved for doctors, technology enabled ever more educated nurses to participate in the structuring and delivery of a kind of care that acknowledged the suffering patient as a human being. This has had the effect of restoring dignity and power to nurses serving patients at the front lines. Given the situation, it was inevitable that leaders would emerge who would insist upon the centrality of nursing in clinical practice.

This is what happened at Beth Israel Hospital in Boston in 1973, when Dr. Mitchell Rabkin, the hospital's President and CEO, hired Joyce Clifford as Vice President of Nursing and Nurse-in-Chief. In the twenty years since her hiring, Joyce Clifford has transformed the hospital hierarchy into a true web of inclusion, altering in the process not only the role played by Beth Israel's nurses, but the entire structure of the hospital itself. Instead of the nurses serving the administration, the nurses now directly serve the patients, drawing upon the resources of the institution as they need them. As Mitchell Rabkin points out, "The nurses are the ones who care for the patients. They are who patients see every day, and they form the largest group of a hospital's employees. In the last analysis, a hospital is a nursing institution more than it is anything else. The rest of us function as support staff for the nurses."

This reversal of the traditional pyramid of power makes Beth Israel one of the classic examples of front-line empowerment in business or industry today, one that a vast number of organizations could learn from. Indeed, were it not for the fact that Beth Israel's example involves nursing, a mostly female profession, the hospital would no doubt serve as a widely acknowledged model for organizations seeking to motivate and enlist the best energies of their front-line people, and Joyce Clifford would be a well-known guru for leaders seeking ways of transformation.

Joyce Clifford does not deny her role as a pioneer, the first top administrator in the country to implement the radical system known as primary nursing throughout the hospital as a whole. Still, she credits the system's development to "a whole group of people" who began to rethink health care delivery in the late 1960s. And she hastens to point out that the system she has put in place did not result from any specific effort to improve the lot of nurses, but rather from a desire to provide vastly better hospital care for patients. "The idea was to make changes, of course, but the *patient* was the focus. Everything else flowed from that." In trying to do right by the patients, Joyce Clifford insists, "we had to get the nurses feeling better about their work. We had to find a way to retain experienced nurses. And that in turn meant changing everything about how the hospital was run."

RECONFIGURING BETH ISRAEL

Beth Israel is a 504-bed hospital that also encompasses an Emergency Unit, an Ambulatory Care Center, an extensive Home Care program, and a large Neonatal Unit. In addition, it serves as a major teaching hospital for the Harvard Medical School. It lies on the border between the city of Boston and the prosperous western suburb of Brookline, in an area dominated by hospitals. Partly because of the concentration of medical schools in the region, few cities in the world have better health care facilities than Boston, and the competition among them is fierce.

Beth Israel began as a storefront dispensary serving Jewish immigrants in the early years of the century; its first permanent home was an old mansion in the impoverished Roxbury district. In those early days, the small professional staff was greatly assisted by a volunteer women's auxiliary, whose involvement extended to supplying sheets and food. As the local Jewish community grew more prosperous, the hospital became a major focus of its philanthropy. Donors acquired the present site, and the hospital moved there in 1928; the names of those early donors are inscribed in stone at the hospital's entrance today. Their descendants have been active in the extensive fund-raising that has fueled the institution's many expansions over the years.

Marjorie Bachmann, an associate in nursing administration, credits Beth Israel's focus on patient care to the close relationship it has always maintained with those it was originally built to serve. "This hospital was built from the nickels and dimes of the Jewish community in Boston," she explains. "The women especially have always been very active. A lot of the present contributors are grandchildren of the people who visited the storefront dispensary, who spent time in this hospital, who probably died here. So there's always been this overlap between those who come here as patients and those who raise the money, which means that the patients have to be well served, or we are going to hear about it." Marge Bachmann points out that Beth Israel today is less Jewish in terms of its patient population, yet it still bears the mark of grassroots traditions and values that shaped it as an institution. "It is very much perceived as belonging to the community," she notes.

However, by the late 1960s, the emerging crisis in nursing was threatening to erode the focus on patient care that had played so large a part in Beth Israel's success. Like most hospitals at the time, Beth Israel was staffed by students who attended its school and worked in the hospital under the supervision of Registered Nurses. RNs themselves rarely performed hospital nursing: they did private work, held jobs as administrators in charge of the units, or taught in nursing schools. The students upon whom the hospital depended for patient care were thus overworked and underpaid, expected only to follow orders. In short, they were typically exploited front-line workers.

Joyce Clifford describes how the old system at Beth Israel worked, while noting that something like it still prevails in most hospitals across the United States. "The nursing aides, who had the least preparation, had the most contact with the patients. But they had no authority of any kind. They had to go to their supervisor to ask if a patient could have an aspirin. The supervisor would then ask the head nurse, who would then have to ask the doctor. The doctor would ask how long the patient had been in pain. Of course, the head nurse had absolutely no idea, so she'd have to track down the aide to ask her, and then relay that information back to the doctor. It was ridiculous, a ludicrous and dissatisfying situation, and one in which it was impossible for the nurse to feel any satisfaction at all. The system was hierarchical, fragmented and impersonal, and overly administered."

Besides being difficult for nurses, the system was unsatisfying for patients. "With nursing jobs broken up into specific tasks, different nurses were always administering different procedures. That made it difficult for any one professional caregiver to form an accurate picture of what was really going on with a given patient—even though the patient was constantly being asked a lot of questions. I've been the head nurse in situations like this, and believe me, the gaps in the information you get are terrible!" Nevertheless, Joyce Clifford points out, most people considered the system to be very efficient. Everyone knew precisely what he or she was supposed to do. Channels of communication, although limited, were clear and well defined.

But the system was becoming untenable, for the same reason that hierarchies of every variety would soon begin to unravel: post-industrial technology was taking hold. The change was particularly abrupt in medicine, in large part because the Medicaid-Medicare bill passed in 1965 by Congress brought a vast infusion of federal money into health care. Suddenly, hospitals had the resources to invest in sophisticated monitoring and diagnostic equipment, the complexity of which demanded that those at the patient's bedside have sufficient expertise to put it to use. Complex technology also demanded that decisions be made more quickly than before, because of increased possibilities for intervention.

Suddenly, hospitals found themselves in need of nurses who were more highly trained and professional—at the very time when there existed a nursing shortage. This meant that high turnover, which had always characterized hospital nursing, could no longer be tolerated. Indeed, hospitals were among the first organizations faced with finding ways to improve the quality of front-line work in order to motivate those who performed it. Improving the quality of the nursing meant more than just improving nurses' salaries, although of course it also meant that. It also meant that nurses' jobs had to be de-industrialized, the range of their responsibilities and tasks broadened, their contact with the patients made more humanly rewarding.

As the need to improve the role of nurses in the practice setting became pressing, academics and administrators worked to find a new configuration, develop models that would satisfy front-line people. Among them, Marie Manthey, the Director of Nursing at the University of Minnesota's teaching hospital, began to experiment with a way to redesign the hospital structure by emphasizing the relationship between the nurse and individual patients. Joyce Clifford, at that time a nurse at an Alabama medical center, became interested in the new system, to which Manthey had given the name "primary nursing."

Joyce Clifford explains: "Marie Manthey figured out that the crux of the problem lay in the way nurses were attached to patients, which was both confusing and indirect. Under the old unit system, which most hospitals used at the time, the nurses were divided into teams that served under a supervisor, who in turn reported to the head nurse. The team nurses were assigned not to patients, but to units or to patient rooms. Also, the system was completely task-oriented: one nurse was assigned to do medications, another was in charge of vital signs, such as taking blood pressure. In essence, each bedside nurse on the unit did only one thing, but for a lot of patients."

After Alabama, Joyce Clifford accepted an academic stint at the University of Indiana; this gave her the chance to study the literature that had begun to proliferate on how to redesign nursing as a profession. Then in 1973, she answered an advertisement for a Vice President of Nursing that had been placed in a professional journal by Mitchell Rabkin. "I was very deliberate about the ad," he recalls. "I asked that respondents write to me directly, rather than contacting the Human Resources department, which is very unusual. And I made it clear in the ad that the Chief of Nursing would have parity on the professional staff. She'd be my colleague, and the colleague of the Chief of Medical Staff." Mitchell Rabkin recalls that he had been reading a lot of books about reorganization at the time, and had concluded that a fresh and innovative approach to nursing would have to be the key if Beth Israel were to become more responsive to the needs of its patients.

Mitchell Rabkin was already getting a reputation as a maverick, an experimentalist. Assuming the position of CEO at Beth Israel in 1972, he had immediately drafted the first "Patient's Bill of Rights" in the country, an effort viewed as heretical by much of the medical profession at the time. "Some people thought it was going to be the end of civilization as we know it," he recalls. However, "I knew the way we were doing things at the time was just all wrong."

He had watched the process at the large and prestigious hospital where he had previously been on staff. "You'd ask the patients about their illness, and they would have no idea what was being done. So you'd ask if they had talked to the doctor about it. And they'd say,

'Oh, no, he's so busy! He just saw me for a minute, and I didn't feel I could bother him with questions.' In other words, they had no one to ask, no one to talk to. They felt no one was really in charge of, or responsible for, their case. The nurses' jobs were totally fragmented, and in any case, they had very little authority and felt almost completely alienated, so the patients couldn't talk much to them. Plus the nurses were always leaving—turnover was atrocious. It was just a bad way of doing things, that was obvious. I recognized that our patients needed to be better served; that's why I wrote the Bill of Rights. But at the time, I could not articulate how to change things."

THE PRIMARY SYSTEM

The colleagueship Mitchell Rabkin formed with Joyce Clifford gave them both the language they needed to articulate change, and transformed the vocabulary of the entire staff as well. But the process of change at Beth Israel proceeded slowly, in incremental stages, evolving as individual tactical efforts proved successful. This approach was used in order to counter resistance, and in order to gather information, for there was no way of knowing what would work and what would not as the new system was put in place. Although primary nursing had been developed in theory, and tried out in individual nursing units, no hospital had ever attempted to implement the system across the board. Charged with transforming how nursing was configured, Joyce Clifford was in uncharted territory, and she would have to draw the map even as she explored it.

What she saw most clearly was that primary nursing could be used as a vehicle to redistribute power throughout the hospital by putting bedside nurses in the position of making decisions that had formerly been made for them. The primary system made every nurse on the floor directly responsible for the care of specific individual patients, eliminating the need for administrators and supervisors to tell her what she should be doing. Each patient entering the hospital would be assigned a single primary nurse; he or she would then become that nurse's patient throughout the hospital stay. The primary nurse coordinates every aspect of the patient's care: she interviews the patient upon entering, gathers all data about his illnesses in the past, and makes an assessment of what he will need each day. She devises a complete care plan. And she talks with the patient's family, seeking both to learn from and to involve them, so that she can devise a realistic plan for the patient's care after release.

The primary nurse then puts together a team for the individual patient, comprised of those nurses who will take care of him while she herself is not on duty—throughout the night, or over the weekend. These co-workers are assigned to the nurse, not to the room or the patient: they report to and take direction from her, provide her with information, and help her to carry out her plan of care. This takes the supervisor out of the nurse-patient relationship altogether, putting an end to the administrative chain of command.

The roles of head nurse and supervisor are assumed by the nurse manager, who devises goals for her unit as a whole, works out its budget, and makes hospital-wide resources available to the nurses. The nurse manager may also help her primary nurses to coordinate their schedules, and may put them in contact with nurse consultants who help them explore new methods of care and treatment. The primary nurse, her position solidified and made professional, consults directly with the doctor, who becomes in essence her professional partner. She makes the daily rounds with him (under the old system, only the head nurse did that), and she provides him with information about how the patient is doing based on her direct observation.

Joyce Clifford says, "What primary nursing really does is to maximize the amount of knowledge that the nurse has about each of her patients. It acknowledges the nurse-patient relationship as *the* primary relationship during the patient's hospital stay, and creates a structure that allows everything else to flow from that. The nurse interacts directly with the patient, with the other nurses who provide care for him, with his family, with the physician. With the nurse fully responsible, conflicts are fewer, because the care plan is drawn up alongside the medical plan devised by the doctor. Most importantly, the patient always has someone knowledgeable to talk to."

Primary nursing was far from popular when it was first introduced at Beth Israel. Mitchell Rabkin recalls the furor. "The system was totally different from anything the physicians were used to, and many of them were very uncomfortable at first. They'd grown accustomed to dealing only with the head nurse, and now they had to deal with different nurses for every patient; instead of knowing just one person, the physician has to work with Laura and Donna and Susan, and he has to deal with them on a more professional and consultative basis. Plus he has to *listen!* After all, the primary nurse knows a lot about the patient, she's been following him since he got here. She's admitted him, she's talked to his family, she knows his history, she's monitored how he responds to medications, so she is bound to have very specific ideas about his care.

"I'm telling you, there was *a lot* of resistance to the new system from the medical staff at first. You'd hear things like, 'I can't be running around and finding all these nurses, dealing with someone different for every patient. It's *much* too complicated, and it wastes my time.' " It was not so much the nurses playing a more professional role that bothered the physicians—although certainly some perceived it as a loss of power—it was more the fear that without a chain of command, things would get chaotic. "The physicians were used to just going to the head nurse and saying, tell me about my patients. Now they couldn't do that, and it seemed inefficient. But after initial resistance, most of the doctors began to really like the new system, because the quality of information they were getting was so superior to what it had been in the past."

As the new system was slowly implemented one unit at a time, resistance began to grow less fierce. "We tried out the changes on a limited scale at first," Mitchell Rabkin recalls. "We wanted to be able to work out the kinks, get new ideas about how to proceed as we went along." Because resistance was limited primarily to physicians and to older nurses who had held positional power under the old order, the tactical approach proved especially effective. "Even people who hated the idea, once they had actually *experienced* it in one of the units, began to see the advantages and to talk about them with their friends. So the general response went from 'I'm not happy with all these complicated changes they're trying to shove down our throats' to 'You should give this a try, it really works.' "

A tactical, unit-by-unit approach was used to implement the strategy, but Mitchell Rabkin and Joyce Clifford were very careful not to present primary nursing as a pilot project. The two agreed that if they announced they were simply going to *try out* the new system, they would be courting disaster. "That's the worst thing we could have done," Mitch Rabkin declares. "It would have been the kiss of death. It would have brought all the kooks out of the woodwork, given them a chance to undermine the system when it was still new."

Instead of piloting a program to see *if* it would work, "We made it clear from the very start that we were totally committed to the new system, that we were going to implement it throughout the entire hospital. We were going to learn as we went along, and make modifications in response to what we learned, but we were definitely going to do it." Joyce Clifford adds: "We let everyone know that we were going to proceed unit by unit, but that we were absolutely going to see the process through on a hospital-wide basis. We weren't interested in creating pockets of excellence. We had a clear vision of what we wanted. The most prepared person—the nurse—was going to be put into direct contact with the patient. Every other aspect of how we were organized would proceed from that."

EVERYTHING HAD TO CHANGE

The implementation of primary nursing throughout Beth Israel slowly but inevitably altered every aspect of how the hospital was run. Replacing a hierarchy with a web—and an internally focused method with one designed above all to serve the patient—required that the way services were delivered had to change. "In retrospect, I realize we had little idea of how enormous the shift here was going to be," says Joyce Clifford. "But once you change your philosophy, once you start to focus on the *patient,* the whole structure that allows you to operate has to change."

One cornerstone of the old system had been the compartmentalization of tasks. For example, a single nurse—usually one with little seniority—would handle the task of administering bed baths to all the patients in a given unit. At another time, this nurse might be assigned to taking vital signs. Chores such as bed baths were viewed as unpleasant and unrewarding, ranking low in the hierarchy of nursing tasks. Since anyone could perform them, it was considered efficient to delegate these tasks to inexperienced beginning nurses. "The whole approach was fragmented and impersonal, focused on the task rather than the patient," recalls Joyce Clifford.

The new system, by contrast, demanded that tasks be integrated. Duties involving patients were no longer viewed simply as tasks, but as opportunities for the primary nurse to spend time with her patient and gain valuable information, so fragmenting and then delegating tasks ceased to make any sense. Bed baths, for example, were no longer viewed simply as routine chores, but rather as a chance for the nurse to observe the state and condition of a patient's skin: whether any circulation problems had developed, how well wounds were healing, if bedsores were becoming a threat. Such indications would then affect the care plan that the nurse was devising for her patient, while also influencing her daily consultations with the patient's doctor. Thus the primary nurse would have a reason for wanting to administer her patients' bed baths herself, or at least assign them to a team member who could keep her informed of any worrisome signs. In this way, the primary nursing system at Beth Israel helped to restore value and dignity to tasks that had borne menial status when assigned in a repetitive and compartmentalized fashion.

Another example of how "everything had to change" once primary nursing was implemented can be seen in Beth Israel's transformed approach to visiting hours. Joyce Clifford recalls, "When I came here, we had these rigid visiting hours, between two and four in the afternoon—the very hours, of course, when most of our patients' relatives were working. But once we made the commitment to patient-centered care, we had to ask ourselves what purpose this almost deliberately inconvenient policy served. Of course the answer was, it served the *staff*. The head nurses in particular didn't want a lot of people wandering around their units. They perceived visitors as getting in their way. In fact, if most of the staff had had their choice, there would have been no visiting hours at all!"

Visitors were viewed as inefficient: again, an Industrial Era attitude prevailed. There was no thought that visitors might be a source of information about the patients, or serve as valuable partners in helping to determine plans for the care of patients after their release. And since visitors were perceived purely as an inconvenience, there was enormous staff opposition to changing the policy that restricted their presence in the units. So Joyce Clifford brought together all the nurse managers to discuss the matter. This in itself was a change, since the nurses were accustomed to policy changes simply being handed down to them. "I told them I didn't want to impose a solution, but I needed to know from them how we were going to meet the social needs of our patients if we stuck to the old rules." Under the old system, of course, nurses had no mandate to consider the social needs of their patients, and as long as that system remained in place, resistance to expanding visiting hours remained strong.

As the primary system took hold in the units, however, resistance began to erode, and nurses soon became active advocates for expanded visiting hours. The transformation occurred because, as nurses became responsible for providing a continuity of care to individual patients, they found themselves spending more time with their patients' families. Nurses interviewed family members about patients' health problems in the past, and consulted them about what kind of situation the patient was going to be discharged into in order to draw up a reasonable program for aftercare. The primary nurse was also responsible for educating family members about what the patient would need after release, so family visits provided a chance to do that kind of education. Dependent upon the family for information and support, nurses at Beth Israel began to *want* the families of their patients to pay frequent visits. Patient families came to be viewed as allies, people whom the nurses had to get to know, rather than as simply "visitors," a faceless and inconvenient mass of people.

Even the way laundry was done had to change. Under the old system, laundry was sent to the units once a day; if a nurse needed an additional piece of linen, she had to go to the laundry, fill out a request form, and sign for the item. The laundry department was virtually run as a separate fiefdom; and supervisors judged its success based on its efficiency and costs. Primary nursing, however, exposed the underlying inefficiency of a system that took nurses away from their patients to go in search of a pillowcase.

"It became clear that we had to make laundry part of the support system," says Joyce Clifford. "We told the supervisors that they had to find a way to deliver items as the nurses needed them. There was a lot of grumbling. The laundry people said they couldn't get their work done if they were servicing nurses ten hours a day. We reminded them, that's not what they were doing. They were servicing *patients,* and they had to be prepared to do that twenty-four hours a day." Under the old system, the link between services such as laundry and patients had been lost; under the new system, it was restored.

Primary nursing enabled Beth Israel to let go of a whole range of supervisory functions. Joyce Clifford recalls that, in the early days of the system, she was asked to define the policy on whether patients needed escorts in order to be discharged. "That's typical of the old way of thinking; the administration makes the rules, and people on the front lines carry them out. But how could I make such a judgment? Why did there need to be a policy on escorts? If the primary nurse was responsible for discharging the patient, shouldn't she use her own discretion?" The old rules and regulations approach had also been a source of dissatisfaction among patients, who understandably came to feel that their care was subordinate to hospital policies that might have no relevance to them. Giving nurses the authority to make a wide range of decisions was a way of showing patients that they were all special cases with individual needs.

Primary nursing thus became the vehicle that put Mitchell Rabkin's Patient's Bill of Rights into effect. Joyce Clifford says, "The primary nursing system was implemented very deliberately as a way of improving patient care. It means nothing if it doesn't accomplish that. Primary nursing was not put in place to help nurses feel better about themselves, although it certainly does that. It was sad to see the nurses under the old system so dissatisfied, so miserable in their jobs. Their frustrations had an impact upon the patients. *That's* why we had to change things. We transformed nursing so it could lead the rest of the hospital in providing patient-centered care."

How It Works on the Front Lines

Michele McHugh, RN, is nurse manager on 7 Feldberg A, a twenty-four-bed general surgical unit at Beth Israel. Abdominal surgery is the most frequently performed type of operation in her unit, and since many of the admitting physicians have particular specialties within this realm, there is a general emphasis on expertise. Nurses as well as physicians develop themselves as specialists, pushing the boundaries of their practice as they take their places on expert interdisciplinary teams.

Michele McHugh explains how the primary system works in her unit. "Say a patient is coming in for surgery on ulcerative colitis. The physician's secretary will fax the information on the patient being admitted, give us all the particulars she has. We'll put it in our log-book for the day the surgery is scheduled, and then the nurses will look it over and decide who among them should take the patient. Their decision will be based on scheduling—who will be on duty at the time of admission—but also on who has experience with that particular type of problem. Then the primary nurse who takes the patient will put together an associate care team, again based on scheduling and who has the expertise.

"The nurses make all the decisions about who will handle which patients and how," explains Michele McHugh. "I don't take that responsibility, that's not what I'm here for. In the beginning, I would run around and try to help them figure out whose schedule might accommodate this or that patient, but I realized that I was over-administrating my role. So I drew back. Now we use staff volunteers to help everyone coordinate the schedules. My role is more to make sure that all the information is in the logbook, and then let the staff negotiate with each other about how they'll use their time."

Once the primary nurse has put her team together for the patient with ulcerative colitis, she will call him at home, and introduce herself as his nurse. She will talk to the patient, make sure he understands every aspect of the procedure he's about to undergo, and answer any questions. She will note down the patient's concerns, and discover any special needs.

Next, the primary nurse develops a schedule and a care plan for the patient. This includes everything from the time of admission to what room the patient will be assigned, as well as the room in which the surgery will be performed. Recovery room time is also scheduled, and a plan for release is written up. If the patient will need home care following the operation, the nurse coordinates that in consultation with his family. She calls in a dietitian to develop a daily diet plan for the patient while he is in the hospital. She contacts the pharmacy and coordinates a timetable for the delivery of medicines in advance. She looks at every aspect of care that the patient will receive. And since the nurse has very likely been developing herself as a specialist—in this case, with an expertise in ulcerative colitis—she has a better idea of what the patient may require than the average nurse.

As unit manager, Michele McHugh's job is to provide the primary nurse with organization and support, rather than supervision. She may help her gather any special resources she needs for a patient, and she is constantly balancing the nurse's needs with the unit's budget. She is also responsible for hiring staff and for allocating money. Very soon, 7 Feldberg A will move to a thirty-bed unit, so right now, Michele McHugh is looking at the dollar figures for other units of that size, calculating what she should imitate, and what she should change. "We realized we'd have to cut some costs, so I brought my staff together and we went over how everybody used their time. We decided we could stand a couple fewer people on the day shift, so we made the adjustment."

Having a primary nurse who understands all the needs of a patient works particularly well for those with special needs. In late 1993, a blind and deaf woman was scheduled into 7 Feldberg A for a hysterectomy. A primary nurse who was interested in the problems of the blind took charge. After interviewing the woman's family, she spent time at a community center for the blind and deaf, in order to be able to anticipate what would be needed.

When the patient was admitted to the hospital, the nurse had an interpreter ready to go through the process and help explain the upcoming procedure. An interpreter was also present in the recovery room when the patient was brought in following surgery, so that the physician and nurse could discover if the patient were suffering any particular pains. What could have been a crisis—"How on earth are we going to communicate with this patient who's blind and deaf?"—was handled smoothly throughout the procedure. "What this example shows," says Michele McHugh, "is that an experienced nurse with real authority can anticipate problems and figure out how to provide for patients in even the most difficult situations."

An even more dramatic demonstration was the recent admission of an oncology patient who had multiple personalities. Michele McHugh: "The admitting physician told me about it, said it would have to be handled carefully. The patient in question was a successful female attorney, but she'd been terribly abused as a child, and when she was under stress, these other personalities would start to come out. We didn't know what would happen to her under anesthesia, with certain medications, or if she were to experience very bad pain. The physician's secretary sent over all the information on the patient, but there wasn't that much—it was untested territory for us."

In this particular case, Michele McHugh did approach one of her staff, a nurse she knew was particularly interested in patients with severe psychological problems, and asked if she would like to take responsibility as primary nurse. "She very much wanted to handle the case. She got permission from the patient to have a psychiatrist present, first in the operating room and then in recovery. She made the psychiatrist part of the team. The psychiatrist visited the patient along with the surgeon, the residents, herself, and the other caregivers."

Because the nurse took the time to familiarize herself in advance with the case, she knew which of the patient's personalities were most likely to come out under stress—she learned their names, and how to talk to each of them. She looked into the patient's long history of medication and figured out what might trigger bad effects. She worked out alternatives to restraints, in case the woman became hysterical, because she learned from the psychiatrist that restraints might trigger a psychotic attack. Despite the complex nature of the undertaking, the woman's surgery was wholly successful, and the patient suffered no major disturbance. In addition, coordinating the admission gave the primary nurse the greater expertise she wanted in dealing with severely disturbed surgery patients.

The extent to which primary nurses take responsibility for addressing patients' special problems can be extraordinary, and lead them in whole new directions in their own careers. An outstanding example at Beth Israel involved an oncology nurse, Donna Miller, whose efforts to meet the special needs of a patient cast her into the role of inventor. One of Donna Miller's duties was providing care for patients with vaginal radiation implants, a device that treats gynecologic malignancies. These implants, which direct radiation internally for several days, must be precisely positioned, and they had always been secured inside patients with adhesive tape. The tape caused extreme discomfort and some tearing of the skin when removed, but it was commonly regarded as the least objectionable way to hold such radiation devices in place.

Several years ago, Donna Miller was explaining the procedure to a patient she had chosen to serve as primary nurse when the patient informed her that she was allergic to adhesives. Trying to figure out ways she might help, Donna Miller stopped on the way home that evening, bought some lingerie, and rigged up a device that would hold the implant in place without tape. She constructed a kind of "artificial skin" attached to a lightweight girdle that would hold the implant without adhesives.

Her improvisation proved a success, and she began mentioning it to patients who were not allergic, since it would save their skin the trauma caused by removing tape. As the new device became popular with patients, the radiation department administrator suggested to Donna Miller that she get in touch with the hospital's Office of Science and Technology. The directors there helped refine the device, and contacted an attorney, who helped her secure a patent.

In the meantime, Donna Miller was experimenting with improving her product. She borrowed a friend's sewing machine, set to work with Velcro and elastic webbing, and developed a high-quality prototype. The Office of Science and Technology then found a company to manufacture and market the product. Donna Miller now receives a thirty percent royalty on the sale of her product. Patients—first at Beth Israel, but increasingly in hospitals across the United States—have benefited.

PROFESSIONAL PRACTICE

Donna Miller's success with her patent resulted not only from the autonomy she was able to exercise as a primary nurse, but also from the clinical expertise she had developed in radiation oncology. That expertise derived in part from the degree of her experience, which was facilitated by the primary system, which supports clinical nurses seeking to upgrade and expand the range of their skills. The situation this creates is almost one of complete reversal from the days when nurses with the highest degree of skill were directed toward teaching or administration rather than clinical practice. The new system's emphasis on developing the expertise of fully accredited RNs who work at the bedside is both a precondition for and a result of the transfer of decision-making power to those on the front lines.

Liberated from the supervisory duties that used to define the head nurse's job, the nurse manager is free to encourage staff development. A good example of this active engagement is Michele Mc-Hugh's role in helping the surgical nurse who wanted more experience working with the severely disturbed to develop a special team for the patient with multiple personalities. In 7 Feldberg A, the goal of providing the highest level of care for patients merges seamlessly with the nurses' desire to gain specialized experience. To further this process, Michele has hired a nurse specialist to serve as a consultant for her staff.

Phyllis West, RN, has the job of helping develop expertise among the unit's nurses. She describes her own grassroots evolution into the role of clinical expert. "It started a few years ago. We had just gotten a new physician in the unit who wasn't used to the primary system, and was not enthusiastic about it *at all*. He came from the old school, where nurses are supposed to dote upon physicians, and he was not accustomed to thinking of us as partners." His arrival coincided with a number of nurses on the staff deciding that they wanted to develop more expertise in gynecological oncology, which is a specialty in the unit. "But because it was also his specialty, we had to take things slow."

Phyllis West had more field experience than any nurse on the unit, so she told the new surgeon that she wanted to develop it as her specialty, and that she would like to accompany him on his rounds. Despite his lack of enthusiasm, she made it a point to accompany him every morning when he saw his patients in company with the residents. "Gradually, he began to trust me. We developed a relationship. And so I started to integrate other nurses along on these rounds. At first, they would just observe. Then after a while, I would start to ask questions, try to anticipate how they could be more active. I wanted to know what kinds of things the nurses could do without having to check with the doctor first. Could we administer such and such medication without having to call you fifty times a day?

"It took a long time before he felt comfortable, but after a while we were able to develop a team of nurses with real expertise as oncology clinicians. They were very knowledgeable, a great asset to the unit." As other nurses got more involved, Phyllis stepped back from active participation on the team, and began to assume more of a consultant's role, coordinating special teams and helping nurses find the resources they needed, acting as their advocate across the hospital. Now the oncology nursing team rounds each day with the attending physician.

"I think he's come to recognize the benefits of working with this kind of team. They can present him with ongoing care plans that are much better than before, as well as very specific and appropriate discharge plans. This makes care more coordinated in general, and cuts the length of time that the patient has to stay in the hospital." As team members developed their skills, they began to assume functions that the physician had filled in the past, cutting costs for the hospital and for the patient. In the past, for example, the doctor had always done the insertions of nasogastric tubes before surgery. Now the primary nurses have taken charge of that procedure. Working with nurses and physicians, Phyllis West helped to write the protocols for the insertions, developing a precise instructional manual and a team of nurses qualified to administer the procedure.

"The great thing here," she says, "is to watch the staff evolve. My position now is almost completely educational." In addition to devising protocols for procedures with which newly autonomous nurses are entrusted, she "focuses on things like communication skills, even body language—a lot of nurses have been trained always to stand behind the physician, as a way of showing respect, underlining their subordinate position. But from that angle, the nurse can't *see* anything, and with her new authority, she needs to watch exactly what's going on!" Phyllis West notes that the kind of training in collaborative skills that she provides is particularly needful because "Nursing schools still don't teach it. They don't understand the concept of the physician and nurse working together."

Her teaching on the unit is also important because "Beth Israel is part of the Harvard Medical School system. Medical students do their training here. So it's important that they have the experience of working alongside nurses who are clinical specialists, although when many of them leave for other institutions, that will be lost." Nevertheless, she notes that some of the younger interns do come to Beth Israel with some experience of primary nursing, so that "in the last few years, we're finding the interns much more receptive to what our role here is, to what we're trying to do."

The teamwork between physicians and the nurses who have developed a clinical specialty in oncology on 7 Feldberg A has helped transform an often adversarial relationship. "At first, when we wanted to round with them, the physicians wouldn't even tell us when they were going out! We'd have to be on the lookout, and then rush to join up. Now the physicians call us at home to let us know when they'll be seeing their patients. They want to make sure that we'll be there." The new situation not only provides nurses with a real measure of autonomy and professional respect, it is also appreciated among the patients. "There's none of that old stuff, where the nurse would come in and ask, 'Has the doctor seen you today?' Now the nurse knows, she was part of the effort."

Michele McHugh points out that the roles of teaching and nursing have become integrated across the unit as primary nursing has become fully established and more refined. For example, the nurses are involved in setting up a Patient Family Learning Center, where families can receive instruction both in how to help prepare a patient for cancer surgery, and in how to follow up on care after release. Primary nursing has had an enormous impact on the approach to and quality of aftercare, because autonomous and responsible nurses coordinate outpatient services. Interview calls to patient and family help nurses learn if the patient will need continual private care after release, or the delivery of hot meals, or regular professional visits. Coordination of these aspects cuts down on the length of time patients must spend in the hospital, and makes it less likely that they will return in the immediate future.

The integration of teaching and nursing is particularly apparent in the Clinical Entry Program, a committee on which both Michele McHugh and Phyllis West sit. Its purpose is to help accustom newly graduated nurses to the unusual amount of responsibility that the primary nursing system at Beth Israel requires them to assume. "It used to be," says Michele, "that a new nurse would come into the hospital and be given a preceptor, a kind of guide who would go around with her for about four weeks. After that, she was completely on her own." Under the old system, many young nurses after the preceptor phase hesitated to ask questions, for fear that they might appear to be ignorant of something they should know. "The way it worked, you basically got no career direction once you had your certification. There was no organized program of staff development in place."

The Clinical Entry Program changed that. Now, a senior nurse is assigned to a newcomer for a full two years. She serves as a mentor, answering questions, coaching the younger nurse, helping her find resources and define her direction. "They create goals together," says Phyllis West. For example: What clinical specialties might the new nurse wish to develop? In what fields might she want to become an expert? And what course of action should she pursue in order to develop herself? The choices she makes will help her to determine what teams she will want to become a part of, and what additional formal education she will undertake.

Michele McHugh notes that young nurses are not the only ones who benefit from this system. "The sponsors have a chance to develop their teaching skills. They take on administrative functions, do the evaluations. They learn a lot about what outside resources are available." In short, the system provides both mentor and charge with greater variety in their roles, thus broadening their skills and providing more opportunities for decision-making.

Teaching and learning among nurses takes place almost entirely in the units. Beth Israel has a profoundly decentralized and flat structure which provides the units with unusual autonomy—nurse managers are directly responsible for their units, and report only to Joyce Clifford. Given the leanness of this structure, the nursing staff began several years ago to recognize that a more wide-reaching entity was needed to further nursing autonomy, teaching, learning, and interdisciplinary teams across the hospital as a whole. And so in 1991, Beth Israel developed the Integrated Clinical Practice program to aid the professional development of front-line nurses throughout the hospital.

The effort is funded by a Robert Wood Johnson Foundation program known as Strengthening Hospital Nursing, which awards grants to help develop outstanding clinical practice. According to Maureen Mc-Causland, RN, the Director of the project, its goal is to take the model for continuity of care established by primary nursing in the units, and make it work more broadly throughout the hospital. "Physicians move across the system," notes Maureen McCausland. "But the whole idea behind primary nursing is that the nurse will stay with the patient throughout the course of treatment. It will be the nurse's face that the patient recognizes, it will be the nurse who is identified as the person the patient looks to at Beth Israel."

With help from the Integrated Clinical Practice Program, primary nurses in obstetrics have now broadened their role beyond the obstetrical unit, and are giving prenatal care and counseling to prospective patients months before they are admitted for delivery. In this way, patient pregnancies are treated as nine-month events requiring continual care, rather than disparate stages being treated as separate events. Of course, involvement with specific patients across such a broad range requires greater expertise of the nursing staff. By helping nurses with cross-unit assignments and broadening the scope of their collaboration with physicians, ICP is configured to help nurses gain this breadth.

Another ICP program has helped alter the entire structure of the hospital's support staff in a way that works to the benefit of nurses on the front lines. Although primary nurses now assume tasks such as bed baths and medications that were formerly delegated to separate nurses, there is a variety of caretaking chores involving patients that are performed by the housekeeping support staff. Previously, housekeeping chores were broken down and distributed among various people: one made all the beds in a unit, another delivered meal trays, a third did light cleaning in the patients' rooms. Decisions about who performed which tasks were made by housekeeping supervisors, whose primary goal was achieving efficiency by routinizing the work.

But, as Maureen McCausland points out, "The old system meant that lots of different people were constantly running in and out of the patients' rooms, which was often disruptive and upsetting for the patients." ICP changed that by de-industrializing the nature of the housekeeping work. Now individual housekeeping staff members are attached to individual nursing units: they are part of the nurses' care team, and report to them. One person performs all the housekeeping chores in a given room for a given patient, making the bed, cleaning, delivering trays. "This does for the housekeeping staff what primary nursing did for the nurses," says Maureen. "It integrates the nature of the work they perform, makes it more varied and far less routine. And it puts them in the position of directly serving patients."

Integrating their various tasks naturally meant that members of the housekeeping staff had to develop higher levels of skill. Not only were they now expected to do more different things, they were also required to make decisions. Maureen McCausland: "Under the new system, they set their own agenda. Nobody tells them, make the beds first. *They* decide how they're going to do their work. Some of them really need help in learning to prioritize—remember, these are people who were given *no* responsibility in the past!"

Because they are far more involved with patients, the members of the housekeeping staff now need a working knowledge of English. "Once we changed the structure of their work, English naturally became a requirement." So the ICP prevailed upon the administration to set up a unit to teach English as a second language at Beth Israel. Thus was born a true staff development program for those who had formerly been regarded as menials, the improvement of whose skills would be of little benefit to the hospital. "Giving these people more responsibility, and then training them to assume it, makes their jobs more interesting and really improves morale. And the new system is cost effective—we need far fewer supervisors than in the past."

The central challenge faced by ICP is that faced by every organization trying to push decision-making power down to the front lines. Decentralization is the key to such efforts, but the organization must still retain some means of coordinating the decentralized units. Maureen McCausland, who wrote the original proposal for the Robert Wood Johnson Foundation grant, has a strong vision of ICP as providing that needed bridge between decentralization and coordination. "The ICP gives us a means to improve support *across* the system," she points out. "That's so hard to achieve when you're decentralized!"

McCausland was initially inspired to devise the program that evolved into the ICP because she's "interested in continuity as a *value*. That's why I came to Beth Israel in the first place. I think we're good at providing it, but still, it's much harder to achieve than it was in the seventies. For one thing, there's a huge emphasis today on shortening patient stays—it's the only hope for controlling costs. For another, technology plays a much greater role." Indeed, while technology has greatly improved both the accuracy of diagnosis and the range of options for cure and care, it also carries the threat of discontinuities undreamt of in the past by substituting the cost-effective processes of the machine for human care. Given the forces pushing against continuity, it is crucial that decentralized organizations find ways to incorporate this value across independent units, strengthening the tendrils that connect them and making the structure more web-like, more coherent, more inclusive.

The final piece in the integration of teaching and nursing is Beth Israel's Center for the Advancement of Nursing Practice, a research facility for nurses. Joyce Clifford points out that, while the teaching hospitals attached to medical schools have traditionally encompassed medical research units, such facilities have been rare when it comes to nursing. Research has traditionally been integrated into the nature of a physician's work: it both advances the practice of medicine in general, and helps to develop a doctor's individual career. But for nurses, research has always been split off from clinical work, isolated in the academic world—following, as always, an industrialized model.

Joyce Clifford recognized that this lack of opportunity for practicing bedside nurses to pursue scholarship and research was discouraging the best among them to remain in direct patient care. The Center for the Advancement of Nursing Practice is meant to remedy this situation, thus helping the hospital effectively to retain highly experienced, well-educated, and ambitious nurses. By providing scholar awards for nurses pursuing various topics (a recent example: "Examining Mental Status Assessment of HIV Infected Individuals"); by offering extensive training in leadership and management skills; and by instituting a Visiting Professorship Program that brings outstanding scholars in nursing from around the world to Beth Israel, the Center enables the nurses on its staff to integrate scholarly pursuits with the applied practice, thus expanding the scope of professional nursing.

HOW DO YOU GIVE POWER TO PEOPLE?

One challenge in the effort to give power to people on the front lines lies in persuading them to accept the responsibility and autonomy that stem from power. Most people have had little opportunity to wield influence or make substantive decisions in the workplace, and many as a result have accommodated themselves to the situation. They may harbor resentment against those whom they perceive as being in control of their lives—the bosses, managers, supervisors, owners, or professionals whom they see as running their organizations. But in spite of their anger, many have, from the long habit of having to follow orders, grown, if not content, then at least comfortable with a passive role.

In few fields has this been more true than in nursing. Until about twenty years ago, nurses were literally instructed to be subservient, drilled in its practice. Trained in ways that undermined the very nature of their professionalism, they were given the message that, despite their labor, they had little real influence in the hospitals that they served. Because of this history, the institution of primary nursing at Beth Israel provides us with an unusual opportunity to observe the processes by which front-line people can be taught to embrace the exercise of broad-scale authority. We can see, in Joyce Clifford's words, "how you give power to people who've never had it."

A first necessary step, she believes, is for managers and leaders to force themselves to let go of making any decision that can be made at a more immediate level. This is difficult, she admits, because "Let's face it, a person doesn't get into a position of authority—such as I am in at this hospital—without *liking* to make decisions, without being decisive and wanting to get in the middle. The hardest thing for someone like me is to sit on my hands, to resist the temptation to do something myself—both because it's easier, *and because I want to!* But I have to realize that part of my job is being decisive, but another part is getting out of the way so other people can find their own answers."

In order to do this, "I try always to ask myself a few questions before I make any decision. Whose decision should this be? Who is in the position to make it? And what preparation, training, and information might that person need in order to make it? How can I help to provide that? And if no one else is in a position to make this decision, what am I doing wrong? When I force myself to think that way" (and Joyce Clifford admits that it's hard), "I discover that the best role for me is playing backup. I need to transform the nature of any given situation so that someone closer to the problem can make the decision, even though it would often have been easier to make it myself."

Easier—and more efficient; which is why decision-making was split off from execution in the first place. Joyce Clifford admits that creating the conditions under which people in the front ranks can make decisions can be cumbersome. In this, she echoes Doug Clifton, the newsroom editor at the *Miami Herald*, who lamented that giving others the opportunity to decide is "So time-consuming! Sometimes my impulse is to shout, *just do it my way because I'm the boss!"* But that impulse must be resisted because inefficiency is the inevitable initial price that must be paid when pushing power down into the ranks. Yet in finding ways to deal with that inefficiency, a manager or leader is forced to confront the reality that efficiency is a diminished value in the post-industrial organization.

"Administrators make a lot of excuses," says Joyce Clifford. "For example, they'll say, 'Our people don't really want freedom. They want to be told what to do.' Of course, in some cases that's true, but usually it's because leaders try to dump authority without helping their people over the rough spots, or being specific about what it is they want to do. I think most leaders aren't clear enough. You've got to be concrete, let people know exactly what you're trying to accomplish, and tell them the reasons you need to do it. And you've got to stay with your people throughout the process, discuss your philosophy and values, share *all* the time, make that part of what you do every day. That's where the leadership lies, in sharing your experiences and beliefs, and providing a model."

All this demands constant, easy, and open contact at every level throughout the organization: only a leader who is readily accessible and easy to talk to can really model for people the process by which he or she makes decisions. An inclusive style is necessary if a transformation such as that which has occurred at Beth Israel can work. Joyce Clifford points out that one particular reason an inclusive leader must remain in constant touch is that he or she represents the point of intersection between the staff and the outside world.

"A big part of my job is to keep the nurses informed on a regular basis of what's going on out there—what the board is doing, what decisions are confronting the hospital as a whole, what the issues are in health care in this country. I also let them know that I'm trying to represent what the nurses here are doing—to our vice presidents, to our board, and people in the outside world . . . to the nursing profession and the health care field as a whole." Bringing information in and disseminating it keeps people in the ranks clear about the larger implications of change, as well as the macrocosmic reasons it is occurring. Without that, they will have difficulty joining in the process.

Joyce Clifford's efforts to institute and then constantly refine primary nursing have been aided by many of the policies that Mitchell Rabkin put into place as part of his effort to provide patient-centered care. Rabkin notes that he has been engaged for a number of years in an effort to "rework the sociology of the workplace," involving people more intimately in the institution that shapes their lives. In part, this involves being direct and open about larger hospital issues, in particular how finances are raised and allocated.

"We are very candid with our people," he says. "We give them a full accounting of our finances, what we're spending on construction, why we are opening a new unit, what we intend to expand, where our money is coming from, what our goals are, what our larger agenda is." Providing this information breaks down traditional barriers that have divided administration and staff. As Joyce Clifford emphasizes, this is an essential step to vesting power in front-line people.

THE ARTFUL EXPRESSION OF KNOWLEDGE

The radical changes that would transform hospital nursing occurred in response to new technology that became available to hospitals across the United States beginning in the mid-1960s. The potential to develop this technology was set free once Medicaid and Medicare were funded by Congress, which brought a massive influx of dollars into the health care system. The sophistication of the technology, and the amount of power and information it provided, demanded that the nurses at the bedside become far more skilled, experienced, and expert. This in turn set off a series of dramatic changes in how hospital nurses were educated and trained, transforming the profession and paving the way for primary nursing.

Technology provided both the impetus for and one of the means to effect the de-industrialization of nursing. The process by which this occurred parallels that which has taken place in a variety of other fields, in which information technology suddenly increased the demands upon, and the opportunities for, front-line people. Over the last decade in particular, many workers in the ranks have been faced with the need to upgrade their skills to a level they might never have dreamed of in the past. The access they have to information, and the experience they have in making use of it, result in their having to *make* decisions as well as execute them. As a result, the nature of their jobs has become more integrated, and the range of the tasks they perform has grown broader, which makes their work more challenging and rewarding.

Shoshana Zuboff, in her fascinating book *In the Age of the Smart Machine,* examines the process by which information technology forces front-line people to develop a comprehensive grasp and a theoretical understanding of their work and their organizations. She quotes a bank branch officer: "The new technology makes you look at the whole. Tasks become more comprehensive as a result. You need to know where to look for what you need and how to get it. You need to see patterns in relation to the whole."

The technology, then, forces front-line people—those who perform what Zuboff calls "practical, acting-*with* functions"—to develop a real measure of expertise, which she defines as "the artful expression of knowledge in action." Doing so creates opportunities for increased power and autonomy among those who labor in the front ranks, making them far more valuable to the organization. This enrichment of front-line work, Zuboff argues, is where the true advantage of computerization really lies. By breaking down the separation between thinking and doing, information technology speeds up functions, focuses resources directly on customer service, and permits the organization to run with far fewer highly paid managers and supervisors. If technology is not used to effect these transformations, the investment will largely have been wasted.

So organizations face a choice. They can automate, using technology to further routinize and fragment the front-line tasks, thus depriving workers of any source of satisfaction, frustrating customers with impersonal service, and assuring a remote and bloated supervisory management. Or they can "informate," Zuboff's rather unfortunate term for using technology to increase information and autonomy at the point where they intersect with the customer. In doing so, organizations have the opportunity to increase the satisfaction of their workers, provide excellent and personalized service, and build a lean and bare-bones structure at the management level all at once. Zuboff notes that organizations that choose to automate are in effect using post-industrial technology to achieve industrial ends—an inherently counterproductive approach.

Clearly, Beth Israel has chosen the path of "informating," of pushing power and autonomy into the front ranks. The primary nursing system is a vehicle to achieve this. It cannot be stressed too much that this decision grows directly out of Mitchell Rabkin's commitment to creating a hospital that best serves the patient's needs. Technology initiated the present revolution in hospital nursing, but Beth Israel is also using technology to continue and augment it.

The hospital relies upon three computer systems: a centralized mainframe from Data General that contains the entire patient data base; an IBM mainframe for administration; and numerous PC networks based on IBM workstations with Novell servers that convey information to nurses and physicians. In every unit, the nurse manager has a terminal with a gateway to both mainframes, which makes both administrative data and detailed patient information immediately available to her.

Beth Israel is presently collaborating with Harvard to develop a Functional Health Pattern Assessment program, designed *specifically* for nurses, that will greatly expand the amount of information available on every patient who has ever been admitted to the hospital or received care in its clinics. The new program will be installed on the mainframe data base, but every primary nurse will be able to access it by entering a patient's ID number into one of her unit's workstations; an electronic signature will be required for security.

The FHPA will include all physician notes on the patient, as well as alerts, attestations, options, lab and radiology reports, family medical history; it will also allow the nurse to view X rays on the workstation screen. It will provide a history of the patient's drug reactions, allergies, special dietary needs, and past willingness to follow prescriptive regimes. It will show how and where a patient lives, what kind of home care was required in the past, which friends or relatives have proven most helpful. The physician can use the program to write orders, and specify what procedures and medications the nurse can administer without special permission—permission that will be delivered on the program. The program will automatically send medication orders to the pharmacy for delivery to the nurse.

Further, the program will provide information on how to find the most up-to-date analyses of various patient conditions, so that the nurse need not undertake a paper chase to find the best available medical literature on any topic. It will also be interactive, answering queries on various patient populations: a nurse can call up the latest figures on Kaposi's sarcoma mortality, or discover if the disease develops at different rates in different age groups. Every primary nurse the patient has ever had in the past will be automatically notified when a patient is readmitted to the hospital—something that has until now been difficult with patients who have been in various units because of the hospital's decentralized structure. This will permit previous primary nurses to visit their patients in other units, strengthening the belief in the patient that she is *their* nurse. The primary nurse's logbook will also be kept on the program, so that caretakers in the future can have access to that.

The FHPA will also be prescriptive. It will provide predictions of the numbers of care hours a patient might need, and a variety of risk factors, based on a cross-index of the disease and the profile of the particular patient: the difference in the typical requirements of a seventy-five-year-old non-ambulatory woman who has had a specific kind of stroke, and the requirements of a forty-nine-year-old healthy man who has had the same kind of stroke. It will show the range of usual outcomes and predict needs for future services—both those the hospital can provide and those that will be needed at home. It will provide listings of what care options can be found in the patient's community: does the neighborhood church sponsor a meals-on-wheels?

This advanced and sophisticated information technology will thus continue the process of integrating a wide range of nursing functions, blurring the line between learning and teaching, acting and making decisions. By making available enormous amounts of information that can be looked at or integrated in a variety of ways, it will enable the nurse to draw up more accurate and effective care plans. Thus the program will transfer to the front lines an even greater capacity to make decisions than has been possible in the past. It is interesting to note that this technology is being developed specifically in response to a survey taken among Beth Israel nurses about what range of information they would like ideally to have. The program's comprehensiveness thus derives both from their needs and from their ambitions, providing an extraordinary tool for the development of nursing expertise.

Six

Making Training Part of the Process: Anixter Inc.

"A key to the future lies in using technologies to deliver mass-produced goods and services to individuals on a tailorized basis and mass scale simultaneously."

—STANLEY DAVIS

KNOWLEDGE IN THE BONES

Complex and interconnected technology demands that everyone involved at every stage in the manufacture, marketing, or sale of today's products and services must develop a more sophisticated understanding than ever in the past of how these products and services work and what they provide. This need for understanding is made more profound and urgent by the kind of mass customizing that Stanley Davis describes, in which every transaction, every purchase, and every sale must be tailored to meet a specific need. It is precisely this ability to tailor-make, to customize on a mass level that will give organizations their advantage in the future.

One inescapable aspect of this customizing is the integration of products and services, which involves bundling them together into a package that provides value at every stage. If, for example, you design a software program to meet a specific need, it won't be worth much to your customer unless you can also explain, install, service, and upgrade it; because the program has been customized, no one else can do the job. Thus the line between products and services begins to blur—even to disappear entirely—as together they get reconfigured into an entire system. And whoever presumes to provide a *system* for a customer had better have a clear and comprehensive idea of how it works and what it can accomplish in terms of meeting that customer's needs.

As a result of this reconfiguration, people in today's organizations need to know a lot about the products and services they offer, which means that they must be trained more extensively than in the past. As we saw in the previous chapter, it was the advent of complex technology back in the mid-1960s that set in motion the dramatic changes in how hospital nurses had to be educated. As Charles Handy has observed with characteristic clarity, "Smart machines need smart people to work with them." But being smart is not enough; people must also be highly trained.

More than that, they must also be trained *continually*, since continual transformative change is complex technology's only constant. And because continual training, by its very nature, cannot be done on a onetime basis, it must therefore be integrated into the ongoing process of daily work. This has enormous ramifications for how training is done in today's organizations, for the role it plays and the importance with which it is regarded. Indeed, the word "training," with its Industrial Era connotations, will probably disappear from our organizational lexicon in the near future, to be replaced by something broader and more evocative of interdependence.

Nancy Badore, who gained her measure of fame in American business by devising and implementing the innovative executive training programs that played a part in the Ford Motor Company's turnaround in the 1980s, believes that the whole concept of training as we know it is becoming obsolete. "Training as it's been done," she declares, "is inherently limited. It's less comprehensive than the idea of learning. As a 'trainer,' you are concentrating on what *you* are putting out there, not on what the other person is absorbing. You hear people say, 'It will take us six months to do the training on this.' Well, that's fine, but the real question is, how long will it take the people being trained to *learn?"*

Nancy Badore also notes that "Real learning is basically about adapting, about finding ways to put new information into a context the learner can use. So by its very nature, it has to be customized, tailored to the person who is going to be using it, adapting it to their work. It also affects the person who provides it—the old Heisenberg uncertainty principle—which means it's reciprocal, always in flux. Learning cannot be thought of as a onetime event, something with predefined limits. It's a process we all do as we go along. So that has to be the way we present it."

Typically, training in an organization has been presented as a class or series of classes intended either to orient new employees to the company, or to prepare them for assuming new positions. Thus training has been split off from regular work, separated out as a distinct function, provided either by those whose job in the organization is to train, or by outside contractors who develop training programs. And despite occasional pious lip service to the contrary, it has also been very much a one-way process, with information dispensed out or down, and the student cast into a kind of dumb terminal role. Yet this purely Industrial Era paradigm, based on standardized presentations, is hopelessly inadequate when it comes to preparing people who must design, market, sell, and service highly customized products.

Formal training departments in large organizations are a fairly recent phenomenon, one very much related to the standardizing of workplace skills that has taken place over the course of this century. As such, formalized training has comprised one of the many efficiencies characteristic of the era of mass production. But before mass production was so firmly in place, the knowledge and skills of work were transmitted directly by more experienced workers to those with less

experience within the context of regular daily work. Rather than being a distinct function, training was thus an inseparable aspect of all
labor, following the ancient dictates of the master-apprentice tradition.

This kind of training was by nature both integrated and continual, an aspect of work as a whole. It required that everyone in the
workplace play a dual role, performing a specific kind of work, but
also either learning it or teaching it as they went along. Education
took place in a profoundly personal and fairly unsystematized way,
with both progress and need judged accordingly. The process was
fluid, loose, shaped by the unique chemistry between teacher and
student. Thus inevitably it was also customized.

As Shoshana Zuboff notes in *In the Age of the Smart Machine*,
such training was often absorbed at an almost unconscious level. Because it was reinforced repeatedly throughout countless workdays,
physical skills gradually became incorporated into the *body* of the
worker; like a knowledge of waterskiing or bicycle riding, once you
had done it, you knew how to do it for the rest of your life. Conceptual skills also were absorbed by the watchful apprentice at a relatively unconscious level, as a result of being in direct contact with a
master who performed a variety of tasks during the course of a day.
Thus complex activities, such as decision-making and delegating,
were transmitted in ways that transcended and went beyond intellectual categorization. Because such skills were taught in the process of
exercising them, the apprentice had the chance to develop an intuition, a *feel* for doing what was right.

Watching complex tasks being handled by highly experienced
people is key if people at all levels are to integrate learning into the
process of work. But opportunities for this are rare in most large
organizations, where people tend to be segregated according to status,
so that those starting out have little opportunity to observe demanding work being done by those who are expert at it. I became aware of
this in the course of researching *The Female Advantage*. On one of the
days I spent with Frances Hesselbein, at that time National Executive
Director of the Girl Scouts, I was present when she invited two very

young women from the media department into her office just before she was scheduled to give a telephone interview to a newspaper reporter. There was no particular purpose for this visit: Frances Hesselbein was simply trying to give these entry-level employees the chance to see firsthand how a good interview was conducted.

As I watched, I reflected how impossible this simple act would have been in most organizations for which I had worked. In them, almost nobody got a chance to see senior executives in action until they had nearly obtained senior executivehood themselves. But Frances Hesselbein was eager to provide the young women with the chance to observe her, for she recognized that watching and listening are all-important aspects of the apprentice role. Thus she was able to provide her staff members with an *experience,* as opposed to a set of specific instructions, experience being necessary for someone to know something, as Shoshana Zuboff describes it, "in their bones."

JUST IN TIME LEARNING

As we move from the era of mass production into the age of mass customizing, the ways in which we train people will radically change. The style and scope of the transformation will be determined by the increasingly sophisticated and integrated nature of products and services, and by the rapid pace of technological change as dictated by Moore's Law. Both of these factors demand that people continually improve and add to their skills, which means that learning and teaching must take place in the context of daily work. Thus the post-industrial workplace will find us returning to an updated version of the old master and apprentice tradition.

It is worth noting that the companies widely recognized in the past as having the best training programs in the world have for the most part been profoundly bureaucratic and many-layered institutions, such as IBM and the old Bell System. These organizations have also been characterized by a plethora of written guidelines and complex procedures that governed the way their work was done. As a result, entrepreneurial spirit and drive have usually been discouraged in these institutions, since such qualities are incompatible with the greater culture, which tends to deemphasize the role of improvisation and individual effort.

Entrepreneurial drive *is,* however, characteristic of many of today's most vital enterprises, with their lean structures and ability to adjust to change. The challenge for training, therefore, becomes finding a way to reconcile entrepreneurialism, with its tradition of by-the-seat-of-your-pants learning, with the kind of deliberate and strategically focused learning that bureaucratic organizations have so excelled in providing. It is only by blending these two traditions that organizations will be able to provide for the kind of continual upgrading of complex skills that will be necessary in order to thrive in the years ahead.

The paradox that lies at the heart of this challenge assures us that we are entering new territory. And yet to some degree we already have a map, provided by our observation of how webs of inclusion work. Because of their emphasis on creating new links and channels across levels, webs of inclusion are particularly useful for organizations seeking to diffuse skills and knowledge throughout the ranks, giving people the chance to watch the experts as they go about the performance of their tasks. Because they work from the grass roots inward, bringing information from the front lines or periphery to the center, webs are ideal for organizations trying to assure that what people need to know flows both ways. And because webs are fluid, expanding and contracting to meet specific needs, they provide the means for a kind of learning that focuses specifically on what the individual learner needs to know at a given time.

Webs of inclusion can thus enable organizations to create updated versions of the master-apprentice system that served the needs of the pre-industrial era, when, as today, products and services were designed and made to meet specific customer needs. It was just this need for customizing that gave Japanese auto companies the impetus to introduce the concept of "just in time" into their management of inventory: since they no longer mass-produced their products, they could not keep huge inventories on hand, and had to develop a more flexible system. Similarly, the web of inclusion offers organizations the means to create what might be called "just in time learning." Such learning would be specifically tailored to hone the skills of people in an organization in the course of performing their daily work—and to do so continually, flexibly, and in real time.

CULTURE AND TRADITION AT ANIXTER

A great place to watch the paradox of an entrepreneurial company trying to make sophisticated training part of its process is at Anixter Inc., a global networking and cabling systems specialist headquartered in Skokie, Illinois. The organization has a colorful history, defined by a driven and independent sales force in which everyone runs his or her own business as an entrepreneur. Anixter has made every effort to keep this individualistic culture intact during an extraordinary period of growth that has taken it from $385 million in sales in the mid-1980s to $1.5 billion in 1993, a fifteen percent average increase for every year. Keeping what is best in its culture has been a particular challenge, given that the fast-growing company has had to hire people at a rapid rate.

In contrast to, for example, Intel, which has its roots in Silicon Valley culture and has been on the cutting edge of post-industrial technology from the start, Anixter began as a family-owned enterprise in a resolutely Second Wave kind of business run on a shoestring in the gritty Midwest. Nevertheless, having from the start identified its purpose as the fulfillment of *customized* wants rather than mass orders, it has positioned itself well for an age that puts an increasing premium on products and services tailored to specific needs.

The company was founded in 1957 by two brothers, Bill and Alan Anixter, who grew up on the west side of Chicago; their father was a boss in the Democratic machine who had lost all his money in the depression. Theirs was a tough world, familiar from the novels of Saul Bellow, in which people prided themselves on having street smarts. The brothers started their company with a $10,000 loan from their mother, part of which they used to rent a 5,000-square-foot warehouse in an industrial part of Evanston. The rest of the money went for the purchase of ten trailer-loads of field wire that the Army had auctioned off as surplus from the Korean War.

At the time, wire and cable were sold by manufacturers to full-line electrical wholesalers, who (in the classic tradition of mass suppliers) carried everything from light bulbs to washing machines. These wholesalers maintained no inventory themselves, but instead relied upon that held by manufacturers. The manufacturers, of course, had little incentive to try to fulfill the comparatively small special orders that the wholesalers were always getting, in particular from building contractors. These contractors therefore had to wait for months to get the specific stock of wire and cable they needed, or were often forced to make do with substitutes. Since there were hundreds of manufacturers but relatively few distributors of electrical products, bottlenecks kept the system tied up at every step.

The Anixter brothers set out to break this bottleneck by acting as middlemen, becoming the first company to specialize in the distribution of electrical wire and cable. They bought product directly from manufacturers, kept a reasonable amount of inventory on hand, and sold contractors exactly the size and length of cable they wanted. Because they specialized in a single commodity, as opposed to electrical products in general, the fledgling company was able to ship its orders much faster than full-line distributors. The business was thus based from the start upon filling customers' orders more quickly and specifically than anyone else. Since Anixter didn't *make* anything—and never sought to be the low-cost provider—its success has depended solely on its ability to provide superior, fast, and customized service.

At first, Anixter was able to buy only remnants. The warehouse, which also served as the company's office, was filled floor-to-ceiling with various lengths of different sizes of wire. Six sales people, including the brothers, solicited orders mostly by phone, and then either found what they needed in stock or scrambled to get hold of what the customer needed. It was a style of doing business that demanded and thrived upon the cultivation of street smarts. Warehouse and shipping tasks were all performed part-time by Chicago firemen, who had twenty-four hours off every few days, because the work was too fitful to justify full-time employees.

Much of what now characterizes Anixter's distinctive culture was there at the beginning. Sales people were given great latitude, not only in developing customers, but also in setting prices for products within a range controlled by their branch managers. As the company expanded, this emphasis on front-line responsibility and independence evolved into the custom of letting people in the units determine the direction of the business, rather than executing it according to some master plan. As a result, strategy at Anixter had traditionally been preceded by tactics, an approach that has strengthened the entrepreneurialism of those in the front ranks.

In addition, the slim margins of profit and the emphasis on individual effort have tended to make people in the company skeptical of professionalized management. Even in the midst of its recent rapid growth, Anixter has been reluctant to hire MBAs, or to bring in outside consultants from companies like Arthur Anderson or McKinsey. Nor has it, until recently, vested much power in people whose specialty is finance. As in the beginning, the power, engine, and essence of the company is its sales force, although this is being modified to some degree by technological change.

Anixter began and has remained relatively unhierarchical and relentlessly informal. Everyone is immediately put on a first-name basis. One of the founders' mottoes was: "No stuffed shirts. No big shots." The organization has retained its entrepreneurial bias by hiring very young people who have not been conditioned by other cultures, and then giving them unusual responsibility and freedom to develop their talents. Anixter also has a history of promoting from within. Even today, a number of top executives have gotten their start by packing wire as an hourly worker in one of the company's warehouses.

The antibureaucratic bias runs deep. Julie Anixter, Bill Anixter's daughter, recounts a story, famous in the company, about her father and uncle trying to borrow money. "It was the early seventies. Things were going great and they wanted to expand. They went looking for someone to lend them ten million. They showed their numbers to a banker from Mutual of Omaha, who seemed impressed, but then asked to see a copy of the company's policy manual. Of course, they didn't have any such thing. But the Mutual guy said, 'You've *got* to have one! We can't give money to some company that doesn't even have a policy manual!'

"So my dad and uncle had this fancy leather-bound cover made up, and then he stuck his copy of the *Up the Organization* inside. They thought that book summed up their idea of policy better than anything else. Then they had 'Anixter Policy Manual' printed on the cover, very official-looking, and brought it to the next meeting and passed it around. The Mutual of Omaha guy picked it up, glanced at the table of contents, and saw all the categories in place—Human Resources, Guidelines, Practices. He never even glanced at the rest of it, that was enough. Anixter had a policy manual, so the company must be all right. My dad and uncle got the loan."

Exemplifying Anixter's continuity, that "Policy Manual" then became the basis for the company's "Blue Book," a tiny pamphlet that states the company philosophy on various matters. An example: "We make our own calls. We answer our own phones. We're never 'in a meeting' or 'busy.' And no one at Anixter ever asks, 'Who's calling?' "

The booklet is proudly devoid of such corporate staples as policies on hiring or promotion. The two pages headed "Organization Chart" and "Job Descriptions" are both completely blank.

Disdain for top-down decision-making done in a vacuum has long been a company hallmark: it's known as avoiding "the Orchard Chevrolet syndrome." Julie Anixter explains: "Our offices used to look out on the Old Orchard Chevy dealer in Skokie, so Orchard became a kind of synonym for an isolated, ivory tower, corporate-versus-field mentality. We always felt we had to be skeptical of any solution that had been thought up while staring out the window. We believe solutions should come from the field, at the level of the people who are actually dealing with the problems. Today, everyone calls that empowerment, but we always just thought of it as the way business should be run—that you should stay away from the Old Orchard Chevrolet syndrome."

The Right Place at the Right Time

Anixter grew steadily throughout the sixties and seventies, helped in part by the rapid spread of television and the boom in electrical appliances. In the mid-1960s, the company went public. In 1984, its fortunes received a major boost with the breakup of the old Bell System. The consent decree that set the terms for divestiture barred the newly regionalized operating companies from manufacturing and selling products, thus opening a competitive market in telephone wire and electronic components.

At the same time, the PC revolution had begun, vastly increasing the need for wire and cable to hook computers and modems into both local and wide area networks. Cable television was also taking off, as were satellite communications. Soon "infrastructure" was being redefined to include the interconnections that held the nation's information systems together, rather than just the roads and bridges that provided glue in a more concrete and observable way. Wire and cable were in the process transformed from a low-end Industrial Era commodity into the very blood and sinews of high tech.

In 1986, Anixter was bought by the Chicago investor Sam Zell and the founders retired. Since Zell's acquisition, Anixter's parent has been the Itel Corporation, which has maintained a hands-off policy in regard to Anixter's business. With vast infusions of capital suddenly available from its parent company for further expansion, Anixter found itself in the late 1980s in the right place at the right time, with the right product and a history of selling that product in the right way. Thus circumstances conspired to encourage the kind of rapid growth that often challenges organizations as profoundly as do lean times.

Since the late 1980s, Anixter has been hiring around three hundred new people each year, and opening new offices and warehouses in cities around the globe. This expansion has meant that, for the first time, the company has had to bring in "outsiders" to fill important jobs, in addition to promoting from the ranks as in the past. Also, thanks to the extraordinary variety of active electronic systems that characterizes the information age—Anixter now inventories over eighty thousand different products!—the company has had to bring in a range of technology experts, thus strengthening the informal expertise culture that has long prevailed.

At the same time, the way in which Anixter markets its products has had to change, as the kinds of full service it sells have grown more complex. In the past, customizing at Anixter meant finding the precisely right size length of wire, made of the right material, and delivering it in the exact amount needed at the right time, and jointly developing cable systems for industrial clients. That level of tailoring sufficed to add real value for the customer during the first few decades of the organization's growth. But customization has become far more demanding: it now means nothing less than the delivery of an entire infrastructure. Providing "one-stop shopping" these days means offering the design, layout, and installation of a network; the maintenance that keeps the system up-to-date; and the physical devices that comprise and connect every part of the network—from cable, connectors, and jacks to intelligent devices like the hubs and routers that transmit information.

All this means that everyone in the company, particularly those who have been newly hired, must have detailed knowledge of the enormous range of communications products and services that the company has to offer, and a sophisticated understanding of how they can be combined—the industry term for this is interoperability. In order to achieve this, Anixter people must be highly trained, and their training must be constantly updated. Yet the antibureaucratic emphasis that permeated the company from its beginnings led it consistently to underplay the need for any formal training.

"Training around here," says Bill Millholland, now Vice President for Marketing Communications, "always used to mean that you threw the Yellow Pages at someone when they came into the company, and told them to go out and scare up some customers. In other words, there *was* no training. People learned by making mistakes, and by asking questions when they had to. We never even had a Human Resources department. Our motto was: you're on your own, we trust you to figure things out for yourself. That whole approach seemed a necessary part of our entrepreneurial culture. Entrepreneurs aren't trained, they learn by doing. We're a company of entrepreneurs, so we've traditionally followed that approach *in spades.*"

Given the vast increase in the complexity of what Anixter sells, however, throwing the Yellow Pages at people will no longer suffice. For one thing, the company's role in providing networking systems means that its sales force must now sell to a higher level than ever in the past. "Our people used to make their sales primarily to procurement staff," explains Bob Eck, who came from Itel in 1992 to head Anixter's first ever Human Resources department. "Wire was traditionally a low-end item, so there wasn't much need for our force to get involved at the corporate level. All that's changed now. We're providing infrastructure for these very complex systems, which involves us in major business decisions. Our people are selling to Chief Information Officers. When you're dealing at that level, you have to be very sophisticated."

The environment is thus challenging Anixter to train its people in a more thorough and systematic way, without diluting the entrepreneurial culture that has defined the company and been responsible for its success. Appropriate training must therefore integrate the traditional emphasis on learning by doing with more formal programs that provide backup and support. As Bob Eck notes, "Our leverage from now on is going to come from how well we develop our people. And we can't do that anymore by just telling them they're on their own. There has to be a context for what they're doing, some kind of systematic approach. Our business has gotten too complicated for the old way of doing things."

FROM FINE ARTS TO THE ART OF TRAINING

Having begun as a family business in a scrappy industry, Anixter still prides itself on being skeptical about how big companies are traditionally run. A rough-and-tumble entrepreneurial culture has long defined the company's sense of "who we are." One result has been the almost scornful lack of interest in any kind of institutionalized training. So it is fascinating to watch Anixter's efforts to find a way to incorporate training into its culture being assumed by one who bears the culture most deeply.

Julie Anixter, the daughter of Bill Anixter, is the only family member who has stayed in the business. She had no thoughts of joining Anixter when she was growing up. "I came of age in the 1960s, and business was not at all my interest. I cared about art, not industry." Leaving home in Highland Park, north of Chicago, she went to San Francisco State, where she majored in fine arts—textiles, with an emphasis on design. "The closest I ever got to the family business in those days," she recalls, "was helping my teachers get a hold of wire for making sculpture. Anixter had warehouses full of the stuff."

After college, she remained in the Bay Area, wrote about art, curated shows for galleries, and sold her own work as part of an artists' cooperative. For a time, she thought she wanted to start a gallery, but she ended up taking a job at a public relations firm that specialized in the fine arts. With that job, "the lights just went on. I realized that I loved business, was fascinated by it. And I saw that I was good at it too. My liberal arts education and the communications skills I'd developed were looked on as being of real value in business, whereas in the art world, I was just one more overqualified person."

In 1982, she returned to Chicago, inspired by the desire to put her public relations experience to work for the company that was then still being run by her father and uncle. "I applied for an entry-level job in advertising. They offered me sixteen thousand a year, and I had to fight like crazy to try to get eighteen. My dad said he had no desire to create high-level jobs for people in the family, and he made it more than clear I would not get special treatment. But *I* knew I had something to offer Anixter. I loved PR and had great experience, and the company really needed that. My dad and uncle had always been the kind that tried to keep their pictures *out* of the papers. But times were changing, and that was no longer a good approach."

Julie Anixter's timing was fortuitous. She began work at the company in 1983, just before the consent decree that broke up the Bell system took effect. Recognizing that this event would give the company a huge opportunity to expand market awareness, she set about building a public relations program for Anixter, concentrating primarily upon the trade press, with which the company had never even had a relationship. She spent the next four years building up a full-scale public relations department, giving Anixter greater visibility in a world where visibility was increasingly important. She enjoyed her work, but she began to feel restless, discontented with being out of the main loop. "In PR, you're basically on the periphery. You're not shaping policy, you're not really at the center of the action. And more and more, that's where I wanted to be."

She saw no path by which she might move to a more central position in the company, however, since executives were virtually always drawn directly from the sales force. Nor was there any particular program she could use to get where she wanted to go. Then a woman manager in the company suggested that Julie take a proactive approach, and try to devise some on-the-job training for herself. She should figure out what she needed to know in order to advance as an executive, and create a program that would enable her to learn it.

Excited by this proposal, Julie Anixter set about gathering information. "From the start, I didn't just think of it in terms only of what *I* needed to know. Instead, I asked myself, what would a training program at Anixter be like? What kind of things do people here need to understand, not just for now but for the years ahead? And how can people learn these things in a way that isn't so rigid and defined that we end up losing our entrepreneurial edge?"

At the time, in the mid-1980s, any training that existed was done informally, by managers at the various locations, or by the company's suppliers. Julie Anixter recalls, "These managers tended to be people who were great at sales and had been promoted because of that. But they didn't necessarily have any aptitude either for managing or for teaching. Training was a completely *ad hoc* process. Yet it seemed obvious to me that this kind of approach no longer made any sense. We were evolving into more of a high-end, high-tech company, and we needed to coordinate the way people learned things. There was just so much that we all had to know!"

While she was thinking about a training program for herself, Julie Anixter went to work on the company's first ever worldwide gathering of managers, which took place in late 1986. She helped with every phase of the event, in particular the workshops and executive speeches. "The conference was just a huge success, and a week or so after it was over, I got a call from an executive VP I'd been working with. He said he'd been talking with other senior execs, and they agreed there was a need for the company to focus more on education, because of the increased complexity of our business. He knew I had a background in education, and he had just seen for himself that I was very good with events, so he proposed I get involved with training. It was just the kind of thing I was looking for, so I didn't even need to think about whether I should say yes."

Julie Anixter notes that she never had a clear picture of what she wanted to do with her life until she discovered training. "Then all of a sudden, it was totally obvious that this is what I was *meant* to do. Training synthesizes everything I have ever been interested in, everything I've wanted to be involved in. It's design-oriented, and I like design—that's clear from my art background. It's also intellectual and challenging, and gives you a chance to work with people directly. It's very much about teaching, and I'd always loved to do that, and it's also about communicating, about engaging an audience. When I was growing up, I used to do choreography and stage-manage plays, and training certainly gives you a chance to do that—it's a kind of theater. Really, training gives me a chance to use every part of myself. So it took a while, but I finally found my passion in life."

THE SEARCH FOR SYNTHESIS

Julie Anixter assumed the job of Anixter's first-ever Director of Training in January 1987. Her friend and then later boss Bill Millholland, who became Vice President of Training and Development in 1988, had had a lot of experience with traditional approaches. He had begun his career in the Army, then spent fourteen years at AT&T, and had come to Anixter from Siecor, a military contractor. These cultures are all characterized by elaborate, rigorous, and carefully designed training programs that could hardly be more different from Anixter's entrepreneurial approach. Nevertheless, Bill Millholland came quickly to be a great admirer of how Anixter did things.

He recalls his own hiring at Anixter. "Siecor was one of Anixter's vendors, so I'd dealt with the company before, signed Siecor's first deal with them. Then I got fired from Siecor—I'd been doing well, but I rubbed the President the wrong way—and the Anixter people could hardly believe it. They kept asking, 'You got rid of *him?*' Bruce Van Wagner (then Anixter's Executive Vice President) called me up, and asked if I'd like to come to work for the company." Bill Millholland was not interested, preferring North Carolina to Chicago, but Anixter remained persistent in a way that gave him an intriguing taste of "just how different this company really was. They didn't have a specific job for me, it was more like 'there's got to be a place here for Bill.' I'd never seen anything like that before." Intrigued, Millholland eventually accepted a position as Vice President of Contractor Sales, and soon discovered the true extent of Anixter's entrepreneurial culture.

"I came in, there wasn't even an office for me yet. Everyone was very nice, but no one seemed to know what I should be doing with my time. I was left completely alone. It quickly became apparent that I was going to have to create my own work. It was a totally different experience for me, but I found that I really thrived on it. At AT&T, they ran you through this whole process, made sure you knew all this stuff before you started work. Here, you either figured things out for yourself, or you didn't." Bill Millholland soon discovered that this kind of baptism by fire worked very *fast*. "You turned into a kind of sponge, and you just learned very quickly. Also, being dropped in like that enabled you to develop at your own pace, to get a feel for what you were doing as you went along. No class, no structured program can provide that."

Bill Millholland began to recognize that Anixter's seat-of-the-pants approach works best with people who are resourceful and independent, which has the effect of encouraging those people to stay in the company. "Really, the whole thing functions as a great weeding-out process, discouraging individuals who aren't highly driven or eager to make their own way." He also notes that Anixter's approach, with its relentlessly grassroots emphasis, enables it to avoid the kind of bureaucratizing that he saw in other companies. Having worked under very different systems, Bill Millholland feels he is able to clearly see and appreciate the value of both approaches to learning. Thus he was able to serve as a resource for Julie Anixter as she undertook the task of synthesizing a kind of training that would preserve what was best in the company.

Just as Bill Millholland had to learn the culture, Julie Anixter had to learn to see beyond it. "I grew up *drenched* in Anixter," she says. "So right from the start, I had a strong feeling for its values. I knew that anything that was too planned, too structured, wouldn't stand a chance in this company. We were used to evolving things as we went along. I was helped by the fact that *I'm* not all that comfortable with an inordinate focus on detail. These days everyone seems to want to be a strategic planner—in their companies, or just their own lives. But I believe in the value of adapting to the challenges as they arise. I'm not bothered when I'm not sure how something's going to turn out, because that's the point at which I really learn things."

In her first year on the job, Julie Anixter was as much on her own as Bill Millholland had been when he had found himself without an office. She was charged to develop a way of training people at Anixter, but she was given little guidance as to what this might entail or how it might be accomplished. "At times, it felt overwhelming," she recalls. "This was the mid-late 1980s, and we had something like forty thousand different products in inventory! The question is, how do you teach some twenty-seven-year-old coming into the company what product the customer needs to use? And how do you help him figure out how to combine that product with exactly what he needs to make a system? It's particularly difficult when the company is just growing like mad, hiring new people all the time. And it's even harder when the inventory is always changing, and new ways of using products are evolving all the time."

From the start, Julie Anixter felt sure that merely devising lectures and classes would never work. For one thing, this approach compartmentalizes learning, restricting it in time and place, whereas Anixter had a long tradition of learning that took place on the job. In addition, the skills demanded of people selling high-end, high-tech products are simply too complex to be absorbed in a discrete, entirely rationalized way. People had to get a *feel* for what they were doing—that was the secret of the old seat-of-your-pants way of learning, which had been successful but which now was perceived as leaving too much to chance.

Julie Anixter quickly saw that the effort to provide integrated training in a way that gives people a feel for what they are doing is essentially limited by our lack of understanding of how people learn at profound levels. As Shoshana Zuboff has observed, *we don't fully understand the process by which people absorb knowledge so deeply that it becomes part of their bodily intuition.* Julie Anixter confesses that, when she accepted her position in training, she had "very little idea how we were going to achieve what we needed to." As a result, she experienced her first year on the job as intensely frustrating at times. "With help from a number of people, I put together some good lectures, but it was all pretty much one-way communication. I was desperate to get beyond that, but wasn't sure how to do it."

She was also aware that she would have to develop ways of

training that were "much more organic, more reflective of the networked, integrated shape of our company and our work. We're very web-like, interlocked with our customers and our vendors. Some of our customers are our suppliers too." As a result of these interconnections, people at Anixter have to know their vendors' business, what they are in the process of developing, where they are trying to go. "This means we have to co-market with them, co-develop programs, and co-train so that we can learn from one another. When I started out, I didn't have any model for how to do that."

Uncertain how to proceed, Julie Anixter "did what I've always done: I searched out the best masters I could find." As a fine arts student, she had made every effort to track down the finest teachers in the world and learn her craft from them. Now she returned to this approach. She had heard about a network of people who were studying adult learning under the guidance of a teacher named Dr. Fernando Flores, the former finance minister in Salvador Allende's government, who had spent years in a Chilean prison before being freed by Amnesty International. After studying computer science at Stanford, Flores had reinvented himself as an educational software designer based in the San Francisco Bay Area. His software, some of the earliest groupware, was specifically designed to allow people to try out concepts as they learned them, both autonomously and in teams. The idea was that discovery combined with simultaneous application could result in knowledge being absorbed at profound and intuitive levels.

Julie Anixter began a three-year graduate program under Flores's tutelage, joining a study group that communicated by e-mail. The experience, she says, "put me in touch with this incredible web of people who were doing imaginative things in business, medicine, design, education, linguistics—people who were studying *how we learn to learn*. This became a source of great power for me: I knew people who were ahead of the game, doing vanguard work. That gave me the confidence I needed to be able to try out things that were absolutely new."

Above all, Julie Anixter learned from her work with Flores "how to initiate the kind of dialogue that helps me to learn from people what *they* need, and then design programs to help them learn what's relevant. People in an organization have a good idea of what they need, the areas where they're lacking; my job was to let myself be guided by that. If you're in training, your real task is enabling people to articulate what they want to learn, and then find a way to help them to learn it."

This was, Julie points out, particularly easy to do at Anixter "because there has always been a group of people here who have lots of ideas and very strong feelings about what it is possible to do, as a result of their five or ten or fifteen years' experience in building a successful company"—people, in other words, with a great deal of nonpositional power. The task, then, for Julie, was to identify these people, and initiate intense and ongoing conversations with them. "A main aspect of Flores's work," she explains, "is the idea that language is generative, not descriptive—it creates our reality, rather than just describing it. If that's true, it means that conversation is *much* more important than we, with our puritan work ethic, have ever imagined! What I had to do, then, was plug into the network of people who had a strong understanding of this company, and engage them in really challenging conversations about the business. That gave me the pulse at the company, and the ideas, energy, and inspiration to concretize what I heard into the design of the training. Good conversation promotes good design, and ensures real-world, *business* common sense results."

Talking with people throughout the company helped Julie Anixter both to identify the primary areas in which people felt they needed more professional training, and to discover what individuals were doing on their own to successfully address those needs. Because of Anixter's tradition of letting people fend for themselves, a number of people in the field had devised their own informal training programs. These were to prove a valuable resource.

Julie Anixter says, "There was all this great stuff happening in the company, but it was being done very casually, very locally, and there was no way for people to communicate about it. More and more, I began to recognize that my role was to scout out pilot projects, and then try to adapt them to serve the company as a whole. Certainly, working through the field wasn't just my idea. Bill Millholland, who was my boss, was insistent about it. He's the one who's always talking about avoiding the Old Orchard Chevrolet syndrome. He made going to the field our religion!"

TRAINING THE FORCE

In late 1987, Julie Anixter was asked by the company's Executive Vice President and now Chairman, Bob Wilson, to find a way to help the sales people increase their sales of entire systems instead of just discrete products. Training the sales force had to be the priority, because sales has always been Anixter's engine; it is within its sales force that the company's entrepreneurial culture has always been strongest. Sales people at Anixter operate with unusual independence, not only selecting and developing their own clients, but also setting prices within a certain latitude, and so determining their profit margins. Every sales manager manages his or her own profit-and-loss sheet, and sells as well as manages. The structure is extremely flat, which augments the power and independence of those on the front lines.

"It was clear to Bill Millholland and me that this was a typical example of why the old approach wouldn't work anymore. You can't expect people to sell products as systems unless you give them a lot of tools and training in how it's done. So Bill and I started looking around the company, trying to figure out what would work. One of the people we wanted to talk to was Andy Chacon, whom Bill had worked with in contractor sales, and had been sent to open a new sales office in Des Moines. Andy had some of the highest sales figures in the company, and he was known for being very creative. We wanted to see if we could learn anything from how he was managing things in Des Moines."

What they discovered was almost a perfect pilot project. "This was back in 1987, before most people in the company were using PCs.

But Andy had been trained as an engineer, and he really knew computers. Well, when we got out to Des Moines, we found that he had bought this terrific graphics program and developed an amazing four-color workbook that diagrammed all the major products that we were selling, and showed very clearly how they could be combined in various ways to work together as systems. It was so beautiful, just a terrific tool. Andy had also created these physical displays of how various kinds of systems worked. These were actual demos that he'd had built, showing all the inside wiring and connectors.

"We saw right away that *Andy was doing system selling*. He'd seen what the problems were, and had figured out how to deal with them himself. He'd developed the right tools, the workbook and the display modules, so he could demonstrate to his customers how their systems needed to work, and he was training the people in his Des Moines office in what he was doing. This gave him a tremendous sales advantage. A typical example: he had a customer who came to him looking for some baluns, those devices that convert coaxial jacks to configurations so you can use them for newer products. Well, Andy pulled out his demonstration materials, and showed the customer how he could do things better, and the customer ended up scrapping his entire coaxial system and going home with thirty thousand dollars' worth of fiber optics!"

Julie Anixter and Bill Millholland listened to a number of such anecdotes from Andy Chacon, then wrote up ten case studies based on what he had done. They then helped him to expand and refine his workbook, using his case studies as a basis for demonstrations, and reproduced enough copies for the whole sales force. "We also reproduced his demonstration modules for our corporate training center, duplicating all of Andy's tools so our force could both train on them and use them. We developed a whole sales course in system selling based upon Andy's success. Then we recruited Andy to co-lead the course. He trained more than two hundred people for us, and while he eventually became too busy to keep it up, he help us launch the program, which is still going strong. I would have to say that this was one of the earliest successful uses of the web of inclusion in the training department."

A more sophisticated challenge involved the upgrading of sales people's technical skills, within the context of meeting their customers' business needs. Rick Keene, the Vice President for the Northeast Region, based in Boston, was trying to address this issue among his people. One of only four regional VPs in the United States, Rick Keene had begun his Anixter career packing wire in a warehouse, then moved on to sales. As one who started back in the days when "they just threw a phone book at you when you came in," he nevertheless appreciated the need for far more sophisticated training as Anixter's products and services became more complex.

"I was getting paranoid that our people might get too focused on technology and forget what we actually *do* for a living. Our real value lies in the fact that we can customize and provide our customers with the highest possible level of service. *That's* the key to our getting these big contracts, not having a lot of high-tech stuff. Anyone can sell equipment. Accenting the technology too much tends to obscure that our real concern is to give our customers *value*. If we forget that, we leave who we are behind."

So Rick Keene got together with a few field people and developed a kind of core curriculum for the sales force that would frame selling Anixter's value within the context of the customers' business. Meanwhile, Julie had been in touch with the Center for Creative Leadership in Greensboro, North Carolina, where she had been studying the concept of Development in Place, which holds that learning is most effective when it occurs through challenging on-the-job assignments that enable people to put what they are learning to immediate use. With that principle in mind, she took the curriculum that Rick Keene's team was devising and added a hands-on aspect, engaging the help of the company's informal network of experts who were *doing* precisely what the training programs were designed to teach. Drawing on their successes, Julie then helped Rick roll out his pilot project across the company.

The first phase of the curriculum they designed begins with a combination of orientation and self-paced training, combined in a week-long workshop called Quick Start. Quick Start brings together twenty-four new employees, usually from the same sales region, in a laboratory setting that introduces them to the business processes they must master in order to really understand and meet their customers' needs. These processes include an introduction to core cabling systems, to computer usage, and to the company's philosophy regarding customer care. Participants are given specific problems—for example, the need of an aircraft manufacturer to create a network that enables it to order parts automatically from suppliers. Working in teams, the workshop participants use the lab to figure out which combinations of cabling schemes would meet the manufacturer's needs. The teams then prepare quotes and present them to "customers" who are played by facilitators, who have all been successful sales people themselves.

The second phase of the curriculum builds on the technical understanding achieved in the first, while also setting it in the more specific context of making sales. Participants, again working in teams, find ways of articulating Anixter's value to the customer whose problems they have addressed in their lab work—and doing so at every phase of the product cycle. "Until now," says Rick Keene, "we've always practiced a kind of stream of thought in sales. That is, our people articulated the needs of the customer as they went along. It's something you pick up in the process of doing business—it's not specifically taught or deliberately passed on. Phase Two makes this process more deliberate. We show participants how to do value audits. We bring in real live scenarios, give them case studies. They thrash it all out among themselves. We don't *tell* them how to analyze the value of a product or service, we let them figure it out. Then they make presentations, so they can all learn from everyone else."

The third phase of the curriculum involves participants in the actual delivery of high-end products. Rick Keene: "We do this phase in the field in conjunction with our suppliers and our clients. The sales person who is being trained works right alongside a technical expert, usually a sales engineer, who goes out to a specific customer site. The expert builds on the formal audit of the client's needs that the sales person has done in Phase Two, and designs an enhanced delivery program based on that. By working with the sales person throughout this process, the expert really functions as an on-site trainer. Also, clients and vendors get very involved in this process. Sometimes, the vendor's expert might be who the salesperson works with. This is where we really function in what you would call a web."

Julie Anixter notes that "In a very neat way, the core curriculum reflects back on the way we *used* to do things at Anixter, back in the days when we just hired people and let them figure things out on the job. It's totally different than just putting someone in a class. What we're doing is making the sales people—working in groups and at their own speed—figure out for themselves how and why something is done. Then they're immediately thrown into a situation where they have to implement what they've learned, on a real job but with an expert's guidance. So people still learn in the process of doing, but within a structured framework that provides support and a path for learning."

The core curriculum thus provides a way to update sales peoples' knowledge of Anixter's complex and evolving products on a continuing basis, broadening their range and giving them a chance to use what they learn as they go along. The key to success in this endeavor is finding a balance between the old seat-of-your-pants approach, with its emphasis on individual need and effort, and a designed-in level of comprehensiveness. The expert assumes the role of on-the-job coach and trainer, which fully integrates teaching, learning, and doing. The final result is a full-blown master-apprentice approach.

THE ROLE OF EXPERTS

Experts play a vital role in making the core curriculum work. These experts may be master sales people, managers, or engineers. Indeed, in recent years, under the pressure of fast growth and with a need to sell more complex products, Anixter has begun to hire more people with specific areas of expertise—technical, financial, and managerial. Rick Keene, as a typical Anixter senior executive whose heart remains in sales, views this hiring of experts as the greatest potential threat to Anixter's culture. He points out that a company top-heavy with experts tends to deemphasize the power of its front lines.

Experts in most organizations tend to be highly paid and have impressive titles; thus they assume positions to which power naturally flows. This in turn often leads the company to emphasize the kind of positional power that Ted Jenkins at Intel warns about. Rick Keene is adamant that the only way to avoid this familiar syndrome is not to put experts into positions of authority, but rather to use them as *support* for the front lines. That is, take advantage of their expertise, but divorce it absolutely from positional power and authority by using the experts for coaching and training.

He gives an example of how this can work. "A few years ago, we began doing these multimillion-dollar bids for very complicated projects—wide area networks, satellite communications, that kind of thing. That was great, but it also brought some problems, because Anixter's culture hasn't necessarily been tuned to developing people who are ready to deal with all the details of such complex products. It became obvious that I was going to have to go outside the company and find a VP of Finance for our region, someone who had a real handle on the kind of complicated leasing arrangements we were getting into. The field sales people just didn't have that kind of expertise."

Rick Keene ended up hiring an executive from Wang, even though he recognized that Wang "has a completely different kind of culture than we do. Lots of VPs, a real chain of command, executives who are used to being *listened* to. Now, say there's a branch manager out there in our region, running a four- or five-million business, very independent, with a couple of people working for him. And say this guy—or this woman—does something for a client that the finance expert I brought in here doesn't like. If that VP were at a company like Wang, you know what would happen: he'd just tell the guy in the field to change what he was doing. But here, things are different: *the*

VP does not have the power from me to tell the guy in the field what to do. All the VP here can do is try to persuade the guy to change his approach. He can't *tell* him how to run his business. He's there to serve the field sales person, so he has to prove his value. What he says doesn't have value based on his position or title."

But how does an expert prove value? How does he or she persuade front-line people, when those people are established as having the final say? Obviously, this kind of persuasion must occur through the continual exposure of the front lines to both the depth and the consequences of the expert's knowledge; in other words, through a process of education. This exposure now occurs at Anixter both within the context of training and through daily contacts that occur as people work to solve specific problems. Used as advisors rather than bosses, experts at Anixter find themselves with little choice but to assume a teaching role.

Rick Keene uses an analogy to describe what he views as the proper role for experts. "I saw this Macintosh commercial where some guy was asked to evaluate two PCs. So he goes out to look at them, and what does he find but one of them surrounded by this crowd of people—the Mac, of course. So I tell the experts we hire: *you* be that, you be like that PC. You're going to be evaluated on the basis of how much people use you. It's just the opposite of most corporate cultures, where the people with big salaries get their power because of their position. Here, they get their power by providing some kind of value. That's the *real* definition of empowerment from down under."

The use of experts as resources has evolved subtly. Rick Keene recalls, "At first, it just seemed like we were having more meetings than we used to. Anixter's always been the kind of place where you didn't have a lot of meetings. But the need for these get-togethers came from the people in the field, who found they wanted to learn more about a new cabling scheme, a new vendor, or a new generation of hubs. So the field sales people would invite some experts in to talk about the products. It soon became apparent that there's kind of a blurry line here. Do these kinds of get-togethers qualify as meetings, or are they really training? It's a kind of learning, that's for sure.

"One thing we really had to work on," says Rick Keene, "was the format these meetings took. A lot of the experts, especially those who had come from outside the company, were used to doing these formal types of presentations. They were big on overheads, and bombarded you with charts. People here tend to be very critical of that sort of thing, because it's boring and all one way. And we're pretty blunt when someone tries to use it on us. In our region, we *fought* to make sure that our meetings played out as discussions. We really worked at being self-policing—we've got a lot of people here who are absolute zealots when it comes to holding on to what this company has always been about."

Systems and Mastery

In pondering how master-apprentice relationships play out in today's organizations, Julie Anixter notes that mastery needn't necessarily be transmitted by a person. "Mastery can also exist in your resources. Really, with technology so complex these days, we have a different picture of what expertise really is. A master can be simply someone who is a virtuoso in knowing what resources to use, and has the power to gain access to those resources."

This definition of mastery fits nicely with Alvin Toffler's observation that, as more expertise gets vested in systems, people on the front lines will find their own authority enhanced. An expert system, by providing a wealth of information to virtually *anyone who knows how to use it,* serves to redistribute mastery in an organization.

These days, much expertise resides in specialized software programs. At Anixter, the potential for mastery among the sales force has been greatly increased by the development of an on-line program known as SALE. SALE enables those who use it to enter orders and build detailed customer profiles in the course of doing their daily work. It also gives order to the sales process, provides an enormous amount of very specific information, and automates most of the clerical aspects of sales work.

Mike Hugos, Anixter's Business Systems Design Manager, undertook the development of SALE with a full understanding of how resistant sales people can be to adapting new and complex technologies. "The split between sales and information systems people is traditionally very wide," he says. "Sales people tend to look at IS people as nerds, removed from the concerns of real business, while IS tends to look at sales as being full of excitable people who are always changing their minds. In many ways, they're the complete opposites." At Anixter, this familiar scenario of opposition was pushed to extremes by the entrepreneurialism of the sales force, with its front-line ability to reject anything they didn't want from corporate headquarters, including the Business Systems team. As a result of this built-in resistance, as well as much mutual misunderstanding, the company entered the 1990s with sales people using software that was ten or fifteen years out of date.

"We had built new programs for accounting, warehousing, operations, and inventory," says Mike Hugos, recalling that period. "But when it came to sales, forget it. Sales people tend to be suspicious of computers; they don't want all their information about a client out there in the open for anyone to see. Also, they thrive on the moment, and they're individualists, which makes them reluctant to cede power to make decisions. They don't want anything to come between them and the customer. And *above all* they don't want to feel overmanaged. If they think a software program compels them to do something—or requires them to do that thing in a specific way—they will respond by hating the computer."

By 1990, the lack of understanding between sales and IS people had reached such an extent that the regional sales VPs attempted what Mike Hugos describes as a "palace coup"—they decided to go off and develop information systems on their own. "The VPs actually demanded a budget so that they could develop software without our help. They were that disgusted with how we were doing things. They said our only role in the company was either to say no or to try to impose our ideas. That gave us a real wake-up call."

At that point, the IS group under the direction of Mike's boss, Mason Rotelli, decided to take an entirely new approach. As designer, Mike Hugos's first move was to get out of headquarters and spend months traveling among twelve sales offices, sitting with sales people at their desk and observing every detail of how they spent their days. In the Saint Louis office, the regional VP dared him to take on the sales job instead of just observing it. "I spent my time on the phone, selling wiring, acting as a conduit, arranging for equipment deliveries to building contractors, doing everything the sales people did. Believe me, it was scary! But it sure gave me an understanding of what's involved."

He continued to look for patterns in how the sales force worked, carefully documenting what he saw. "Sales people will tell you, every day is different, but the *process* of sales tends to be the same. You *do* tend to ask yourself the same questions. What does the customer need? Do we have it in stock? What's the time frame on this delivery? What's the value to the customer of this product? What else might the customer need to enhance the way this product works? Remember: we're not selling naked commodities, we're selling *systems,* so we have to know how things fit together. And with eighty thousand products, software that shows the combinations can really help!"

Mike Hugos's time in the field proved invaluable. "First of all, it enabled me to look at things from the sales point of view, to know what was useful to them and what would just complicate their job. Also, I was no longer just perceived as a techie from corporate trying to impose my will, but as someone sympathetic, a kind of ally." His stint in the field completed, Mike asked each of the regional sales VPs to give him one sales person who would attend a three-day session every few weeks. The idea was to include these people as collaborators in developing a new sales software program—an example of the web in action.

Mike Hugos was emphatic about the kind of people he sought for this role. "What I was looking for were colorful characters, the kind of experienced line people who have been in the company for a long time and commanded a lot of respect because of what they know. The kind of people who have big reputations and a lot of subtle influence in the field. Real *live wires,* people who are very individualistic—not necessarily loudmouths, just people who are very confident. These people *exist,* especially in a place like Anixter, where you have a lot of freedom and everyone tends to stay with the company for a long time. People like I was looking for can be difficult, because they're skeptical and blunt. But you can't bluff them. I wanted those people for my project, because I knew that if I could get them to buy into the program, everyone else would too. People listen to them, so they can sell the field."

Mike Hugos's description of the role that "colorful characters" played in his effort echoes Ted Jenkins's words about the role at Intel of people who wield inordinate power by virtue of their connections, their personal charisma, and their expertise, rather than by the precise level of their position within the company. Mike also shares Ted Jenkins's idea that such people are usually long-term employees, and thus symbolic of the company's culture as a whole. Mike's understanding of the importance of these people when it comes to getting buy-in for a difficult project also recalls Dave Lawrence's recognition that the *Miami Herald*'s diversity committee, in order to be taken seriously, had to include precisely those people who were most vociferous on issues, because those are the people that "everyone knows can't be bought. If they say the effort is real, people believe them."

In the monthly three-day sessions, Mike Hugos took his group through the process of developing a program by presenting it as a kind of game. "I got them to break down their various activities in sales and look at each as a game, involving a set of skills, rules, and an object. Then we just brainstormed away, using keyboards and screens, refusing to censor any ideas. We *welcomed* bad ideas, because often they're the ones that get you thinking—they trigger something, a sense of play." The group worked in intense, hour-and-a-half bursts, breaking frequently, allowing one idea to lead to another, and going out together at night.

During the brainstorming sessions, Mike Hugos discovered that his roles as facilitator and designer merged. "One thing I learned is that the people who will be using the programs really know what they want, but they only know it in pieces. You have to pull those pieces out of them—that's how you get your pattern. So you use the technology both to figure out what people want and to teach them about it at the very same time. You can only create an interactive program by using an interactive process. That's why the teamwork concept is so important in organizations today. The technology not only enables but also demands that you work on things interactively, all in one process."

Mike Hugos was trained as an architect, and he compares the techniques he used in developing SALE with those that architects use with their clients. "As an architect, you try to get your clients to reveal their expectations. They know what they want, but only in an intuitive and emotional way. They can't exactly describe what the final product would look like. So your job is to pick up their intuitive needs and try to feed them back, using models and renderings. That gives them something to react to, and helps them articulate better what they need. Then you can go back and make that work."

Designing software, he observes, is much the same. For just as architecture defines a physical space, so computer systems define a psychological space. "You can use architectural analogies to describe what you're doing when you design software. What the client, the person you're designing the program for, sees on the screen is his emotional and intuitive wants expressed concretely. You use renderings and prototypes, models to do this. Once the person you're designing for sees something illustrated, he can see what he contributed: 'that icon on the screen, that was my idea!' That's when they start to get excited, and become more articulate about what they need. It's all just education. You kind of plant the seed, show them what the system is capable of doing for them. Then they come alive, and figure out how *they* want to use it."

Mike brought the programmers who worked for him out to field sales offices. "I had them put on telephone headsets so they could plug right in and listen to how the sales people dealt with their customers. As we began rolling out the SALE system to the field, the programmers would sit with the sales people so they could watch how the sales person worked with the system. The process of testing and refinement is so important: again, it's how an architect works. You need to continually refine and improve the details. That's how we had to present our program to the sales force. We had to convince them that this program is here to help them make money, not to turn them into trained monkeys ruled over by some machine."

Because the "colorful characters" involved in the development of SALE had such a capacity to sell the program to people in the field, Mike Hugos wanted to use them to do the initial training. He worked with Julie Anixter's team to develop a way to do this, and also to integrate training into the fine-tuning process—another example of Development in Place. The sales trainers worked alongside programmers, who served as experts, identifying potential problems as they observed people learning SALE. "The sales people have new ideas all the time, and by having the IS people work with them in training, we've been able to constantly improve the software," Mike observes. "But of course the programmers also needed training in order to be able to do this, especially in terms of working with people, and Julie gave me help on that. We tried to teach them never to defend themselves, or make excuses when one of the sales people criticized the program. They should always just say, what do *you* want? How could this software be more helpful? How could we make it less confusing?"

The SALE program as it developed unfolds in three basic steps. First, it helps the sales person to locate the item that the customer has requested by checking stock throughout the company. "It's especially helpful if the customer doesn't know exactly what he wants," Mike Hugos points out. "If, say, he just asks in a general way for some fiber optic cable. SALE gives the user seven ways to figure out what kind of cable he wants. He can find it by entering the attributes—the fiber count, the manufacturer, or the application, how it will be used. With so many products, it's invaluable to have this kind of expertise available in the software. Even the most experienced sales person doesn't know all eighty thousand products!"

Next, SALE helps the user to develop a price quote by tracking what other customers are paying for a given product on any day, as well as showing suggested volume prices for different-sized orders. The system also suggests other items that might be sold along with those specifically requested in order to customize the product, and develops quotes for these as it goes along.

Finally, the program prints a complete quote that the sales person sends to the customer, and tracks it until it either becomes an order or is canceled.

Mike is careful to point out that the program does not compel the user to use the quote that it suggests. "It helps you develop one, but it doesn't lock you in. The sales person decides on the final quote, not the computer." This flexibility is a major reason that SALE has been accepted by the sales force. Mike notes that people are likely to feel well disposed to computers only when the programs they use don't take away their power to make decisions. "People feel bullied when that happens. They perceive that the value of their own skills is being diminished. That takes away from the pride they feel in their work."

Shoshana Zuboff makes much the same point when she observes that software that abrogates decision-making makes people cynical about their own human value, subordinating intuitive human processes to the rigidity of the machine. Mike Hugos is convinced that programs that people enjoy using on the job are those *that automate only the repetitive and clerical aspects of their work,* rather than those aspects that demand human skills. Thus he was aware from the start that if he wanted the sales people to use a program, it would have to be one that let them stay in command. "That's especially true in a company like Anixter, where sales people are given so few guidelines. People just won't use programs that make them feel bullied or diminished."

SALE also assists the drawing up of customer profiles, one of those tasks of sales work that often remains undone because while it is important it is rarely urgent. Because SALE allows the sales person to quickly type in the elements of every customer conversation, the sales person can easily refer to them during later transactions, building a record of interchange over the course of time. SALE also stores and shares information about customers' business strategies that can help the sales force in other regions when prospecting for new business. "Say you find out that 3M is opening a new branch in Austin, Texas. You type that into the program. Then Anixter people in Austin pick that up, and start accessing information about what we've sold them in the past, what their base products are. Those are the products we'll want to pitch."

Working together, Julie Anixter and Mike Hugos developed a series of nine training modules so that sales people can learn the SALE software interactively and on-line, at their own speed and discretion. "Basically, the modules teach you how to use the program within the context of becoming an outstanding sales person," Mike notes. Thus SALE qualifies as part of Development in Place, which provides learning for people within the context of their daily jobs. As part of Development in Place, Julie Anixter has developed a large catalogue that lists courses, computer programs, and video- and audiotapes and other tools that people throughout the company can use on the job in order to constantly upgrade their skills.

Bill Millholland likens certain aspects of Development in Place to basic training. "The military," he notes, "is really about training people on a continual basis. You're always either acquiring new skills or upgrading those you have. You never get past the training stage—it's a process that never stops. The goal is always optimal self-development and readiness. That kind of approach is exactly right for a complicated company, where the nature of what people are being challenged to do is always changing."

Mike Hugos points out that working with Julie's team on the SALE modules has convinced him that what integrates training with daily use is always *design*. He observes that this notion is implicit in the work of Christopher Alexander, the principal author of *A Pattern Language,* whose writings have influenced Mike's thinking. "In *Notes on a Synthesis of Form*," says Mike, "Alexander describes design as 'the process of organizing form under a complex variety of restraints.' " One primary constraint, he believes, is the need to make things obvious.

"For example, when you walk into a building, it should reveal itself to you *naturally.* You shouldn't need a manual or formal instructions in order to get around. You should be able to grasp intuitively where the door is, or how to get from one floor to another—that is, you should learn how to use the building *in the process of using it.* It's the same with software systems. You should be able to figure out how to enter, and how to get where you want to go: as much as possible, the system should teach you how to use it. Like good architecture, good software is intuitively obvious to human beings. That's really the essence of good design. If you're designing software for a specific kind of job, it should fit that job so well that if someone knows how to do the job, they'll know how to use the program."

THE 70/30 BALANCE

Cindee O'Leary, who manages Anixter's Evanston office, notes that many managers in the field have felt the need for greater structure in recent years. "We used to run our offices pretty much as we liked, but as the company has expanded and we've had to hire a lot of people, most managers have felt they needed more direction. "We need policies on things like maternity leave and other HR issues."

Sales managers still hire their own staffs, which gives them a great autonomy, and keeps corporate bureaucracy and policy-making under control. But Cindee points out that the growing need to sell cabling systems instead of products has created a far greater need for teamwork. This is especially true since Anixter has been hiring experts in finance and technology to work alongside the formerly freewheeling sales force. "We've got to develop skills in how to build and manage teams. What this means is we need a lot more training."

Global expansion too has brought a need for policies and guidelines, since business is conducted differently in different countries. Cindee O'Leary points out that, in the United States, fears of conflict of interest have reached the extent where a company's sponsorship of a golf tournament in which customers compete may be perceived as a problem. By contrast, in some Asian countries, a sales representative is expected to arrive at a customer's office on the initial call bearing a heavy load of expensive gifts. "The field managers need to know how much to follow Anixter's way of doing things and how much to go along with the local customs. People can't always make these kinds of decisions on their own."

As the company expanded, it found itself under pressure to institute guidelines for regular performance feedback through reviews. "In the past," says Julie Anixter, "we had no policy on this. Any evaluations were casual and verbal, and were done at the discretion of the sales manager who ran the office if they were done at all. It was all part of our informal culture. But as we began hiring more people from outside the company, we found that these people expected formal reviews, so they could monitor their own progress in the company. They wanted their managers to tell them how they were doing, and they wanted some specific means by which they could improve the level of their work."

Julie Anixter felt convinced that any performance review system at the company should be integrated with the training effort; indeed, she saw the review as a useful tool that an individual employee could use to target the specific areas in which he or she needed to develop. In trying to discover what kind of review process would be most helpful in such an effort, Julie Anixter set about trying to find out if any managers in the field had developed a successful program for their staff. This was the same approach she had used with Andy Chacon in Des Moines, when she was looking for a way to train people in system selling.

She discovered that Gary Conrad, then an area sales manager in

Chicago, had devised a particularly successful review process for his people. At the time, Gary was studying for an advanced business degree, and he wanted to try out some of what he was learning in his office. The system he created for his unit was based on a joint review, in which he and the person he was reviewing sat down on a regular basis and discussed how that person was developing and where he or she wanted to go.

"What impressed me," says Julie, "was that Gary's process was not so much an evaluation or critique as a means to help guide his group's development. He used it to coach his people, but gave some structure to that process—there was continuity, and it was done on a regular basis. Mainly, the reviews enabled Gary and his people to set goals together, which made the sessions something to look forward to, rather than something to dread." Since the reviews were made jointly, they deemphasized the gulf between boss and employee. In this way, the performance reviews reinforced the relationship of master and apprentice and defined the staff structure on the basis of teaching and learning.

Working with Gary and a key group of senior managers, Julie Anixter adapted his methods to serve the company as a whole. This resulted in the Performance Development Process. Julie and Gary made a video to explain the PDP to managers, so they could implement it among their people. The training team then devised a workbook that offered managers specific criteria by which to identify both people's strengths and the areas in which they needed to develop more expertise. Those being evaluated would also use the workbooks and share their own observations of their work with their managers. The managers were trained in the process by other managers who had gone through the program, rather than by members of the training team. "The development was a collective process," says Julie. "At one point we had thirty-five department managers in for a brainstorming session, where we discussed our various options in detail. This way, we were able to get real-world feedback before we arrived at a working version. This kind of widespread ownership in the process meant that PDP was embraced very quickly once we rolled it out."

Bob Eck notes that the PDP at Anixter is distinguished from similar efforts in that the use of ratings is optional; managers are free to use only concrete observations if they like. The review does not rely on any kind of point system, nor are composite scores given. Also, the PDP plays only a minor role in determining an employee's compensation: one does not hope for a "good score" in order to get a raise. "The idea is guidance and open discussion, not simply a critique," Julie explains. "The whole thing is really just a way of designing a constructive coaching conversation. It creates a gap, a kind of space, where people can step back and discover what they need to learn. Then they work with their manager to create a kind of action plan, specific steps they'll take to get the expertise that they need."

Julie stresses that the purpose of the PDP is seventy percent development tool and only thirty percent evaluation. "Also, there's no idea that you ever get a perfect score, not because you're always falling short, but hopefully because you're always learning. You might be a master when it comes to developing accounts, but a beginner in understanding finance, and at an intermediate level in understanding how a router works. As I mentioned before, being a master is often a matter of knowing how to leverage resources. The PDP helps employees pinpoint exactly what resources can help them achieve what they want."

SUGGESTIONS FROM THE FIELD

Not all training programs at Anixter have resulted from pilot projects in the field that Julie was able to uncover and adapt. A healthy number were suggested directly by people in field leadership positions who felt the need both for improving specific skills and for pushing the company in new directions. By keeping herself open and convincing people throughout the company that she is eager to listen to their ideas, Julie Anixter has created an environment in which people at every level feel comfortable asking her help in designing innovative ways of training their units.

A vivid example can be seen in the program that has developed for support staff. This effort is particularly worthy of note because most organizations make training available only to people in management and sales, while those in administration are rarely given more than tips on telephone etiquette or classes in the new software program. By contrast, Anixter fully integrates training into the support staff structure, which enables people at the grass roots to expand their expertise. It is worth pausing to examine how support staff training functions—and perhaps more important, how it came about—because it gives us a picture of what Julie Anixter calls her "strategy of inclusion," and demonstrates in particular how such a strategy can be useful in speeding the deindustrialization of the workplace.

The initiative began when Melanie Thompson, then Executive Assistant for the Vice President of Marketing, began thinking about the problems she saw among the other secretaries. "I'd worked in a few big companies, always as a secretary or an admin person, and everywhere I went the support staff people were always overlooked," she says. "They felt powerless, absolutely *out* of it, so they wasted a lot of time just griping, which is what people do when they have no power. Most of them would have liked to grow in their jobs, because that would have made them more secure, but there was never any path for them, never any way for them to develop."

At Anixter, however, Melanie Thompson thought it might be possible for support people to get beyond these traditional limitations. She approached her boss with the notion that executive assistants should be given more professional and systematic kinds of training. At the time, such training as they received occurred haphazardly, with a more experienced person helping out a newcomer. "It's not the kind of suggestion I would have made in any other company," Melanie says, "but my boss was a very liberal guy, and he trusted me. Right away his attitude was 'what a great idea!' "

Melanie's boss suggested she talk with Julie Anixter, since Julie had recently begun canvassing the business units on what kind of training various sales and management people felt they needed. "I typed up a list of suggestions. Most of it was stuff I had noticed was a problem in my own work. Julie was *very* receptive. She told me she had thought that support staff might need more attention, but the idea had got pushed to the back burner because technical training for sales was just so urgent."

But what most amazed Melanie Thompson about Julie Anixter's response was that she didn't say, "That's a good suggestion; my department will develop something." Instead, she asked Melanie to gather a team of support staff people together to develop a training program that would address the specific needs of their colleagues. "Julie said she'd be glad to help, but that *I* should put the thing together," Melanie recalls. "Because I had a better idea of what support staff people needed to know. It makes sense, but I had not foreseen being given that kind of responsibility. It really changed the way I thought about my job."

Melanie Thompson knew little about what formal or systematic training for support staff might entail, so she asked Julie Anixter if she could attend some training sessions for support staff being held in Chicago by Dun and Bradstreet. She got a lot from those sessions. In particular, she learned that it was important to identify areas where people felt dissatisfied with or confused about their jobs, and then develop training that addressed those points of weakness. At this time, Melanie asked Tina LaPelusa and Stefanie McLaughlin to join her efforts; both were executive assistants whom she had helped informally to train when they first arrived at Anixter. Working together, the women tried to identify problems among support staff, so that they might devise training programs tailored to them.

The women found that confusion about what resources were available in the company was a common complaint. If an executive assistant was helping an executive to prepare overheads for a presentation, for example, she had no way of knowing if the graphics that illustrated a particular piece of information had already been done by someone in the company, which would save her the effort of having to create new ones. Because most support people were attached to a single executive, they had few means of discovering information that existed in other parts of the company. The channels of communication simply were not there.

So the group decided to develop both a presentation library and a resource file, and then train all executive assistants in how to use them. This would help people to avoid time-wasting redundancies in their work, while also enabling them to prepare more professional presentations. To be useful, both the library and the file would need to be maintained and constantly updated, which meant that executive assistants would need to manage them together as a team. In the past, building flexible teams and communicating across channels had been considered management skills, but the demands of managing the library and the file now meant that support staff wanted some training in these areas. So Melanie Thompson's group began sitting in on management team-building sessions to determine how these might be adapted for support staff.

Melanie Thompson's team also found that support people wanted to be more included in decisions that affected how they worked, in particular those relating to technology. As technology becomes more complex, and support people are trained in a wider variety of programs, it makes sense to include them in some of the decisions. As Tina LaPelusa noted, "This company spent an absolute fortune on workstations for the tenth floor, and then found they didn't fit the way they were supposed to! Well, why didn't they ask me or some of the other admin people if it was going to work? We could have saved them a lot of money!"

The desire to be involved in such decision-making made it obvious that support people needed to know a lot more about Anixter's business. They had not in the past: indeed, Tina LaPelusa recalled that she had been working at Anixter for months before she had any idea of what the company actually did. "No one tells you, and usually you feel too embarrassed to ask, 'Oh, by the way, what kind of business are we in?' " Stefanie McLaughlin had a similar experience. "When I came in, there was no welcome booklet, no orientation—I had no idea what anyone did. I felt isolated. What I learned, I had to learn on my own. My boss was very supportive—he said, 'I trust you to figure things out,' and he gave me plenty of authority. In a lot of ways, that was helpful. But the only reason it worked is because of what *I'm* like; I'm very inquisitive, and I don't mind asking questions. A lot of people aren't comfortable being like that. What happens to them? They get lost in the shuffle, and never find out what they need to know."

Technology expertise, decision-making, understanding the business, working in teams: it soon became apparent that the support staff's training needs overlapped with those of others in the company. The group Melanie Thompson brought together thus had to figure out a way to adapt a broad-scale approach to training for support people, one that could be integrated into the daily process of doing their jobs. The Performance Development Process, formerly reserved for management, was extended through the company to meet needs at the support level. Again, its main purpose was to suggest paths for future development rather than to evaluate performance.

The Anixter catalogue of courses and self-paced training modules was also sent to support staff; in the past, only managers had received it. They were expected to share, but somehow the catalogues never reached administration people. Now support staff managers work directly with their teams to help individuals plan programs that help them expand their skills and gain more specific expertise. Support people without long experience are also given mentors, who help guide their learning and introduce them around the company. When anyone new is hired, he or she is given videos and computer programs that describe the company's work in detail.

Stefanie McLaughlin notes that this level of involvement helps support staff feel like part of the company. "But it has a lot more value than just making us feel good. I don't know how admin people can be good in their jobs if they don't even know what the company's trying to accomplish! Now we have training that helps us find and use resources in ways that make us much more efficient. Julie's always talking about resources, but one thing I've realized: in this company, *we're* resources too! A lot of us are getting to be very expert at certain things, like using color graphics programs, or really understanding how DOS works. So people call on us all the time for help—not just people in our departments, but other managers who might be on the floor. Before you know it, we're *training* them in what we know. So we have a much wider base in terms of who we help."

Stefanie McLaughlin believes that training for support staff has greatly improved Anixter's ability to get the best from its people. "It used to be, if you wanted to learn a lot, you had to be the assertive type. If you weren't so nervy, you got lost in the shuffle. I was always comfortable asserting myself. I knew that I had my own voice, and I knew how to use it. But other people aren't always so comfortable speaking up." Such people had a hard time developing themselves. "They weren't the kind to go to their boss and say, 'I want to become an expert on spreadsheets.' But with self-paced training, and a mentor working right alongside you, you don't have to be assertive to get really good anymore. You don't have to come in already having a voice. The training helps coax one out of you!"

The women in Melanie Thompson's group point out that the changing nature of technology makes well-trained and professional support people valuable in ways impossible in the past. Their observations of why this is so are fascinating, because they reflect the profound changes presently taking place in the very nature of how we conceive of and do our work.

As noted earlier in this chapter, Alvin Toffler has observed that expertise vested in systems redistributes power in an organization—whether the organization intends this to happen or not. Stefanie McLaughlin's description about what occurs when support staff people develop their skills and then find their voice in the process of being trained provides a vivid picture of the far-reaching consequences of this redistribution.

As specific administration people develop skills in programs like spreadsheets or advanced graphics, more people in the organization want to take advantage of what they know. In order to make use of their diverse and often specialized skills, support people begin to pool their talents, thus widening and deepening the skill base of the entire unit whose work they support. They become a team of specialists, rather than a collection of individuals providing generalized support to those with management rank. The support staff's expertise, as well as their increasing tendency to work as a team, reconfigures the structure of their organization, and contributes to the professionalization of their own work.

Meanwhile, information technology returns to management some of the tasks that had been assumed by support staff in the industrial system. The women on Melanie Thompson's team were all quick to note how profoundly the nature of secretarial work has changed since the advent of the personal computer. Says Melanie Thompson, "These days, everyone has to know the basics. Once executives started using workstations, they couldn't get away without knowing how to keyboard. That made a big change. Our exec VPs even do their own correspondence now, which means that fewer of them need or have their own secretary. That leaves support people free to do other things." Melanie cites the example of a former executive assistant who has begun managing Anixter's data base. "We didn't need to hire some outside expert to do this: the support staff can handle the job."

And so the huge gap that once yawned between support and management, so characteristic of the Industrial Era, begins slowly but inexorably to close. Until recently, support work was deliberately dumbed down, fragmented, broken into single repetitive tasks that demanded little training and that almost anyone could perform. Today's technology, however, serves to "smarten up" support work, reintegrating tasks and broadening roles. Rigid distinctions between thinking and doing, between making decisions and executing tasks, begin to blur as a result. Management and support grow more interdependent as web-like connections form at points of need.

A prime example of how expert systems reintegrate tasks can be seen in what happened to Tina LaPelusa, an administrator who provided support to the marketing staff. She had developed an interest in graphics, and availed herself of self-paced modules in order to develop a sophisticated range of skills. She did all the overheads for a large marketing meeting being held in Dallas, and worked on coordinating the sessions as well.

"When it came time, I told my boss that I really needed to be there. The whole thing was complicated, and I was the person who had put it together. He agreed, but it got to be a real controversy. People said that admin people weren't supposed to go on junkets. They were looking at the whole thing as if it were a perk. Believe me, I've never worked so hard in my life. But it was great, and things really went better because I was there. Also, I met a lot of field people that I'd been talking to on the phone for years, and it's been helpful for me to know who they are in person. But the best part was that I got to see the project I'd been working on through to the end, instead of seeing only one little aspect of it. I got to see the *results*." There could be few clearer definitions of what happens when technology and reorganization force the deindustrialization of support work.

High Reliability at Anixter

Bill Millholland believes that much of Anixter's success has been based on its speed and reliability in delivering the right product. "When you think about it, one way you could describe us is as specialists in emergencies, because that's what infrastructure providers these days have to be. We've got to be very *precise*. With these complicated, highly computerized systems, even the smallest mistake can become a major disaster. You can't afford to make an error! That's why this company is so well run. It *has* to be. If we make a mistake, it affects our customer's entire business."

This emphasis on precision, on being prepared for emergencies, brings to mind the high-reliability organizations mentioned in this book in Chapter 2. High-reliability organizations have been defined as those in which the potential for mistakes to escalate into catastrophe is so high that unusually low rates of failure are mandatory just for survival. Such organizations are technologically complex, and characterized by the ability configure as webs whenever danger arises. Intense, continual, and integrated training is the other common characteristic feature of these organizations.

It is noteworthy that, as Anixter's business has grown increasingly complex, and its products more sophisticated, its training process has become intense, continual, and integrated, in line with high-reliability principles. Bill Millholland is concerned that everyone at Anixter—from warehouse workers to senior management—have a basic understanding of how products move through the system. He describes this understanding as a core competency, the basic information everyone must know.

Core competencies result from an understanding of logistics and the product flow. They demand that people at every level in an organization have a broad enough grasp of the business that they are able to help keep errors almost at zero. As Julie Anixter notes, people in the company "have to know a lot, and also must be prepared to react, to respond to glitches no matter where they occur in the cycle." One way in which she tries to ensure this level of preparation is by gathering people throughout the company on a regular basis in quality-of-service sessions and getting them to deal with the persistent question *what if?*

She makes it into kind of a game, really, and it is played in teams. Participants are handed cards describing hypothetical situations, then they brainstorm among themselves to develop helpful answers. What if HOT RUSH FED EX didn't ship? What if the order was for four pair but the warehouse shipped six pair? What if the yard is covered with ice so the forklifts can't operate? What if the tubes go down? Along with these exercises, people play another game using cards and a board to map every step of the order flow. The purpose is the constant exercise of solutions.

This process is akin to the high-reliability exercises described by the Berkeley researchers, in which the entire crew of an aircraft carrier participates in a walkdown, looking for bits of debris that could make a landing fatal. The hallmarks of the process are precision, anticipating potential problems, figuring out in advance what might be done to solve them, teamwork, and participation across levels so that everyone thinks of the enterprise as *theirs*. Anixter is incorporating these aspects into its culture by using a wide-ranging web of people to co-develop and co-lead training programs for areas in which they have expertise. In this way, training functions are spread throughout the organization, rooted in and owned by the people who use and need them. As the company's products get reconfigured into systems, Anixter is beginning to assume more high-reliability characteristics and threading the process of training into how people do their jobs every day.

SEVEN

Building Outside
Alliances: Nickelodeon

"What we are witnessing is the double convergence of large- and small-firm structures."

—CHARLES SABEL

"As various parts reorganize into a new whole, the system escapes into a higher order."

—ILYA PRIGOGINE

In previous chapters, we have watched the unfolding of web-like and inclusive groups or divisions *within* larger structures, which then help to transform the organizations of which they are a part. This is an internal process, one that originates at the grass roots, and enables companies to evolve in response to the knowledge and experience of people at every level. It is a process that broadens the base of talent and ideas upon which the organization may draw, while fostering changes tailored to specific circumstances, cultures, and needs. Thus it is particular to the organization, rather than generic.

But what happens when companies that are themselves small and web-like reach beyond their own parameters to form outside alliances with very different kinds of cultures? This is a crucial question, for as organizations become leaner than in the past, they are finding that strategically conceived partnerships provide a way for them to develop their strengths, while compensating for what they cannot afford to do on their own. Indeed, much of what American organizations have sought to learn from the Japanese in recent years has centered around the need to nurture and develop close and stable relationships with partners—be they subcontractors, suppliers, or marketers. The ability to form strong alliances offers advantages in terms of broadening scope and leveraging power, but can also pose dangers for lean organizations, which may have difficulty retaining their integrity when paired with partners of unequal size. In the convergence of large and small firms, those which are smaller sometimes get swallowed whole.

Because of their flexibility, permeability at the edges, and emphasis on open and diverse channels of communication, webs of inclusion provide a useful structure for organizations seeking to establish relationships with those on the outside. Far from permitting small organizations to be overwhelmed, webs can help them to influence hierarchical partners to adopt different ways of operating, while at the same time enabling the smaller organizations to learn from their partners. In the process, the alliance itself gets reconfigured as a learning system, giving both organizations a chance to evolve.

A good example can be found at Nickelodeon, the highly regarded and exceptionally profitable cable television network that specializes in children's programming. During the decade between 1984 and 1994, Nickelodeon moved from being a money-losing operation with a staff of twenty, which offered well-meaning shows largely acquired from other countries, and had a 0.5 rating that defined the bottom of the market, to being a major force in the entertainment industry. The network now counts $250 million plus in revenues, achieving an extraordinary forty-four percent margin on profit. Nickelodeon's reach, which extends into 62 million homes, and its history of award-winning original programming have made it one of television's most successful presenters of children's entertainment. Nickelodeon also publishes a humor magazine for children and offers a line of video- and audiotapes and books, as well as a fast-growing range of activity toys.

The lean staff and tight operating budget that have characterized Nickelodeon from its earliest years have forced it to rely on an ever-increasing web of partnerships in order to achieve this rapid growth. The company's partnerships, often made with entrenched hierarchies whose operating styles differ from its own in nearly every regard, have presented Nickelodeon with opportunities unusual for a company its size, while also posing a threat to the company's tight focus on its mission and goals. Nevertheless, Nickelodeon is managing to navigate around this threat, maintaining the clear identity and consistent voice that have been its source of strength in the marketplace. How the company has managed this balancing act presents an instructive story, one that illustrates yet another useful facet of the web.

EARLY DAYS AT NICKELODEON

Nickelodeon today is a member of MTV Networks, which also includes MTV and VH-1. Along with Showtime, they are owned by Viacom, which recently acquired the entertainment giant Paramount. The large-scale corporate environment in which Nickelodeon now must thrive is a far cry from its scrappy beginnings, but the philosophy and vision that define the company have varied hardly at all during the years of its rapid growth. This is thanks largely to its President, Geraldine Laybourne, a vivacious blond woman in her middle forties, who from the outset of her tenure has been determined that the company hold firm to an operating style and culture that is based clearly upon the principles of the web.

Walking into Viacom's office tower in midtown Manhattan, one takes the elevator to Nickelodeon and finds oneself in a domain where the emphasis is on children—or "kids," as they are unvaryingly referred to in the company. Cartoon characters and activity games fill offices and hallways, colors are cheerful and bright, and everyone is eager to show off the toys that have accumulated on their desks.

Nickelodeon's workspace, spread out over three floors, has recently been redesigned to be more open, circular, accessible, and flowing. Offices are of mostly similar size, and grouped around larger common spaces that provide big tables, great views, and places for cooking. Prestigious corners are given over to gathering rooms that everyone uses. The open plan is saved from feeling barnlike or impersonal by close attention to craftsman-like details such as one would be more likely to find in a home.

Gerry Laybourne sits in her not especially large office close by Nickelodeon's newly constructed "town hall." One of the ideas behind the workspace redesign, she explains, "was to get me off the pedestal that too many executives who have been successful get elevated onto. I don't *want* to have a corner for myself, I want to be where people can find me. And I don't particularly want the perks that executives use to make a statement about how important they are. My office has relatively bad sightlines, and my view is of Times Square rather than the river."

If Gerry Laybourne sits at the literal center of her organization, she sits at its figurative center as well. She has been with Nickelodeon since 1980, less than a year after its initial start-up. Back then, the company was a backwater cable venture owned by Warner-Amex, a conglomerate that would disband by the middle of the decade. Nickelodeon was not particularly important in Warner-Amex's scheme of things, but more of a way for the company to establish a foothold in cable television.

Gerry Laybourne came to Nickelodeon with experience not in entertainment, but in education and the nonprofit sector. She had been an open classroom elementary teacher, had instituted a media program at a New England prep school, had formed a media resource library for schools, and had worked with a group that evaluated supplementary material for teachers. "My commitment, as you can see from my background, has always been to kids. I came to Nickelodeon because I was interested in doing something that would serve *them*. I wasn't all that interested in television. After all these years, I'm still basically distrustful of the marketplace, especially as it has been defined by the entertainment business."

Nickelodeon had a staff of five people when Gerry Laybourne arrived, but despite its small size the company was run in a hierarchical manner. "The head guy was very much in control. Everybody reported directly to him—there were no group meetings, so you never knew what anyone else was doing. He kept all the information to himself, because he believed that information was power, and he didn't want to share any of that power. And he made sure that everyone knew that he was in control of all decision-making." This executive also had what Gerry Laybourne describes as "the typical broadcast mentality—that is, he basically assumed he could feed his audience whatever *he* wanted. There was little interest in trying to figure out what kids were interested in, what would appeal to them."

In addition to this inward focus, Gerry Laybourne was troubled by the pervasive lack of ambition that she felt permeated the company, the failure to recognize that a children's network offered a great opportunity. "The goals for Nick were *so* low! The expressed view was that all we should worry about was being on time and on budget. There was no notion that we should be trying to figure out how to relate to kids, or delivering something to them that they couldn't get anywhere else. There was no recognition that we might be able to turn the network into something terrific, if we worked hard enough and were creative about it."

In her first few years at Nickelodeon, during which she served as Program Manager, Gerry Laybourne basically kept her eyes open and took a lot of notes. She says that she learned most of what she knows about managing a network by watching her boss and the other executives very closely, and figuring out what they were doing *wrong*. She was always asking herself how she would do things differently if she were in charge. From the start, she was thinking in terms of how she would run the company.

One of the specific things she noted was "the extent to which the whole hierarchical style is built upon the belief that if one person is up, another person has to be down. I would have these meetings with my boss, but what they were really about was about him showing how much smarter he was than me. I would always leave those meetings deflated. I could feel my effectiveness and motivation drain out of me as a result. So I figured that if *I* felt that way, the impact on people who were not as confident must be devastating. What you really had, then, was the boss creating this environment in which people had low motivation. Plus, they were so afraid of making mistakes or looking foolish that they were too inhibited to be creative."

Watching this process, and being a part of it, Gerry Laybourne resolved that when she got an opportunity to lead, her own approach would be very different. In 1984, she got her chance. Warner-Amex, going through one of its periodic shake-ups, elevated Bob Pittman, one of the creators of MTV, to head its group of networks, and the chief of Nickelodeon subsequently resigned. Gerry Laybourne found herself moving into the sudden vacuum created by her boss's departure. Presented with this unforeseen opportunity, she decided that she might as well try to run the company the way she thought it should be run, even though she was only temporarily in charge. Aware that Warner-Amex was actively searching for someone to assume the reigns at Nickelodeon, she nevertheless resolved not to let that affect her. She made it clear to the corporate heads that she had a vision for Nickelodeon, and that she wanted to pull the staff together and make it a team. Her motivation wasn't so much the desire to head the company as to see if the ideas she had been thinking about would make the network successful. As time passed and the brass at Warner-Amex grew more comfortable with her vision, the company abandoned its search for a new head of Nickelodeon, and put Gerry Laybourne in the spot.

She began her efforts at transforming Nickelodeon by inviting its twenty staff members off-site for an intensive full-day brainstorming session. It was the first time people had met together as a group. "I told everyone, okay, we've all been here three years, so we know what our problems are. Now we're going to have a chance to *fix* them. But if we want to do that, we've got to find a new way of working together, of really being a team. If you want to be part of that effort, this is your chance."

Basically, she was testing the staff, trying to determine who had the enthusiasm and energy needed to make a quantum leap. The problem was, she had no idea what the staff could *do*. She didn't know who could work as part of a team and who could not, because people had always worked in isolation from one another. She felt it was particularly important that she learn what people's individual strengths were, since she would have to build the organization by drawing on those strengths. "As an open classroom teacher, I had learned that you can really unlock kids when you identify their strengths, and then provide an individual curriculum that helps those strengths develop. I bet it was the same with managing people—you just had to figure out what an individual was good at, and then give him or her tasks tailored to developing that."

During the off-site sessions, it became apparent that some people were not going to function well in the kind of environment Gerry Laybourne was trying to create. They were too preoccupied with turf, they refused to share information, they were divisive, and they complained a lot. She attributed these problems to their having grown up in a hierarchical situation, in which they had become accustomed to operating from feelings of powerlessness and fear, thus becoming obsessed with trying to shift the blame.

"Warner-Amex had told me I had to let people go if I was going to succeed. But when I presented them with the list of people who I thought were hampering efforts, their response to each was 'this person has a perfect record, you can't let her (or him) go!' " However, perfect records were not what she was seeking, but rather people who liked being part of a team, who knew how to share information and ideas. "My response was: 'First you tell me I'll fail if I don't get new blood in here, then the personnel records say I can't change things. The problem is, I'm not interested in failing.' " At last, the company agreed, so Gerry Laybourne worked to get good severance packages for those she wanted to leave, and then counseled them to move on.

This put her in the immediate position of having to be very tough right away, but she believes that a leader must operate from a framework of discipline in order to run an inclusive and open organization. Part of this discipline involves resisting people who won't work in an open and inclusive way. "Toughness must *balance* openness, or everything will get muddled. It's easy to make fun of the style of management we try to practice at Nickelodeon—at our best, we're consultative and team-oriented, with people able to freely admit their mistakes. That often gets perceived as being weak or soft. That's why being disciplined and clear is essential. It gives you credibility, makes your openness seem viable." Gerry Laybourne also points out that, to be effective, toughness must be combined with directness, since going behind people's backs or letting them find out bad news from others is not so much tough as autocratic and unfair. "I was always extremely open about why I wanted certain people to go."

REACHING OUT

Prior to 1984, Nickelodeon was the last resort for kids. The network had a 0.5 rating. It didn't have a cohesive identity or recognizable voice, but instead just presented a collection of shows. However, with Bob Pittman now in charge of all Warner-Amex's networks, Gerry Laybourne was eager to learn some lessons from how he had shaped MTV, which had pioneered the idea of creating a network-wide identity. MTV's strong and clear voice was apparent in everything it did—its graphics, programming, characters, and style. Although it was not an appropriate voice for Nickelodeon, Gerry believed that her people could learn from how MTV had put together the elements to create one, and embraced consultants from network TV into its web.

Nickelodeon needed a voice that was right for *kids*. It had to be cohesive, but it also had to be a voice that would allow for variety. Standard wisdom at the time didn't go much beyond "kids like cartoons, so give them a steady diet of cartoons." But Nickelodeon set out to prove that kids, like everyone else, would respond to a whole range of things—drama and comedy, quiz shows and news. But in order to hold this variety together, the network would need an overall identity that could transcend the diverseness it sought to provide.

Nickelodeon faced other major problems beyond its lack of

voice. It was not yet profitable, and although it was on-air from 7 A.M. to 8 P.M., different shows were on at different times of day, creating a confusing checkerboard. Together, the staff decided that in order to address these pressing needs, Nickelodeon had to discover what its audience wanted. The first step was to initiate a series of focus groups for children all over the country, with staff members participating directly.

Gerry Laybourne: "We needed to figure out what kids wanted, but without pandering. So we talked to them about their lives. What did they like about being a kid? What didn't they like? What were their concerns? We found that a lot of them were scared of growing up, getting older. They had heard a lot about things like teen suicide and teen pregnancy, and they were worried. The world out there did not look all that friendly to them. One thing was clear: they wanted childhood to be a safe haven—like most of us had when *we* were growing up. They wanted a place where they would not be accosted by violence and pain, a place they could be lighthearted and express themselves. They wanted more *humor* in their lives, but they wanted humor that was smart, that didn't condescend, or assume they were stupid."

What repelled kids the most about Nickelodeon at the time was the network's insistence upon telling them that its programming was fun. "We had this very male, adult broadcast voice saying, 'Come on, kids, watch us because we're fun!' " Over and over, the focus groups revealed that children resented this approach—they said that if the programming was fun, they would be the first to tell us! The researchers discovered that kids were very resistant to any kind of hard sell, which they took as an insult to their intelligence. They wanted to be approached as if they could make their own decisions about what they did or did not like.

Nickelodeon also found that children were made uncomfortable by preaching. "One early mistake," recalls Gerry Laybourne, "came because, in our eagerness to do good, we got too earnest and turned kids off." The network had developed a program about stellar role models—"you know, the kind of kids who seem to do everything right. We thought the show would inspire our audience, but instead we found that it made the kids who watched it feel bad. They felt they could never possibly compete with these paragons." Again, Gerry Laybourne was forced to go back to what she had learned in the open classroom—"that you inspire people by looking for and building on their *strengths*. When you put them in a position where they feel they are being negatively compared with others, they feel bad and withdraw into themselves."

Building on this realization, Nickelodeon began to develop a philosophy, a mission. "Basically, it says that we are here to accept kids, to help them feel good about themselves. It's a philosophy that impacts everything we do. It impacts casting: we don't look for gorgeous kids, we cast kids who are fat and kids who are skinny, kids of all colors and nationalities, every kind of kid. We don't give out the message, this is what a cool kid should look or be like. The philosophy impacts our marketing: we don't market based on gender, because that implies exclusion, which is not what we are about. If we want to make kids feel good, we have to embrace them all." Nickelodeon's philosophy also mandates a refusal to show violent material, Laybourne insists. "Of course, kids will watch violent shows, but we've found that they don't always like the way it makes them feel. So because our mission is to make kids feel good about themselves and provide them with a safe place, we won't undermine them by presenting violence."

From Nickelodeon's philosophy came the voice the network needed to distinguish itself in the marketplace—a voice that encourages kids to enjoy just being *kids*. The company's battle cry became that Nickelodeon stood with kids against anyone who found them "unbearably loathsome" or sought to condescend to or undermine them. This voice gave the network a means to develop a style of comedy built on opposition to pompous or mean authority figures—bus drivers who yell at kids, anyone who treats them unfairly. In this regard, Nickelodeon's distinctive voice has not been uncontroversial, for some critics have viewed it as undermining the respect children should show adults.

Gerry Laybourne's team at Nickelodeon took over in May 1984. By the following January, the network had a 1.0 rating. "We doubled our ratings in just six months by moving from a hierarchy to a team!" What she concentrated on during that first year was changing the way the company was managed, changing its processes in order to reflect its goals, encouraging communication across levels, and including everyone in decision-making. Laybourne feels that these difficult efforts were made easier by the fact that the company was so small at the time, and because it didn't have all that much at stake. It wasn't profitable, and it didn't have any original programming, so there was nothing the company could not afford to throw away. Operating in an environment in which they had no vested interests made people very loose, encouraging them to present new ideas in areas outside their functional responsibilities.

During that first year, the Nickelodeon team focused on "including kids in our web, putting them at the center of everything we do. From that focus came our mission: 'to connect with kids, and to connect kids with their world through entertainment.' Notice that our mission is *not* to be the biggest network for kids, or to have the highest ratings—it never has been and it never will be." Holding to its goals, Nickelodeon was able to reposition itself in the marketplace, defining a voice and philosophy, and putting in place a predictable, week-long schedule. With improved ratings, the network was then able to begin soliciting advertising for the first time.

EXTENDING THE WEB

The new team, small and flexible, thrived in an inclusive setting, but ran up against a wall when it first tried to extend its operating philosophy beyond its own narrow borders. In 1985, when Nickelodeon began to solicit advertising, it had to rely on the staff that sold airtime for all the networks owned by Warner-Amex. Harvey Ganot, head of advertising sales for all MTV networks, remembers those uncomfortable early days as emblematic of what can happen when a small internal web meets its first ferocious resistance within the larger organization.

"Sales is usually the most hierarchical part of the organization, because sales people are the hunters and providers," says Ganot. "They are typically type A's, competitive and individualistic. The emergence of a more inclusive culture is often hardest on the type A's, because they tend to thrive on defining where they stand in the pecking order. So you have this natural potential for antagonism."

Harvey Ganot points out that Nickelodeon's relationship with MTV's ad sales department was particularly difficult because the sales staff was skeptical of Gerry Laybourne as a leader. "They perceived her as being weak because she wasn't afraid to admit when she didn't know something, and then ask questions in order to find out. Whereas the sales guys were like men who refuse to ask for directions even when they are completely lost. Also, Gerry's people were running around with all these wonderful, noble, and innovative ideas about entertainment for children, and the ad sales staff at the time could have cared less about that. Add to that their misogyny: there was all this grumbling about Gerry's staff as 'those bitches down the hall.' So what you really had was a bunch of people in sales who had an investment in *proving* that what Nick was trying to do would never work."

Still, Gerry Laybourne persisted, holding weekly meetings with the head of ad sales in which her ideas were constantly ridiculed. Abusive and obscene language was used to irritate and taunt her, and to try to make the point that television was a nasty medium with no place for idealists. "It was so frustrating," she says. "Not just the ugliness, which was bad enough, and which required me to focus a lot of energy on trying to deflect it and show it up for what it was. But I was also having to deal with this very destructive short-term focus. All the sales people seemed to care about were the quarterly CPMs, or cost per thousands, and here we were, trying to build a network! Plus

I knew that the idealism we had at Nickelodeon was a great potential asset, but as idealistic as we were, they *hated* it, hated us for that." The structure of the relationship as well as the personalities involved lay at the heart of the problem: "My people had absolutely no access to the sales staff. Everything had to go through the head guy. I had this idea that our staffs could benefit from working together, but that was unheard of. It was just assumed that the creative and business people should be on opposite sides."

Finally, crisis intervened. According to Harvey Ganot, "1986 was the critical year. The MTV network had always been successful, but then suddenly it began to bump up against limits. The organization could not cope with adversity, people had grown too arrogant for that, too unaccustomed to listening. The sales staff was a perfect example. In the shakeout of August 1987, every one of the senior sales staff got fired."

Ganot, who then took over Nickelodeon sales, was excited about Gerry Laybourne's vision of the creative and business sides working together. "She wanted to know *everything* about ad sales, and was always asking questions, and she encouraged her staff people to learn more about what the sales people do. There was none of that familiar attitude that the creative side of the enterprise was better." This inclusive approach, the eagerness to extend Nickelodeon's web to include the sales staff, would shortly prove invaluable. For the company was about to embark upon several projects that, as Ganot recalls, "everyone in the industry was one hundred percent sure would never work."

Nickelodeon steadily expanded its programming in Gerry Laybourne's first years as director. In 1985, the network added an evening format known as *Nick at Nite*. "We *had* to extend into prime time if we wanted to be a serious network," she explains, "but we had no idea of an appropriate way to do it. Evening meant an adult audience, and we didn't want to put anything on that was not for kids: we knew that would dilute our identity. Debby Beece, who was head of on-air promotion, was working with a swat team at the time, and she came up with the idea that we should feature old shows that adults had watched when *they* were kids, so that they could now watch them with their children."

Nickelodeon proceeded to buy up old programs such as *Drag-net, I Love Lucy, The Dick Van Dyke Show,* and *Mr. Ed*—shows that evoked the innocence and values of another era. It was the perfect idea: inexpensive, obvious, easy to do. It is also a good example of what can result from an inclusive approach to brainstorming. It was hardly part of Debby Beece's job description to think up an evening format for the network, but once she floated it at a staff meeting, everyone agreed that it was a great, and very appropriate, solution. Debby was soon thereafter promoted to head of programming.

In 1986, Nickelodeon moved into original production, Gerry Laybourne having realized that if the company wanted to be a real network, it was going to have to produce its own material. It could no longer continue to buy everything from outside sources or syndicators. "Our first effort was a quiz show called *Double Dare,* which was invented by a team of people from on-air promotion, Bob Mittenthal and Mike Klinghoffer, our executive producer Geoffrey Darby, and a development executive, Dee LaDuke, who had actually started working at Nick as a receptionist. The concept was based upon a childhood game that various people on the team had played, a truth or dare kind of thing. The team members took an office together, and developing and refining the game became their mission. They had a rule: anyone who came into the office for any purpose had to play the game. Pretty soon, people were playing all the time." After a few weeks of this, the company taped seven pilots, and then put *Double Dare* on the air with no advance marketing and no promotion. The premiere was on a Monday: by Thursday, the show had tripled its ratings, and by the third week it was the highest-rated original series in the history of cable. Nickelodeon then offered the show for syndication, and met an enthusiastic response. At last, the company began making money.

Original production was clearly the right direction, but it was also very expensive, and there was little money for a big push into it at the time. In 1985, Warner had bought out its partnership with a division of American Express, and the next year, Warner spun off its group of networks as a single public company. That company remained public for only a few months; it was quickly bought up by Viacom (then pronounced vee-a-com). "This group never really focused on developing the MTV networks," says Gerry Laybourne. "They were more preoccupied with attempting a management buyout. So basically, we were paralyzed about our future."

Then in 1987, Sumner Redstone, one of Viacom's shareholders, convinced that the company was being undervalued, assumed enormous debt and took it over himself, changing the pronunciation of the name to vy-a-com. "Everyone at the time thought he'd paid way too much for the company," says Gerry Laybourne, "although the way things turned out, both the company and its debt were very well managed and so did well." Nevertheless, in 1987, with new ownership installed after years of corporate tumult, there was no money for Nickelodeon to expand into producing a whole line of original shows. It was at this juncture that the company began its practice of forming internal and external webs in order to achieve what conventional wisdom held could not be done.

"We needed a lot of revenue," says Harvey Ganot, "in order to cover the costs of producing new shows. But revenues for children's advertising have always been low. We had to find a way around this, so Gerry got the idea that we should sell our first-run, original programming for a premium price, and use the extra revenue to fund production. Now, this is absolutely unheard of in cable. Except for a few exceptional programs, such as sports events, you sell time slots, not shows. And you do *not* charge higher rates for a certain kind of programming. Nickelodeon was undervalued in the marketplace: it was also identified with quality in children's entertainment. That meant if something was original, we should be able to put it on a pedestal, give it an aura of being the very best. *And* get advertisers to pay for the association."

The concept required the sales staff to create a separate price structure for its original programs, and then persuade the marketplace to accept it. The new approach inspired a certain skepticism. Harvey Ganot: "Our clients were saying to us, 'Last year we paid one thousand dollars a unit for this slot, and this year you want us to pay five thousand? What do you think, we're out of our minds?' This reaction was tough on sales staff, because our people are naturally protective of the relationships they've built with clients over the years. And not only were we trying to convince our advertisers to spend the extra money, we were trying to make them feel *good* about doing so, because it meant that they were associating themselves with the best. All the experts said it would absolutely fail. This is a business where advertisers look first at *costs*."

The key to success, says Ganot, was getting total buy-in from the sales force. "They had to understand *in their bones* why these shows were so special, why they were worth paying extra for, why it was to the advertisers' advantage to be associated with them. The sales staff could not convey the enthusiasm needed to persuade the clients if they did not have that outlook themselves, if they didn't appreciate all the subtle nuances of what Nickelodeon was trying to do. We had to put a halo around these programs, and coordinate that effort across the board, using press, promotions, and marketing. We had to convince the world that we were not selling spots, but a trademark with concrete value in the marketplace. And we couldn't do that unless *we* were believers, unless we had a passion for the product, unless we knew how much it was driven by a vision of innovation and quality and fun. To carry it out, we had to make it a kind of justice, a crusade. It's an attitude you can't buy or fake."

There is no way this attitude could have been instilled, Ganot insists, if Nickelodeon had not already taken great pains to establish a collaborative way of working with the ad sales staff. "Resistance on the part of ad sales people was overcome because they were made a part of the process, because nothing was ever shoved down their throats. If Gerry hadn't made such an effort at the very beginning to change the relationship between programming and sales, we could never have carried out her plan. But she had created this web, made our staff part of the overall vision, and that's what made this happen."

The sales staff meets regularly with the heads of programming at Nickelodeon to share in developing ideas. This gives the sales force ownership in what they're trying to sell. As Harvey Ganot explains, "The network takes us into their confidence about what's in the pipeline, so we can figure out in advance the best way to sell it. They ask us, 'What do you think of this? What do you need to know?' And in turn we tell them about our processes, how we sell. Now, that's really unusual—most sales people like to keep their techniques secret. They view that as the basis of their job security. Getting them to share it is about instilling trust. But without that trust, they're never really going to be inspired about the product."

Gerry Laybourne says, "What we've tried to do is to establish a kind of R&D for programming, so that we can create a much higher level of entertainment for kids. Our advertisers have to be part of it, since we need the revenues they provide if we want to do something exceptional. That means we need a really strong ally in sales, a force that is very committed, and getting that takes a lot of work. You've got to include your sales staff right into your process, bring them along on everything, if you want to build credibility and to get people invested in what you're trying to do. If you don't take that time at the beginning, they're going to drop the ball along the way, because they aren't heart and soul in the effort. It takes a *lot* of time to get this commitment, and it's tempting to get impatient—in a hierarchy, you don't have to take the time, you can just tell people what to do. People who manage that way have very little tolerance for putting in a lot of work up front—really, they don't have the discipline for it. But if you invest the time, you can accomplish amazing things. We were able to change the price structure for cable television because we took the time to get our sales staff committed!"

Talking about the amount of time inclusive leadership demands up front, Gerry Laybourne sounds like Dave Lawrence at the *Miami Herald*. She also echoes him when she notes the absolute importance of tearing down the barriers that commonly exist between the creative and advertising sides of business. "At most entertainment companies," she observes, "ad sales doesn't work with the creative side. There's a wall between them, and everyone feels they have an interest in seeing those on the other side as the essential problem. All the sales people want is for you to set a budget, tell them the compensation structure, and then cut them loose to do their job. Their attitude is, let us do it, just don't make us explain. Sales people don't like memos, explanations, meetings—that's not how they work. But we said, we *have* to do things differently, we have to include you in how we work. We need you to understand what our goals are, in terms of how we represent ourselves in the market. We're trying to change the dynamics of kids' TV here, not argue about percentages. And the only way we can do it is if you're on the team."

A Platform for Production

Persuading advertisers to support Nickelodeon's move into original production by paying higher rates for these shows resulted in award-winning programs such as *Clarissa Explains It All* and *Eureka's Castle,* a variety show for pre-schoolers. Nevertheless, as Nickelodeon expanded from one original program in 1986 to six by 1988, the company began to suffer from not having a studio of its own. Productions moved from city to city, which put wear and tear on the staff, and made it difficult to achieve continuity. But Viacom, still struggling under the debt assumed for its leveraged buyout, was not about to build a studio for the network. So the people at Nickelodeon began asking the underlying questions upon which strategic relationships are always built: What do we need? What can we give? And who might need it?

What Nickelodeon needed was a state-of-the-art production base in a place visited year-round by children from around the country. What the network could offer was an enthusiastic audience and access to publicity on a regular basis. "Orlando," says Gerry Laybourne, "was the obvious place for a studio. Disney World brought children in from all over the country. So I had an idea about that in the back of my mind. Then one day, I read in the trade press that Universal was thinking of building a studio in Orlando. I asked Sara Levinson, then head of new business development for MTV, to set up a meeting with MCA. Our meeting was basically a cold call—Universal had no idea who or what Nickelodeon was. These were people consumed with the idea of building a theme park. They didn't particularly care what we were trying to do. But they *did* know they had to attract kids in order to be successful in Florida.

"We said, this is just the germ of an idea—what would you need for it to work for you? We didn't go in with any formal presentation. Our approach was about listening, about hearing what *they* might need. Once they gave that some thought, we could look for ways to come together." She believes that many organizations, in seeking strategic alliances, make the mistake of approaching potential partners with a full proposal neatly worked out. "They go in with overheads, with facts and figures, eager to be very persuasive, but they don't leave any room for the partners to figure out what *they* might need." In time, it became clear what Universal was looking for: an audience it could count on daily, rather than one bound by the on-and-off of production schedules. "That gave us the idea. If they would build us a studio, we would use it not only to tape all our original shows, but also to hold auditions. Kids would flock to Orlando if that meant a chance to get on TV. And Universal would get airtime to promote their park."

Throughout the process of building the partnership, Nickelodeon was determined to maintain its own operating style, so as not to get swamped by the strong identity of Universal. Universal was run very much as a top-down hierarchy, with decisions made at the top, and formal, agenda-driven meetings. "We were *so* different!" says Gerry Laybourne. "And we knew that if we started doing things their way, the partnership would never work. We were going to be producing *our* shows down there, so we had to keep our voice. That was crucial." Since Nickelodeon's voice derived from its way of operating and its sense of mission, it could hardly change how it did things without diluting that voice.

Gerry Laybourne worked to make inclusiveness part of the daily process, bringing together a diverse team from production, operations, and legal, and making them part of the meetings with Universal. "We didn't announce we were coming, we just showed up with this *gang*. So Universal started including people too—if we showed up with six staffers, they would bring a similar group. The Nickelodeon people were very vocal, and would make a lot of suggestions, because that's what they were accustomed to do. Pretty soon, the people Universal brought started speaking up too instead of waiting to see what their boss would say.

"At our first really big meeting in Orlando, I brought almost the whole company along with me. The idea was to have this open brainstorming session. Well, we got to this huge auditorium, and here were all the Universal people in their suits, and the Nickelodeon people dressed in shorts. I was sure it was going to be a disaster, but I told myself, just have faith in people! So I took a breath, and set the ground rule for the session: *there's no such thing as a bad idea.* Well, the Universal people weren't used to working like that, to being very free and speaking up, but it worked because our people were so experienced at brainstorming. We divided everyone up into groups of seven or eight, with no leaders, and we mixed people across every level. That blew them away—they weren't used to that at all!"

She recalls another early gathering in which Rich Cronin, one of Nickelodeon's senior vice presidents, presented a Nickelodeon marketing plan to a group from Universal. At first, no one made any comment, so the senior Universal executive stood up and started to demand that his people respond. "He wanted them to have answers immediately. They were all saying, give us a minute, but he kept shouting that what they should now suggest was so obvious. I said, if it's so obvious, why don't you share it with us? He flew into a further rage, and said, 'That's not my job, that's why I'm paying them. If you want my idea, I want two weeks of their pay.' From that experience, we learned to actively appreciate what this group was faced with. We made sure they were prepped for future meetings."

One of Nickelodeon's concerns was to set limits on the negotiating time. Big studios are known for dragging deals out for years, using teams of lawyers and haggling over every detail. Gerry Laybourne: "We knew that to get the deal done, we should take advantage of MCA's scheduled press conference to announce the theme park." The press conference at that time was just three days away, and Nickelodeon was able to get an agreement. They would negotiate night and day with MCA over the next three days, but if they couldn't reach an agreement within that time, the deal was over. "Whenever anyone started to nitpick, I jumped in and cut it short." A number of Nickelodeon's tactics proved surprising to their partners. Gerry Laybourne: "At one point, Geoffrey Darby, our executive producer, argued eloquently on MCA's behalf for something he didn't think would serve their best interests. I don't think they'd ever experienced that before, but we were here to set terms for the marriage, not the divorce. I've never done a deal so fast, but if we had cut them any slack on timing, we could never have got it done."

Although Nickelodeon asserted its own methods, the company also learned a lot from Universal, particularly about managing the process of production. Gerry Laybourne says they also learned a lot about the need for follow-through, particularly in dealing with complex projects. While Nickelodeon is very good at getting people excited and enthusiastic, worthwhile ideas sometimes get lost in the shuffle. Since follow-through is something that bureaucracies often shine in, Nickelodeon was able to learn from being in partnership with Universal. After the Orlando negotiations, the company began scheduling more checks into its process.

THE PERILS OF CROSS-PROMOTION

Working with Universal, Nickelodeon learned the basics of how to form a partnership with a larger company in ways that permitted it to retain its identity and continue to serve its mission, thus building upon what had made it successful in the marketplace. The Universal experience has proven invaluable over the last few years as Nickelodeon has begun the work of transforming itself into a children's entertainment juggernaut by dramatically extending its range of partnerships.

One of Nickelodeon's early ventures beyond the network was a humor magazine for children, first published in-house in 1991. Gerry Laybourne admits that the first attempt was not a real magazine but rather a cross-promotional marketing vehicle for the network, neither strong nor distinct enough to stand on its own. In its haste to get out a magazine, the company had gotten away from its basic principles, which were above all about connecting with *kids*. But the magazine was not about children, it was about selling and promoting Nickelodeon. After two issues, the company shut it down.

To redesign the magazine, she hired a consultant named Anne Kreamer, who had previously headed advertising sales for the iconoclastic humor magazine *SPY*. Kreamer saw her mission basically as giving the magazine the same level of diversity, excitement, and unexpectedness as the network—*that,* not a marketing connection, had to be the tie. "You don't build a complex relationship with your customer by simply exploiting your brand name," Anne Kreamer insists. "If you do that, the name will soon mean nothing. Every media has to be true to its own attributes, but also have an identity that derives from common principles. *That's* what makes it all work."

Anne Kreamer hired a staff of twenty-eight, and began turning out a magazine in which ninety-five percent of the material is now original. "We retain continuity by means of the emphasis on creativity, and by the fact that we give kids what they don't get elsewhere." The magazine does a lot of humor based on history, as in a recent issue which was devoted to what U.S. Presidents were like as kids. Nickelodeon wanted to use material that preserved some kind of relationship with the past, and to tap into parents' memories of what had interested them, so they could feel comfortable with what their kids were reading instead of alienated by it. Basically, it's the same principle that inspired *Nick at Nite.*

Six months into the magazine's redesign, Gerry Laybourne asked Anne Kreamer to join the company's staff and create a division to oversee all of Nickelodeon's licensing operations. The big push for

partners in the future was going to be in such joint ventures, and
Gerry Laybourne believed that Kreamer's emphasis on preserving
long-term trademark value would permit Nickelodeon to expand
without losing its identity. She also liked the way Anne Kreamer
worked. "She is very fluid. She understood from the start how to
work within a web, moving across barriers and letting projects develop in response to people. If you come to work at Nickelodeon, you
can shape your own destiny and change the nature of the place by
doing what you do best—you don't wait for an external force to tell
you what you do. It's a very organic process: no one here is just filling
a slot. Anne's job evolved because of what Anne could do." Within a
year of joining the company, Anne Kreamer had built four operational teams, hiring the staff for each and developing distinct missions
that nevertheless reflected a continuity of principles.

In retrospect, Anne Kreamer's background would seem to have made
her role with Nickelodeon a natural. Arriving from Kansas City via
Harvard, she had a brief stint at a Manhattan bank, which she says
served as her introduction to "Soviet culture." She then landed at the
Children's Television Workshop, where her ideas about what constitutes an effective organization were formed. "At CTW, *everything* we
did was related to core values. There was a strong ethic about including kids in urban centers, embracing those who felt disenfranchised
from society. So everything we did was about inclusion. That was
reflected in these very inclusive teams—editors, producers, writers,
and marketers all working together. I saw very clearly that, to be
effective, team management *has* to derive from a sense of shared values. A team can't be a monolith, it has to express diverse perspectives.
That makes it imperative that everyone operate from the same basic
assumptions."

Her next job, as director of development for education and publicity at CBS, brought her "back to the hierarchy, where I saw it all
again—the aversion to risk, the conformity, the emphasis on the low-
est common denominator." In 1986, she joined *SPY,* which her hus-

band was just starting with two partners. "I didn't know anything about advertising sales, but I said I'd give it a try. There were only six people on staff—obviously, no HR department, no policies or guidelines. We had to figure everything out as we went along, so I had a chance to test what worked and what did not."

At SPY, Anne Kreamer put her energies into making sure that the barriers that traditionally divide the creative and business sides of such an enterprise never had a chance to develop—a concern shared by Gerry Laybourne as she built her network. Kreamer notes that SPY initially had a terrible time attracting advertisers, and credits this adversity, along with the very small size of the initial staff, with helping bring the advertising and editorial sides of the magazine together. Indeed, when the magazine finally expanded and had to move into larger quarters, they waited for months until they could find a space where everyone could continue to share the same floor, rather than separating ad and editorial staffs as usually happens. When she came to Nickelodeon, Anne Kreamer was determined that the departments of the magazine she was brought in to redesign also "live together," so that they could not become entrenched as separate fiefdoms.

In her first year at Nickelodeon, Anne Kreamer launched operating units for electronic publishing, video- and audiotapes as part of a partnership with Sony Music Entertainment. In its alliance with Nickelodeon, Sony operates through a division known as Sony Wonder, which Anne Kreamer describes as a cross-divisional group within Sony's corporate headquarters that was configured for the sole purpose of developing services for kids. In structuring the alliance, Anne Kreamer's team both relied and expanded upon what Gerry Laybourne had learned while putting together Nickelodeon's first major partnership, with Universal. Primary among these lessons was the necessity for Nickelodeon to control the way it interacted with its more hierarchical partner, in order to retain its own voice.

Working with a start-up division made this control easier to achieve, since, as Anne Kreamer notes, "Sony Wonder is basically structured a lot like we are. It's very inclusive, a web-like team, which makes it easier for us to work with them in ways that we are comfortable with." Maintaining its mode of operation is crucial, Anne Kreamer believes, "in order for Nickelodeon to control the marketing and packaging of all the products we develop with Sony. And we *have* to keep this control, because it's in the presentation that our identity could most quickly be diluted. We have to determine process, product, and presentation if our mission is to remain intact. And if we do not remain intact, what's the point?"

THE DEEP STRUCTURE OF TRUE PARTNERSHIP

An alliance with Mattel to produce a line of Nickelodeon activity toys was already in place when Anne Kreamer arrived at the company, but the nature of the partnership was the antithesis of what she believed it should be. "The agreement was really just a standard licensing arrangement, driven by a short-term desire to bring in money. At Nickelodeon at the time, we had no infrastructure in place to support the partnership—no design group, no product development people, no marketing experts. No one was giving any thought to developing consistency of product, to creating toys and games that made an emotional connection with who *we* are."

She describes Mattel as very much a large hierarchy, with a rich history and traditions and a strong sense of itself—the kind of company that could easily swallow "the little Utopia we've established here at Nickelodeon. We had to find a way of working that would enable us to use the enormous amount of information about children that Mattel has access to, while still exerting enough leverage to keep what is powerful in our own culture. Everything associated with our name has to provide enrichment, so that licensing *adds* to our trademark. That means we have to control design and marketing for all our licensed products."

To make its partnership with Mattel successful, Nickelodeon had to establish a way of working with the company that broke down barriers instead of respecting them. The archetypical relationship between a manufacturer and a licensee doesn't leave much room for interaction. Usually, the manufacturer develops the product and sends a prototype to the licensee for inspection; the licensee then sends it back with a few comments. After some back and forth, the manufacturer's distributors put the product into the stores. Thus the manufacturer both creates and markets the product, while the licensee merely oversees it. It's a fairly rigid process, one that adheres to established channels and respects barriers, rarely permitting either organization to learn from or influence the other.

The process leaves little room for the free-flowing creative brainstorming upon which Nickelodeon has always thrived. As Anne Kreamer observes, "Our whole method has always been about building these very creative teams and then giving people permission to let themselves go by providing a situation where they can be fluid and spontaneous and interactive. You can see it at work in the way careers develop here: the company evolves in response to the talents and ideas of individuals, rather than requiring the individual to fit into positions or roles. More than anything, *that's* what makes us function inclusively. It's the basis for how we run things. We have to run our licensing like that, or the products we do won't reflect who we are."

With the Sony Wonder team, Kreamer's team established a method that reflected how people at Nickelodeon liked to work by basically creating a subset within Sony that works in a similar way. Achieving this at Mattel proved more difficult, partly because the partnership had already been established when Anne Kreamer arrived, so that what she considered some unproductive ways of working were already in place. The difficulty was compounded by the real differences between the companies. As Liz Sheppard, a member of Anne Kreamer's team, observes, "A major aspect of Nickelodeon's identity has always been that we don't do gender-specific programming. And here suddenly we are working with Mattel, a company organized by boys' toys and girls' toys divisions."

Not only is Nickelodeon's programming gender-neutral, its advertising is as well, so any products it licenses must be developed with that in mind. By contrast, Mattel designs most of its products specifically for boys or girls; those that appeal to both genders are marketed to boys, on the assumption that boys will not buy products advertised for girls, but girls will follow the lead set by boys. "That assumption is widespread in the toy industry and is the rule on network television," says Gerry Laybourne, "but we've always stood against it. Since our mission is to make kids feel good about themselves, how could we possibly accept advertising that leaves out girls?" Similarly, if Nickelodeon permitted Mattel to advertise their jointly created products in its conventional way, a key aspect of its own identity would be destroyed, which meant that the company had to control the advertising of its licensed products.

From her years at Children's Television Workshop, Anne Kreamer had become convinced "that you can't do teams well unless you're operating from a set of principles that everyone understands and shares." In setting parameters for work with Mattel, therefore, she first set about training her group "to get very clear about who we are and what we believe. That means being specific. For example, we hold to a philosophy of quality, of variety, of self-discovery for kids. We believe that boys and girls should be treated as equals. We expect the unexpected. And we seek to build a bridge for kids with the past, with what their parents did, that connects them to the whole history of American childhood."

Liz Sheppard notes another defining principle. "Our commitment to making kids feel good about themselves means we have to encourage play that is open-ended and creative. We don't think there should be a right way or a wrong way to play with something, whether it's a toy or a game. With Candyland, for instance, you have to follow the rules, or you're playing *wrong*. So we could never be involved with a game like that." Going through the process of self-definition, says Sheppard, "made us a lot clearer about what our parameters are. It's too vague just to say, we want products that reflect the identity we've established on-air. Also, that's internally focused. We have to be *precise* about what we stand for, so we'll know what to turn down."

■ ■ ■

In order to bring about a "mid-course correction" in its relationship with Mattel, Anne Kreamer scheduled an intensive two-day off-site retreat and brought in a small consulting company named Proteus to run it. Both her own team and the activity toy and game developers and marketers at Mattel were invited to the event. Mattel trusted Nickelodeon to shape the retreat. The purpose was to define the nature of the joint relationship and spell out common goals.

Gerry Laybourne describes the off-site retreat as "Anne's way of taking a shortcut to get the partnership on the right wavelength *fast*. Just going through the process of that retreat, all that interaction, established a new level of communication. Everyone suddenly got more comfortable asking the big questions: Where are we going? How are we going to get there? What kind of differences are standing in our way?" One reason Gerry Laybourne believes the off-site was so successful is that Jill Barad, Mattel's President and COO, gave it full support, and even joined in as a participant. "She handed over control to Anne on this, which is rare for someone in her position. There's something different about Jill's management style. She's willing to let go when there's a need to."

Anne Kreamer says, "At the off-site, we went through the histories of both Nickelodeon and Mattel. By this I mean the unofficial histories, the ones that are transmitted orally in every organization—through stories, anecdotes, warnings, and gossip that gets repeated and handed down until it becomes a common legacy. People in different organizations usually aren't familiar with one another's traditions, so they can't appreciate what the other has to give. The whole exercise took a lot of time, and people might look at it as a waste, but it established this familiarity at a deep level. And I've always found that putting a lot of time into a relationship up front makes things go much smoother down the road."

In sharing histories, people began to discover that they weren't always talking the same language. Anne Kreamer: "You know how in organizations people always have their own private lingo, their particular way of phrasing things. Little phrases and sayings serve as a bond to hold people together—they're part of institutional memory, a way of declaring that you share something in common. In terms of building a close-knit organization, *language is a key*. One trouble in partnerships is that people from different companies *don't* share a language. So we decided we were going to get together and create a specific vocabulary, a way of expressing what we wanted our relationship to be."

Tom Ronig, the EVP of Marketing at Mattel, believes that developing the shared language has been crucial to the partnership's success. "Specific words have a way of bringing back the memory of what you've shared together and what you're trying to achieve. They're a kind of emotional trigger that reminds you of your common purpose. So inventing a vocabulary together really cemented this bond."

The partnership vision for Nickelodeon and Mattel is in fact written in the form of a list of its shared vocabulary. For example:

MONDO! Nickelodeon and Mattel create great things together . . . lots of growth and profit, a global presence, influence in the industry.

FRED AND GINGER: We dance together, sharing resources, information, and ideas; trusting and supporting each other's "moves" and expertise.

TOTALLY GAK: We create fun, innovative products that break ground in a kid-focused, "Nick" way—that come up to a "Gak standard."

FIFO: Fun In, Fun Out—we have fun working together, we recognize the importance of fun in our partnership—and the end product is fun things for kids.

"We really *use* these words," says Liz Sheppard. "In our phone calls and when we meet, and especially in our e-mail." E-mail, she points out, is a medium with a special affinity for particularized language, for identifying handles and idiomatic phrasings; thus it has great potential as a tool for organizations seeking to form a shared culture. Sheppard notes that "When you think about it, language is what really defines a culture. So by making up a specific vocabulary, we define a culture as ours."

With Mattel, Nickelodeon has concentrated on developing a wide range of activity toys that can be used in open-ended ways, and that hark back to what Anne Kreamer calls "the classic experiences of an American childhood. That's what we really want, to make a classic. Look at Crayola. They connect with the way kids in this country actually spend their lives. Plus they have such a strong and distinct identity that they can expand into fat crayons, paints, and coloring books without losing any sense of who they are."

Nickelodeon's hopes for creating classic products start with Floam and Gak, malleable substances that can be molded into shapes and which reintroduce the concept of creepy crawlers. Liz Sheppard describes how Nickelodeon worked with Mattel on these products. "Mattel's research people developed the compounds—they have the best inventors, and they're great at that. But we were involved every step of the way. We had ideas about how the compounds should look and feel, how they'd smell, what colors they should be, their packaging, how to promote them in ways that captured the Nick spirit. We were in constant contact with Mattel, always splitting into groups. We built all our teams around tasks, ignoring categories, not looking at who's who on the work charts. We kept notebooks in which we wrote down our promises to each other. Or we put wild ideas in them. And we expressed our ideas in our new vocabulary."

More than anything, Sheppard says, the partners at Nickelodeon and Mattel tried to maintain a sense of spontaneity and fun. "Most adults have forgotten how to play. They don't touch, experiment, or do things that are silly. But all that's *essential* to how we work. We were always bringing stuff home to watch our kids play with it, and that would give us ideas. But we also kept stuff in the office and played with it ourselves. We were always *messing* with it. That's how we developed extensions, things like Floamatic, which comes with shapers and cutters, so you don't have to use just your fingers. For Gak, we came up with the bladder pump, so you can make the stuff slither up through a tube. The idea came from imagining what kind of disgusting noises the stuff might make. That's the kind of thing that makes kids laugh."

Nickelodeon can use the strength of its trademark to forge alliances with a variety of partners, but only if it does not dilute what it stands for. The way the company can accomplish that, according to Anne Kreamer, is to be willing to say no, and say no often. She notes that a successful brand is always going to be under market pressure to license products that have nothing to do with what the organization is really about, products that may make money in the short term but will ultimately dilute the brand's identity in the marketplace. To resist that, an organization must focus on the long term. But it can do that only if both the organization and its partners have a firm and clear sense of precisely why it exists, how it is unique, and why it is of value.

GOING GLOBAL

Nickelodeon has expanded greatly since 1984, when Gerry Laybourne assumed leadership of its staff of twenty. The company now has about two hundred people in New York, forty in the U.K., and another few hundred in Orlando—as always with studio production, the number of people varies. Nickelodeon also maintains satellites in its various sales regions. Counting everyone who works on the company's behalf, the numbers go up into the thousands.

This poses a challenge, especially when it comes to maintaining an identity predicated on being run in an inclusive fashion. Gerry Laybourne: "We've always worked as a web, including people in, emphasizing process, letting the organization evolve in response to people. When we were a handful of pioneers, going up against the mainstream culture, it was easy to have that orientation. But when you have seven hundred people to consider, it's not so simple. You bring outsiders in—either through expansion or partnerships—and they bring not only needed skills, but also their own values and ways of working. Often they're very different. So how do you include *them* without destroying what has made you successful?"

One essential problem caused by the web of inclusion, Gerry Laybourne believes, is that it also creates a web of exclusion. For when an organization defines itself in terms of its mission, it also defines itself in terms of what its mission is *not*. This breeds an us-against-them mentality, apparent at Nickelodeon in the us-against-the-broadcast-world, us-against-conventional-wisdom attitude that prevails. The question thus becomes, how can an organization hold on to its distinctive way of operating without shutting others out in the process?

The question is particularly crucial when, like Nickelodeon, an organization is seeking to expand beyond national borders, into places unfamiliar with its basic principles and assumptions. How can strong and specific organizational cultures be translated and made to work in different countries? How do partnerships based on mission work across national borders?

The key, Gerry Laybourne believes, lies in remaining committed to letting the organization evolve in response to what the different individuals within it bring. She reiterates that, as a teacher in an open classroom, she became convinced of the power of individualized instruction, of the need to identify your people's individual strengths, and build upon them by providing tasks tailored to their development. "With Anne Kreamer, for instance, I know that she's got to be constantly challenged. She *thrives* on that, needs it to make her happy. So my challenge is to make sure Anne is challenged. Otherwise, I won't be using what's best about her. And the organization won't evolve as it should. She won't be able to see her own footprints. And we might lose her."

Laybourne's challenge as she contemplates going global, looking toward Planet Nickelodeon, is not unlike that faced by Anixter Inc. as it seeks to take its warehousing and distribution system worldwide. At Anixter, the complexities of the global push are being met by a commitment to integrated training. Nickelodeon is using a similar approach. Laybourne observes: "Those of us at the core of the company are in the position of having to teach what we have learned. But we also have to *keep* on learning, so we can stay ahead of that curve! To do that, we're using a workshop or apprentice approach. Take the U.K., for example. We bring people over here for apprenticeships, so they can get steeped in Nickelodeon tradition. They *live* with us, absorb our methods and language, what we're about."

But true learning must go both ways. At some point, people who are new to an organization need to be able to find their own direction, rather than continuing only to absorb old lessons and duplicate past efforts. When the U.K. launch began, the Nickelodeon staff in New York got very nervous: they kept wondering if their British counterparts really understood all the nuances of the Nickelodeon concept, and if they could repeat their success.

Finally, Jeff Dunn, the head of strategy and business operations, pointed out that the expansion would never work if the new unit couldn't function as an independent group, with its own mission, its own reason for being. As a result, Nickelodeon quickly embraced Nickelodeon U.K.'s desire to be a laboratory for interactivity. Not in the high-tech sense, since televisions in England don't have that capability, but rather in the more conventional sense of providing lots of ways for children to call in and connect directly with a live host on the air. Because the U.K. is in a single time zone, it provides an ideal laboratory for this kind of thing. The new unit is thus leading the company in discovering what kinds of programming will inspire its audience to get directly involved, so that when interactive television is available, Nickelodeon will already have a strong idea of what really works.

The difficulty, as Gerry Laybourne notes, is "to find ways to resonate with kids in our distinctive voice, while expanding beyond just American culture. It's something we're just starting to learn about." A similar imperative is faced by every variety of organization today. Nickelodeon, for example, has long been characterized by an attitude of insouciant irreverence. But how will this translate in Asia, where children are taught to revere those in authority? How will its accent on open-ended play fit in cultures where a premium is placed on people learning how to do things in a single proper way? "The thing we need to keep in mind as we move onto a world stage is that our voice comes from our method, our process. It comes from our recognition that, if we include kids in everything we do, we're going to produce a product that serves them better. But inclusion is a radical concept in most other countries—people aren't comfortable with it yet. So it's by keeping to our *process* that we're going to push the frontiers of change."

PART III

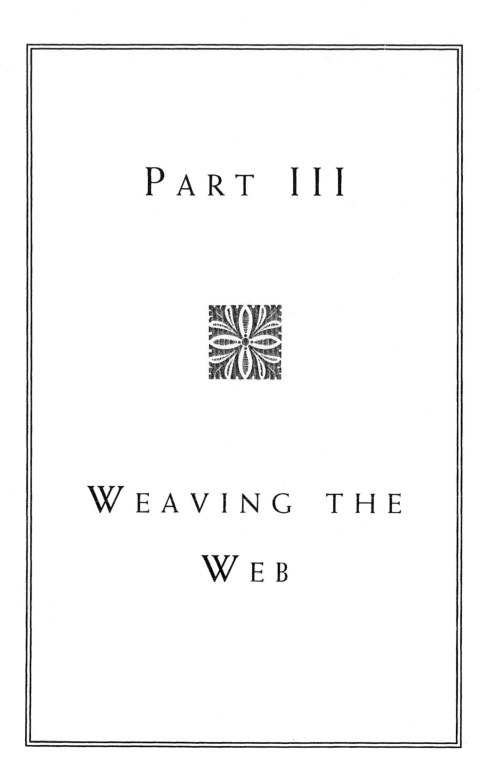

WEAVING THE
WEB

EIGHT

The Hearth, the Hub, and the Working Club

As I watched people at the *Miami Herald* struggling to build a fairer, more inclusive, and flexible workplace—one in which people at all levels could participate in a range of vital decisions, and communicate more directly—I began to recognize the extent to which one major aspect of how we think about organizations is overlooked in even the most painstaking and thoughtful efforts to restructure them. This aspect has to do with the physical design of workspace.

We need to ask ourselves a few questions:

What do our buildings look like?

How does it feel to be inside them all day?

What kind of behaviors and attitudes do they inspire?

Although rarely mentioned in the plethora of writings that deal with organizational change that have appeared over the last decade, physical design is a vital aspect of workplace culture. How we use our workspace reflects our presumptions about our work—its purpose and meaning, how it should be accomplished in time. Indeed, an organization's physical space is the most truly tangible metaphor for the company as a whole; it is the *place* we visualize when we think about our work. And yet it is common for these physical places, even in the most innovative organizations, to remain mired in Industrial Era presumptions, contradicting any message about inclusiveness and change.

The *Miami Herald* provides a vivid example. One Herald Plaza, which occupies a spectacular piece of harborfront real estate in downtown Miami, is a long, low-lying building from the late 1950s, with the painted cinderblock walls and low ceilings typical of institutional structures of that era. Five floors sprawl along corridors that connect offices and meeting rooms, converging around a central elevator shaft. The newspaper presses are housed within the building, so that one side is dominated by a huge delivery truck garage. On the other side is the in-building parking lot reserved for executives that stirred such resentment among the staff. Between these is a wide, cheerful lobby, with a security booth, a rotating display of photos and awards, and no real place for anyone to sit.

The building is isolated from its surroundings, fronted by a vast open parking lot, and approachable only by the dead-end road it shares with the towers of the Harborplace Marriott. There is no access from the building to the waterfront, which therefore functions only to provide a view; nor can you visit nearby shops or restaurants unless you first retrieve your car. With few other options, most employees eat in the vast and gloomy cafeteria, an uncongenial and noisy setting in which few choose to linger. There is also a hushed but cheerless executive dining room with full table service.

The top floor of the building is occupied by the Knight-Ridder group, the *Herald*'s parent company, and by the newsroom of *El Nuevo Herald,* isolated behind an infamous glass wall. The wall is perceived by many on the *Herald* staff as serving primarily as a buffer that spares the corporate brass from having to listen to Spanish being spoken all day. On lower floors, people are divided according to function—the advertising department occupies the second floor, editorial the fourth. In both departments, people below senior rank perform their work not in individual offices, but in platform spaces open to general view. Here scores of desks are grouped, each with its own computer terminal; when everyone is busy, the place is very loud.

The private offices that open off these spaces vary greatly, with size determined more by rank than by the kind of work actually being done within them. The largest offices, along the rear wall, offer a grand view of the waterway that divides Miami from Miami Beach; the smaller offices at the front of the building are either windowless or look out over the parking lot. None of the private offices connect, so that, while employees in the lower ranks lack privacy, those of senior rank are isolated. This is particularly true of the publisher's office, which, cut off by heavy wooden doors, is enclosed within a suite, in the front room of which sit executive secretaries and receptionists. A large meeting room is attached, and private washrooms.

The *Herald*'s offices are thus constructed in a way that reflects Industrial Era notions about the transcendence of hierarchical rank, the necessity of supervising the rank and file, and the importance of compartmentalizing tasks. As a result, people at the paper must go to work each day in a physical environment that undermines the very essence of their efforts to decompartmentalize tasks, decentralize decision-making, and break down rank-based barriers to communication. Because traditional assumptions about the nature of people's work and how they use their time are *built right into the* Herald's *physical plant,* they inevitably undermine efforts to develop the more interconnected and fast-paced ways of working that define the architecture of the web.

Still, the *Herald* building is by no means a particularly terrible example of late twentieth-century workplace design. Certainly, it is neither as aggressively hierarchical nor even remotely as soulless as many of the large towers that serve as corporate headquarters in our cities and suburbs today. There is no gratuitous wasting of huge amounts of space on pseudo-impressive lobbies, no gigantic vice presidential offices separated by scores of floors from the cubbyholes of people who report to those same vice presidents. And because the *Herald* building is primarily horizontal, its corridors provide space for random encounters, which helps inspire familiarity across levels. Nevertheless, the profoundly compartmentalized notions implicit in the physical design of the building stand in opposition to Dave Lawrence's efforts to push his staff to adapt a more web-like and inclusive workplace structure, one that emphasizes direct communication, the integration of tasks, flexibility, and a relative disregard for rank.

The contrast between how space is used at the *Miami Herald* and how it is used at Intel could hardly be greater, and it illustrates how physical design can help facilitate the formation of webs. As has been noted, the scorn for hierarchical privileges and perks that is a legacy of the individualistic Silicon Valley culture is evident as soon as one approaches Intel's huge complex, and discovers that there are no parking places reserved for executives. This designed-in egalitarianism extends to the way space is apportioned throughout the five-story glass-walled building, where everyone sits in a cubicle, including the President. The almost total lack of correspondence between one's position in the organization and the size and location of one's office emphasizes and encourages the development of the nonpositional power that is so valued an aspect of how the company functions.

The well-laid-out cubicles at Intel, with their sound-absorbent and comparatively high walls, provide a mix of privacy and quiet, diminishing both the isolation that is a feature of private offices and the chaos characteristic of open platforms. And because personal workspace is allocated in accord with what people need to accomplish their tasks rather than in order to reflect their rank, space is not viewed as a perk that helps to define status. Absent entirely is the "from Versailles to the pigsty" syndrome notable in many organizations, in which the top executives' offices, the boardrooms, and the building's entrance are wildly luxurious, while rank-and-file employees labor in inefficient squalor. Intel's use of cubicles also permits an unusual degree of flexibility: the dividing panels can be shifted to enlarge or diminish an office's size, or to accommodate a new assistant or a new group of tasks. This facilitates Intel's policy of continual reorganizations, enabling people to change jobs without having also to change offices.

Perhaps the most noteworthy aspect of Intel's physical design is its cafeteria, a large and light-filled space built on a variety of levels, so that it feels open and intimate at the same time. Everyone in the company eats in the cafeteria, from the Chairman to the security guards, as well as workers from an Intel manufacturing plant that shares the headquarters' grounds. Tall glass doors open from the main room onto a landscaped courtyard, with a fountain, flowers, and plenty of trees, as well as tables and benches, so that people can enjoy their meals outdoors if they choose.

More striking than its humane and cheerful design, however, is how the Intel cafeteria is actually *used*. Remaining fully open from eight each morning until six at night, it serves as a meeting and conference room for people throughout the company. "Since private space is limited, we come here when we need to stretch out and talk to someone," explains Carlene Ellis. "It's especially helpful when you need to discuss something with a couple of people; the cubicles are too small for that. The cafeteria makes getting together easy—you don't have to schedule a conference room, you just tell someone to meet you downstairs. It's relaxed and informal, and you can get coffee or go outdoors if you want. There are days when I spend most of my time here. If anyone wants to find me, this is where they look."

Carlene points out that being interrupted is not a problem, for scattered around the room are small signs that say "One on One." Putting one of these on the table signals that a private conference is in session. "If people see a sign on your table, they won't stop to chat. So you can be very private even though you're visible." The cafeteria thus permits privacy to flourish within a public space, blurring the usually rigid distinction in organizations between what happens in private and what occurs in public. This helps to vanquish the unequal balance that prevails in most companies, where privacy is the privilege of those who wield positional power—and is also indistinguishable from isolation.

The Intel cafeteria, as a large and highly visible central gathering space shared by all, creates a feeling of community. And by encouraging ongoing informal interaction among people at various levels, it diminishes the distance between top executives, mid-level managers, and support staff. Ultimately, the space serves a function similar to that of the large central plazas in European and Latin American towns, which create a sense of shared identity and interest among all citizens, rich or poor, by offering them a common and accessible spot in which to meet. In a business organization, the sense of shared identity that such a space creates can help people in the ranks to focus on the company's greater mission, rather than getting stuck in isolated concerns. A common space provides a common ground, and common ground is essential if webs of inclusion are to flourish.

Although Intel makes use of its physical design to encourage a sense of belonging within the organization, it does not use space in ways that reach out to the larger world. As one of thousands of large commercial and industrial buildings spread out along Route 101 as it surges north from San Jose, the Intel complex is isolated from everything that adjoins it; it can be reached only by means of an access road from the highway. As at the *Miami Herald,* Intel employees must use their cars if they want to run errands on their lunch hour or eat outside the complex; the supremely compartmentalized fortress mentality of suburban development prevails. And so despite Intel's thoughtful use of internal space to promote web-like and inclusive values, the exigencies of sprawl prevent it from relating to the larger physical landscape or the greater community of which it is a part.

OF SPACE AND TIME

Watching life swirl around me one afternoon in the Intel cafeteria, I recalled an observation made to me by Nancy Badore, at the time Director of Executive Training for Ford. "The real *stuff* of work," she noted, "gets done mostly in downtime, during those informal moments when people just happen to run across one another, or start up a casual conversation that meanders along until it leads to some new idea." Nancy Badore believes that organizations can achieve great benefits by trying to encourage this kind of casual interaction—in particular, interaction that occurs between people at various levels. But she also notes that, in order to achieve this, organizations must begin to provide "lots of inviting places where people feel comfortable just hanging out."

Such an approach amounts to institutionalizing what might be called "the watercooler factor," the natural desire of people in organizations to come together in casual settings in which an *element of randomness* predominates and the feeling of being on downtime prevails. Meeting in this casual mode puts people in an entirely different frame of mind than coming together in formal and scheduled meetings, for which preparation is imperative, indeed the entire point. In random encounters, one is not required to be prepared but rather free to be spontaneous. And spontaneity is the key to freeing the creative imagination.

For any creative work, preparation and spontaneity must achieve some kind of balance. People must be able to structure some of their work time so that predefined tasks can be done, while leaving other time open to pursue the kind of free exchange that plants the seeds for new ideas and ventures. In most organizations, time used to complete tasks has traditionally been more highly regarded, with the result that preparation is valued over spontaneity. This out-of-balance approach is a legacy from the old Industrial Era view of work as a series of discrete and sharply definable tasks, conceived by supervisors and executed by drones. But as technology and the global marketplace increasingly demand innovation, the valuing of preparation over spontaneity becomes increasingly obsolete.

The way in which an organization conceives of how its employees should be using their *time* is probably the primary influence on how that organization allocates its *space*. If people are expected either to be working alone at their desks or attending scheduled meetings, workspace will be rigidly divided between private offices and formal meeting rooms. Undefined space—cloakrooms, or the spot where the coffee machine and refrigerator are housed—will be cramped and uninviting, conveying a clear message to employees not to linger and chat. Organizations that apportion space this way make it clear that their leaders do not believe that unstructured conversation among employees could ever result in ideas that would be of value to the organization as a whole.

Mistrusting their employees, such organizations discourage random interactions, controlling how people spend their time by limiting the space in which random encounters might occur. Perhaps one reason companies tend to discourage such encounters is simply that they look like so much fun, being by nature an exercise in personal freedom. Also, because the value of spontaneity is difficult to quantify, it is hard to justify the value of downtime space. Yet if spontaneity is discouraged, creativity will not easily flourish; and the most creative employees will feel the most hemmed in.

THE HEARTH

In designing Ford's Executive Training Center to encourage spontaneous interaction, Nancy Badore had the offices built around a large common space, located at a crossroads where people were apt to pass through. Along one wall, she set up tables where fruit, muffins, and beverages were always available, for she recognized the vital role food plays in encouraging free exchange. Eating and drinking often provide a means of delineating the difference between free and structured time, allowing people to take control of what they are doing in trivial but psychologically satisfying ways. By providing an alternate focus that takes pressure off, food gives people's imaginations a chance to roam, as well as stirring echoes of human communion that have been with our species since its beginnings. Eating or drinking with others cements an elemental bond and implies a basic trust.

The importance of food in establishing common assembly or gathering spaces emphasizes another aspect of their function: in the most basic terms, such spaces serve as collective hearths. In ancient cultures, the collective hearth of the city-state or village served as its central and defining space: people gathered around the communal fire to cook food and to share warmth, but also to hold councils, exchange tales, and make decisions that would affect the group as a whole. In such spaces, the values and traditions of the clan or citizens were formulated, learned, refined, and handed down. The hearth defined in spatial terms "who we are."

Louis Kahn, the great American architect, understood this. In creating his exquisite designs for institutions, he made a careful study of how assembly space was used in the ancient world. He was particularly intrigued by public spaces in early Greece and Rome, sophisticated venues where political and economic business was transacted, but where sacred flames still burned, signifying that these public spaces still functioned as communal hearths. Kahn concluded that the true value of these gathering places lay in "their ability to encourage the notion of a collective of individual beliefs." That is, by acknowledging the sacred and traditional character of common ground, the builders of ancient institutions instilled within the individuals who used them a sense of being part of something *larger than themselves*. In a similar way, public spaces that function as hearths today can help to balance the values of the individual with those of the group, reconciling the demands of public and private, sacred and profane. Both physically and spiritually, the hearth is the heart of the organization.

I first became aware of the central role hearths could play in organizations while researching *The Female Advantage: Women's Ways of Leadership*. Watching the daily unfolding of business in the women's companies, I could not help but note how often vital exchanges occurred in informal but comfortable communal spaces that defined the true image people had of their organization. I imagined these spaces as kind of "organizational kitchen tables," since in many homes today the kitchen table serves as the true domestic hearth. I received many letters about this from people eager to describe the "kitchen table" that formed the center of their own workplace, symbolizing for them the true essence of the organization of which they were a part.

Since then, I have been intrigued by the role that purposefully designed hearths can play in helping to transmit and reinforce web-like and inclusive values in a variety of organizations. Pentagram, an industrial and graphics design firm with headquarters in London, New York, and San Francisco, serves as a good example. The company's airy and well-laid-out offices in a large loft building in Manhattan are centered around a kind of open lounge in which long tables are surrounded by shelves filled with reference books on design. The space serves as a research resource, but also as a conference room where people can talk with clients or gather for impromptu meetings.

At the noon hour, caterers come in and set up an expansive buffet in the lounge for whoever wants to join in. As at the Intel cafeteria, senior partners and support staff eat together in this common space, along with visitors and clients, who are thus entertained "at home" instead of at nearby restaurants. It is faster, more efficient, less expensive, and, as partner Colin Forbes observes, "It gives our clients an idea of who we really are. All of us, not just the partners." After the caterers clear lunch, the space once again reverts to serving as a place for research and informal gatherings.

This central space defines the company: it is the image, the internal symbol of Pentagram, the means of defining "us." That both the lounge's design and the way in which it is used de-emphasize the importance of rank is not coincidental, for that is a bedrock value of the organization. Pentagram's structure is unusual. Its sixteen partners work individually as heads of their own small businesses: there is no common strategic plan since, in the words of partner John McConnell, "the company is individual-driven rather than market-driven." Each partner's business is run as an independent profit center, each partner dealing directly with his or her own clients, while also serving as a mentor to the apprentices who make up his or her team. Yet despite the emphasis on individualism, profits in the company are split equally, with tolerance extended when one of the partners is having a bad year. No one gets rich this way, but the business as a whole remains solid. The structure and style of functioning are both web-like and inclusive—values given spatial expression by the way in which the organization's offices are designed.

■ ■ ■

The hearth both expresses and helps to shape the true values of an organization's culture. By integrating individual and common values, hearths are by nature inclusive, expansive in their definition of who comprises "us." Thinking back to my early experience at the *Village Voice*, I realized that Dan Wolf's office served as that organization's hearth. It was both accessible and intimate: you entered as an individual seeking guidance and/or wanting just to talk, and you came away with your concerns given a concrete form that could then be developed as a project for the paper. You entered the hearth-realm as "me" and came away as part of "we." You absorbed the values and the culture at the source.

A similar principle operates by entirely different means in the offices occupied by the *Utne Reader* in a rambling old commercial building in downtown Minneapolis. The *Reader,* a monthly compendium of articles culled from obscure or alternative journals supplemented by original articles that reflect a particular monthly theme, was founded by Eric Utne in 1984 on a shoestring. As of 1993, the magazine showed the greatest percentage increase in circulation growth of any monthly publication in the United States, as well as one of the strongest demographic profiles.

Trained as an architect, Eric Utne is a passionate advocate of the ideas about balanced and evolving design found in *A Pattern Language.* He keeps a copy of the book—"my Bible"—always on his desk, and he referred to it constantly while designing the *Reader*'s offices, a task he assumed himself. The design is above all web-like. Individual offices are private but accessible: all the doors are made of glass, which gives the rooms the feel of porches, casual and airy. The offices radiate out from a central library, by far the largest room in the complex, which is used for research and weekly meetings of the magazine's staff. By criteria of shape, position, and usage, the library fills the function of the organization's hearth.

The paper's true and most individual hearth, however, seems to lie in another part of the rambling building: in the Loring Cafe, which occupies the ground floor. Here Eric Utne and four or five members of the *Reader*'s staff gather for monthly conversations with a group of invited guests. Deliberately free-form, these gatherings are both web-like and inclusive, drawing from an ever-widening matrix of teachers, writers, artists, environmental activists, business people, and political leaders who either live in the community or happen to be passing through town. These "salons" form the essence of the *Reader*'s culture, defining what is unique about it, for the subjects and themes addressed in the magazine evolve directly from these extended conversations.

The purpose of the gatherings is "to find out what people are thinking about," on the presumption that these same topics will be of interest to the magazine's readers. Eric Utne explains: "We never do reader surveys. We totally avoid the market analysis approach, which tries to figure out what the reader wants and then deliver it. That approach is viewed as inclusive, but look what it really does: it imagines the reader as 'other,' as someone outside the magazine, whose interests must be discerned and then catered to. We take the opposite approach, and try to look inward: What interests us? What interests the people we know? What do we like to read? What do we find ourselves obsessing over? We start from the presumption that there's not much difference between us and our readers: we figure that what we care about will also interest them. So instead of trying to isolate our readers or predict trends, we look within and try to discover what's universal. In doing that, we acknowledge and assume a commonality."

Eric Utne's philosophy as an editor strongly echoes that of Dan Wolf, and the means used to translate it into concrete product is also the same: people come together at the organization's hearth in order to synthesize their private vision with that of the larger whole. The hearths at the *Utne Reader* and the original *Village Voice* are thus functionally similar, although also profoundly different, in that they reflect the different personalities of the editors who shaped them. Dan Wolf preferred to hold his long and searching conversations in private, with just one other person, while Eric Utne clearly finds stimulation within a larger group. But both of the hearths they configured reflect the notion in *A Pattern Language* that true flexibility in an organization demands the willingness both to use unexpected spaces and *to build traditions as one goes along.* The same holds true for Pentagram's lounge area and the Intel cafeteria: all follow Nancy Badore's dictum that "the real stuff of work" gets done in downtime, and that space is best used to encourage an atmosphere that fosters spontaneous exchange. These differing spaces also reflect Louis Kahn's belief that institutional hearths are where individual ideas and beliefs are integrated into the collective whole.

THE HUB

Hearths reflect, sustain, and strengthen values within the organization. Thus they look inward, and bear echoes of communal values, of village life. But to be both web-like and inclusive, an organization must also look outward, must find ways to strengthen the filaments and tendrils that connect it to the larger world. Organizational architecture today must therefore not only strengthen and declare identity, but also encourage flexibility, evolution, communication in all directions, and quick response. In terms of physical design, organizations can achieve this by making use of the principles of the hub in addition to those of the hearth.

We can see the hub principle most clearly at work in global organizations that function very leanly, having dispensed with the notion of a large centralized corporate headquarters where all major decisions are made. Asea Brown Boveri, the Swiss-based electrical power manufacturer, provides a classic if extreme example. Although it is a truly global corporation with 220,000 employees and yearly sales of $28 billion, a mere 140 people are based out of its headquarters. The headquarters is more hub than home base: it links up resources rather than providing them, connecting suppliers with markets and subcontractors. Radically decentralized, ABB is profoundly web-like in that it places primary emphasis upon the spokes and radials that bind its myriad operational units together, rather than upon the central entity that serves as the point of connection.

The hub principle is reflected and made manifest in how physical space is used. ABB's headquarters is almost aggressively modest, a squat five-story building in suburban Zurich that might be mistaken for a high school or a small manufacturing plant. The operational feel of the place is not coincidental, but in keeping with the organization's emphasis on operational units. The notion of headquarters as an impressive and luxurious monument that proclaims the success and power of the organization as a whole would be entirely inappropriate to its purpose. ABB's headquarters does not even serve as the site for top managers' meetings; these are held every three weeks in various cities around the globe.

Physical design thus reflects values of flexibility and leanness, and helps downplay the role of top management. A look at the architecture makes clear the difference between ABB's operations-based structure and the more centralized approach that still obtains in most large organizations. The prototype of the old-style corporate structure was devised and given form by the extraordinary Alfred Sloan during his forty-year tenure as president of General Motors. Beginning in the 1920s, Sloan reorganized his company according to principles that served as a corollary in managerial terms to the production techniques pioneered by Henry Ford on the factory floor. Working in their separate arenas, the two men managed to create a system that served the needs of mass production through the postwar years.

In Sloan's system, organizational units were decentralized, but staffed and overseen from a single headquarters, which judged performance by looking at the numbers. This entirely rational means of measuring success enabled managers to make decisions without having to know much about operations. The uncoupling of judgment and specific expertise led in turn to the professionalization of top management, and the consequent separation of decision-making from the implementation of tasks. Sloan thus carried the principles of division of labor into the managerial arena; principles soon given concrete expression in the use of physical space.

Whereas operational units in most organizations continued to maintain a somewhat factory-like ambiance, headquarters and staff offices began to be designed in ways that gave executives the feeling of being above the fray. The numbers, after all, were expected to be reviewed in detachment. The separation of professional and line management led to the practice whereby a professional manager's dignity and importance were reflected in the lavish "impressiveness" of the space in which he worked. Corporate headquarters thus came to be viewed not simply as serving the needs of the business, but also as giving symbolic expression to the power and prestige of the top brass —and by extention to the whole of the company's enterprise.

Modern corporate architecture thus derives from the rigid division of managerial and operational labor that Sloan put into place. It is an architecture that reflects mass production values. Yet long after the heyday of mass production, extravagant corporate buildings have continued to carry this almost purely symbolic burden. From the 1960s through the 1980s, the most representative corporate buildings were designed on the assumption that the wasteful and ostentatious use of space and materials declares an organization's importance in the world. And although such an organization might pride itself on being rational and efficient—relentlessly "bottom line"—it in fact uses space in ways that are neither. Indeed, the patent irrationality of grossly unequal allocations of workspace is usually interpreted by employees as proof that only people at the top are valued, while those who have not reached high rank are held of little account. It is a profoundly demoralizing message, and one that runs counter to the structure of today's increasingly flat and lean organizations.

In addition to being demoralizing and implicitly hierarchical, many workspaces today are too rigid to meet the needs of rapidly evolving organizations. Trying to run an inclusive and flexible operation based on multidisciplinary teams in a physical space that virtually embodies Industrial Era values has become a real source of stress. How can continual reorganizations take place without massive disruption if everyone has to move each time they change their job? How can the constant updating of technology be accommodated when every change means the redesign and rewiring of everyone's office? How can teamwork be encouraged when everyone is either walled off in separate units, or expected to work in chaotically noisy open platforms? How can markets that expand and shrink almost daily be served when space is inflexible, a fixed cost that remains always the same?

The corporate towers that have become so familiar a part of our landscape over the course of the last thirty years are increasingly obsolete from an architectural and design perspective. As the writer and entrepreneur Stewart Brand points out in a forthcoming book, *the* most important characteristic of organizational space in the future will be the "loose fit," the extent to which our buildings enable people to move around. To fulfill this requirement, Brand believes that buildings should be "low road"—sturdy, but minimal and spare, like the lofts and garages in which most of the world's work is done. They will be versions of what the architects Robert Venturi and Denise Scott Brown have called "the decorated shed," and they will invite the people who work in them to think in terms of add-ons, changes, subdivisions—anything that enables them to adapt their spaces to new ways of working. As Brand observes of such buildings, "function melts form." Since function is always changing, form must be able to follow suit.

Workspaces such as the old MIT annex known as Building 20, where the Digital Equipment Corporation developed much of its pioneering technology, will increasingly serve as prototypes. They have what might be called good bones, but little finish. The money spent on them goes into basic structure and services (plumbing and wiring) rather than into the skin (outer surfaces) or the set (interior design). They are in fact *under*-designed, which permits them to evolve with the changing needs of the enterprise. They evoke images of line and operations, rather than professionalized management, breaking down the barrier between the two erected by Sloan. Such images have a direct effect upon organizational performance. Space that is always in process encourages fluidity and improvisation.

Loose-fit workspaces present a total contrast to the kind of "high-road" buildings that still commonly serve as corporate offices, in which the finish is so polished that the structure cannot easily be altered. As Brand observes, high-road buildings are in fact commonly very cheap as basic structures, while little expense is spared in the creation of dazzling surfaces meant to impress the beholder—obviously a bad investment for the buyer. In order for a building to be flexible, it must *by definition* be under-finished, since the surface elements are the first to change when a plan is altered. Because of their attention to finish, high-road buildings are resistant to tinkering, to letting the people who work in them have a say in how they want to use their space. It is hard for people in high-road buildings ever to make their space their own, to infuse it with a measure of their personality or tailor it specifically to their needs. This situation affects the organization, robbing people of control over their work lives, discouraging improvisation, and lowering morale.

No doubt in part because high-road buildings have proven so high a fixed cost, some organizations are trying to take the step of dispensing with the office altogether. The "virtual office," a subject of speculation and fantasy in the past, is being tested in a number of organizations, most famously Chiat/Day, the advertising agency known for introducing the Apple MacIntosh.

The idea behind the virtual office is to encourage employees to divorce the concept of work from the notion of a specific place. Since laptop computers, modems, and cellular phones now make it possible for people to work in hotel lobbies, client offices, coffeeshops, private automobiles, and airport lounges, the formal office has become for many people less important than in the past—it is *a* place, rather than *the* place, of work. Given the parallel between the use of space and the use of time, the uncoupling of work from place also implies that work can be done at any time. Since this notion meshes with the increasing desire of so many employees to be able to structure their own days, the virtual office is being touted as the ultimate in both flexibility and convenience.

According to Chiat/Day's chief executive, Jay Chiat, the virtual office encourages people to take responsibility for how and when they work, as well as fairly pushing them to interact more directly with the agency's customers. Instead of a headquarters, Chiat/Day has built in Los Angeles what it calls a high-tech "campus," with project rooms, a media center, even a "student union" where people can plug in the Powerbooks they pick up at the company store. For private conferences, the center provides an area furnished with vintage amusement park cars, creating a kind of workplace theme park that seems rather awkwardly intended to spur creativity.

But rather than being under-designed, as Stewart Brand suggests workspaces in the future will have to be, the new Chiat/Day workspace is in fact hyper-designed. People can move around, come and go at will, but the spaces themselves are unusually rigid, designed and wired to serve a specific purpose. Employees thus may be more in control of their *time* than under the previous system, but they are in many ways less in control of their *space* than they would be in an ordinary office. In addition, many company employees lament that they have gone from having cubbyholes to having nothing of their own beyond a locker—a situation that *feels* to them like a demotion. For all the theme park touches, this depersonalizing of individual workspace pushes the abstraction of the working environment to the limit, and seems to go against what we know about how human beings actually *do* things.

The disjunction may exist because, although the virtual office reflects many of the principles of the hub, it entirely ignores the principles of the hearth. By failing to provide a space that is both "mine" and "ours," that defines both "I" and "we," it provides no way for the individual to mesh his private identity with that of the larger organization. Without a hearth, there is no *there* there, no kitchen table, no informal center that inspires spontaneous exchange. No way of being part of the organization.

The hub and hearth, it would seem, must maintain some kind of balance if an organization is to be both web-like and inclusive. As Nancy Foy observes in *The Yin and Yang of Organizations,* institutions need both spiders and butterflies—spiders being those who stay at the center and retain information; and butterflies being those who deploy their energies outward in order to obtain clients, resources, and contracts. The philosopher Ginette Paris compares the spider and the butterfly in modern organizations to two mythic Greek divinities: Hestia, the goddess of the hearth, the flame at the center of any communal space, and Hermes, the ever-mobile messenger. Paris goes on to observe:

> Organizations, especially if they are subjected to a decentralized political environment, must develop new ways of concentrating the energies of multiple human networks. Institutional decentralization, like changes involving new technologies of communication, may perhaps have the paradoxical effect, not of anarchy, but of a new confederation of institutional hearths, each animated and warmed by its own Hestia.

THE WORKING CLUB

What Ginette Paris identifies as a confederation of hearths, the economist Charles Handy describes simply as a federation. Handy posits that a kind of new federalism, evolving in both politics and business, will in the future provide the means to govern our increasingly complex organizations. He points out that, as a structure, federalism has the ability to address today's paradoxes of power and control: the need to make things big while keeping them small; to encourage autonomy while keeping it in bounds; to reconcile variety with shared purpose, individuality with partnership, local concerns with global ones, regional interests with those of the nation-state.

As part of this emerging federalism, Handy discerns the existence of what he calls "electronic shamrocks," multileaved organizations branching out from a central core. He sees such shamrocks as being bound and defined by a common purpose; a purpose made manifest by how the organization makes use of its people and its physical space. His conception of how workspace functions in shamrock organizations points the way to integrating the principles of the hearth with those of the hub. Handy believes that work in the future will not take place in offices as we have come to know them (mere "apartment houses" for work), but rather within the confines of a variety of "working clubs," clubs being "places of privileged access to common facilities."

Handy describes one working club, headed by a friend of his named Walter:

> Walter runs a design and consultancy business with a staff of around one hundred professionals—quite big. He runs it from a converted warehouse, except that he hasn't converted it very much. There are no offices in it. There are meeting rooms; there is a superb farmhouse kitchen; there are drawing-boards scattered around; there are word processors, telephones, and computers abounding, but no one, not even Walter himself, has any particular private space—except for the secretaries, who are really not secretaries as such but project coordinators, each assigned to work for a project rather than for an individual.

All the elements are there—the obvious loose fit, the flexibility, the low-road design, Denise Scott Brown's notion of the "decorated shed." Walter's working club fulfills some of the functions of the virtual office, for employees are encouraged to do much of their work at home, in clients' offices, or in airport lounges—wherever doing their work will be efficient. However, the impersonal element of people logging in for needed space or "renting" equipment from the company store to use at a drop-in center is forgone, as is the rigid organization of various kinds of spaces that characterizes the redesign at Chiat/Day, for the working club is conceived above all as a gathering place. Handy quotes Walter's description: "People come here to keep in touch. We lay on the best breakfast in town in our farmhouse kitchen, and there's always a bottle of wine open and waiting for anyone who might drop in after 6 P.M."

In Nancy Foy's terms, the working club serves both the spiders and the butterflies within the organization, integrating the center with the radials and tendrils that reach out to the larger world. In Louis Kahn's terms, the working club serves as physical space that can reconcile the organization's collective purpose with the talents of its individual members by recognizing the human need for affiliation and belonging. A similar balancing of private and public is implicit in Handy's definition of the club as a *privileged* space held in *common* by its members.

Pentagram's lounge, Intel's cafeteria, and the *Utne* salon achieve this integration of communal and individual, and so lend to these organizations the ambience of working clubs. But perhaps the best example of how the working club aesthetic might define a company can be found at Fitch RichardsonSmith, a design consultancy based in Worthington, Ohio. Fitch RS's flexible and imaginative use of physical space reflects its continually evolving structure, which makes use of multidisciplinary teams to design consumer products, graphics, and retail interiors. Driven by its structure to rethink entirely Industrial Era presumptions about the use of space, the company points the way to a far more integrated, flexible, and ultimately humane approach to design.

Fitch RS occupies a group of five old farmhouses set together on fifteen acres of rolling meadow. Each farmhouse has a variety of rooms that connect with one another, and each has a small library spun off from one that used to be centralized in a single place. The kitchens in the various houses play an important role: lying at the crossroads, they provide a place for people to congregate informally, but because there are five of them, they encourage a maximum of interaction. Since work in the company is done by teams, workspace evolves to fit each project: a team might take over one of the larger conference rooms, or split up and occupy more informal spaces, or connect a series of rooms to accommodate different tasks. People needing to work alone might make use of the private upstairs rooms that were originally for sleeping, or stretch out at one of the picnic tables scattered around the property. If two departments are working together on something and need to be in closer contact, one or the other of them may simply move.

Space is not static at Fitch RS. Walls, windows, doors, and halls are constantly being changed, remodeled, and moved around, not as the result of what some design consultant suggests but because an employee thinks doing so would be helpful. "The idea is to let the workers shape the space instead of letting the space shape the workers," explains CEO Martin Beck. Employees are encouraged to tinker with their space in order to tailor it more specifically for their needs—some people like antique desks, others minimalist slabs; some like low walls, others value privacy. Some want to "own" their space, others prefer to locate their identity in some communal spot.

Because the nature of each project dictates how space will be used, overall design is always in process: yet the basic farmhouse structure remains. That Fitch RS occupies a group of farmhouses is in fact a fitting metaphor for the company's effort to move beyond an industrial approach to space. The farm was the basic economic unit in pre-industrial times, and the farmhouse—particularly its kitchen—served as the communal hearth. Thus in moving forward to adapt space to today's needs, we may also find ourselves moving back in time, resurrecting earlier ways of doing our work in the physical world that give more scope to the human spirit.

SOME MODEST PROPOSALS

Fitch RS teaches us that no single way of using space will prevail in the future. As hierarchies evolve into webs, design will be both various and ever changing, with architecture reflecting opportunities rather than defining roles, and providing backup rather than declaring fixed identities. Tactical efforts at redesign will be best led by ordinary people within the organization, who have the most accurate idea of what might work for *them*.

Keeping in mind the need for both variety and tactical improvisation, it is nevertheless possible to discern a few guidelines for the organization of physical workspace in the years ahead.

1. GIVE PEOPLE MORE CONTROL OVER THEIR ENVIRONMENT.

The architect and town designer Peter Calthorpe notes that hierarchical organizations often commission spatial designs that prevent employees from exercising even minimal control over their environment. In particular, buildings that give people no choice about how much light and air they may enjoy reinforce the organizational message that even petty decisions must be made at the top. Stewart Brand points out that denying people at work the power to so much as open a window places them in an almost entirely passive relationship to their environment. Sealed buildings, in addition to being often unhealthy, deny people control at one of the most basic human levels.

This both exacerbates people's feelings of powerlessness and exaggerates the differences between their workplace and their home. Under such conditions, the notion of a working club can never flourish, since the whole point of a club is to serve as a "home away from home." The club thus helps to bridge the dichotomy between public and private that prevailed so rigidly in the Industrial Era. Decompartmentalizing work, encouraging people to integrate it into their lives, demands that we begin building workplaces that give people control over the most basic aspects of their daily lives.

2. KEEP EVOLVING TECHNOLOGY IN MIND.

A primary selling point of sealed and highly finished buildings has been that they offer a single system for heat and air, which are thus regulated and made uniform throughout the structure. But this uniformity comes at the cost of structural inflexibility, which renders the buildings static and frozen in time. With interdependent services built right in, it becomes hard to alter the design of such buildings; their skins are simply too polished. This inflexibility did not matter so much when technology was evolving slowly, coaxing us from the manual to the electric keyboard over the course of fifty years. But as new generations of equipment become available in ever-speedier cycles, such buildings prove more and more challenging to rewire. Loose-fit workspace makes upgrading technology an easier and far less expensive undertaking. It acknowledges the prevailing truth that a building's systems will soon be obsolete.

3. DESIGN MUST INCORPORATE THE NOTION OF MANAGEABLE SIZE.

The authors of *A Pattern Language* stress that, as among natural organisms, every social organism has its ideal size. Every town, workplace, or neighborhood cannot grow beyond a certain limit if it is to achieve maximum efficiency while continuing to serve human ends. The Industrial Era concept of economies of scale forced organizations to ignore this fact of organic development and find ways vastly to expand. Efficiency then demanded a centralization of systems that often worked against human needs, creating bureaucratic and even irrational structures.

Lean production techniques, mass customization, and the flexible ways of managing that these demand have made economies of scale obsolete. As hierarchies shrink in response, and evolve into more web-like structures, organizations will begin to focus on finding a sustainable size. The federalism advocated by Charles Handy envisions whole webs of loosely connected organizations that are comfortable remaining inside their organic limits. Once we begin thinking in terms of sustainable size, we must become more open to designing spaces that are manageable, humane in scale, and better able to represent the values and spirit of the hearth.

Nine

Moving Outward into the Metaweb

I once worked as a speechwriter for a large telecommunications company—let's call it BigCo. One of my most vivid memories is of a woman on my floor. She was a mid-level manager, and I used to see her at intervals throughout the day, usually when I stopped by the women's lounge. She seemed always to be there, smoking or talking with colleagues, and she always greeted me—and I suppose everyone else—with a variation on the same comment. If it was nine-thirty in the morning, she would shake her head dolefully: "We've got the *whole* day ahead of us." If it was eleven-thirty: "Not too much longer till lunch." If it was two-thirty, she would sigh with exhaustion: "*Three* more hours." If it was four-thirty: "Just one more hour to go."

I used to wonder what was so compelling about her life at home that she literally counted each hour at work as it passed. But of course, her attitude was in no way evidence that her personal life provided any extraordinary satisfaction—perhaps all she did at night was watch TV—but rather revealed only that she was bored stiff by her work. Despite her evident frustration, she never seemed to consider leaving the company, which paid salaries that were more than competitive. In fact, seven years later, she is still at BigCo—putting in her hours, collecting her paycheck, and no doubt counting the years until she can retire. There are many like her, in that organization and in others: people who have capitulated to the deadening assumption that work constitutes drudgery, and true enjoyment is to be found only in private life.

Other people I knew at the company have long since left; I, of course, am among them. Those who went voluntarily were among the best and the brightest. Unlike the woman I used to see in the lounge, they were unable to sacrifice themselves to the notion that the only purpose of work is to earn a paycheck. They were simply more demanding than that. Those I've talked to who left BigCo wanted work to be more satisfying and rewarding than it was in that large bureaucracy, where many employees were demoralized, great ideas inevitably got watered down, and an Industrial Era division still prevailed between the big shots who made all the decisions and everyone else who carried them out. Many of those who left wanted the pleasure that comes of putting their own ideas into action. They wanted to see their footprints, know that they'd made a difference.

Of course, such people are *precisely* those that BigCo is in dire need of now, as it tries to navigate the complexities that have evolved over the years since the breakup of the Bell System and take advantage of the opportunities presented by new technologies and global competition. Yet BigCo seems to have perfected a system that separates the wheat from the chaff—and an unerring ability to retain the chaff. It is hardly alone.

In *Beyond Potential,* an unpublished manuscript, the author Kelly Morgan interviews scores of people who abandoned good jobs in thriving companies, often in hopes of striking out on their own. Morgan is fascinated by the fact that the best people are often the most eager to leave their organizations, and tries to answer why this should be so. She concludes that frustration is particularly intense among those who have the most to offer *because they are the most committed to finding satisfaction in their work.* The men and women she interviews talk about the risks they took in leaving, but say that a measure of uncertainty is preferable to remaining in organizations that deny them scope for autonomy and self-expression.

Autonomy and self-expression. This is what people with high expectations seem to want most from their work. They want to be real participants, citizens in their organizations. They want to feel ownership in the places where they give their labor. They want to be able to implement the solutions that they devise, and have the power to tinker with those solutions until they get things right. They are willing to trade a degree of risk for the satisfaction that comes from having real responsibility for getting things done.

Those who feel this way are the most valuable people in any workplace; and yet for the most part they are also the most poorly served by their organizations. This is true in every arena of public life —not only in business, but in government and our major institutions as well. The disjunction between what people have to give and what organizations are structured to permit is creating a crisis of historic proportions. The effects are to be seen everywhere: in the precipitous destruction of America's consumer electronics industry, in the fractious decline of companies like General Motors and IBM, in the decay of the nation's infrastructure, in the poor performance of the nation's public schools, in the uncoordinated attempts to address the confusing realities of the post–Cold War world.

Few would deny that we need new mechanisms, new structures, new architectures, if our common life is to flourish in the years ahead. We need to create organizations that have the capacity to retain their very best people, draw wisely from their talent base, address issues that are truly important rather than just urgent, prepare for constant change, and provide the training appropriate to meeting these challenges. And we need to find ways for organizations to both reflect and take advantage of what today's powerful, decentralized, and interconnected technologies enable people, working on their own, to do.

The web of inclusion gives people at every level the opportunity to exercise both autonomy and self-expression. It makes citizens of an organization's people by helping to put in place what Carlene Ellis of Intel calls "participatory democracy for the organization." This is because the web enables people not only to address challenging issues directly, because they believe they can find a solution, but also to do so *in a way that changes the nature, scope, and form of their organization*. This is an organic and reciprocal process, the result of constant and shifting adaptations between organic parts in relation to one another. It works incrementally, by means of individual improvisations, and because the process is piecemeal, it is easy to tinker with, and less disastrous when specific solutions prove to be wrong.

In the web, people are free to take individual action, and the organization changes because they do. By enabling the parts to determine the shape of the whole, the web permits people at every level to leave their mark on the organization. This is precisely why Gerry Laybourne at Nickelodeon talks about the need to build an organization that adapts itself to serve the particular talents, interests, and skills of the people who are a part of it at any given time. It is what Bill Millholland at Anixter saw when he was hired because people in the company liked him—and then left alone to discover what *he* might want to do. Bill Millholland notes this approach works best with people who are resourceful and independent, which has the effect of encouraging them to stay at Anixter. Thus the open and inclusive structure of the company serves as a tool that enables Anixter to retain the very best among its people.

True webs are different from teams because teams are configured specifically to address specific problems; they do not have the power to transform the organization as a whole. This is why webs may be defined as *teams that go the distance.* At the *Miami Herald,* we saw how what was originally configured as a team to address diversity issues evolved into a web because, in the process of doing their work, the team members began breaking down barriers between the business and editorial sides of the paper, thus reconfiguring how the organization as a whole was run. At Beth Israel Hospital in Boston, we saw how the introduction of primary nursing changed the nature of not only the nurses' jobs but those of everyone else, turning administrators into support staff and doctors into support professionals.

In the cases examined in this book, the form of each organization and its concerns were shaped by the individuals within the organizations—individuals whose *positions* did not necessarily reflect the influence they were able to exercise. These people changed their companies by their very presence. What they accomplished was a direct expression of *who they are,* and would not have been done in the same way or had had the same effect if someone else had done it. Ric Giardina tells us that he joined Intel for this very reason, because he sensed that it was "the kind of place where you could create something on your own, be imaginative, really leave your mark."

The entrepreneur and writer Paul Hawken notes that a prime source of satisfaction in starting a business lies in creating something that reflects who you are. He writes:

> I am suggesting that the best idea for a business will be something that is deep within you, something that can't be stolen because it is uniquely yours and anyone else trying to execute it without the (perhaps unconscious) thought you have given the subject will fail. It's not basically different from writing a novel. *A good business and a good novel are both faithful and uncluttered expressions of yourself.*

Successful entrepreneurs have always known the satisfaction of this kind of expression; even unsuccessful entrepreneurs feel it in some measure, because they are responsible for what they create. But people who work for mainstream organizations today also need the chance to know this satisfaction, if their work is to be rewarding and their best energies engaged. Describing the creative process, T. S. Eliot wrote, "In dreams begin responsibilities." In Industrial Era organizations, responsibilities became uncoupled from dreams, as conception was divorced from implementation. Web-style organizations, by contrast, enable those who dream to assume responsibility for putting their dreams into action, and so return the joy of true participation to daily work.

Being shaped by the individuals who comprise them does not mean that webs of inclusion are characterized by any looseness of purpose. On the contrary, open, task-based structures work only when the organization is dedicated to achieving a specific and clearly articulated purpose, mission, or goal. Gerry Laybourne: "It is because we are profoundly focused on our mission that we can let people find their own way. Everything we do derives from who we are." Joyce Clifford, who brought primary nursing to Beth Israel, concurs: "We set out to do one thing and one thing only: provide our patients with the best possible service. All the changes we made here derived from our intense focus on that."

THE TECHNOLOGY OF PARTICIPATION

The web of inclusion provides a means for individuals to affect their organizations, even transforming them when circumstances demand it. By giving scope for individual improvisation within the context of group endeavor (remember the parallel to the jazz band), webs resolve the tension between autonomy and relationship, and even exploit the potential dynamism at the heart of that tension. Marilyn Ferguson notes that networked technology also resolves issues of autonomy and relationship, by providing "a matrix for personal exploration and group action *at the same time.*" Thus the web of inclusion may be characterized as the expression of the network in organizational space, while the network may be described as the expression of the web in cyberspace.

Networked technology, by its very shape, emphasizes and gives power to those in an organization's grass roots. Similarly, the web is essentially a grassroots structure, one that emphasizes the citizens rather than the leaders by vesting the capacity for action in those at the periphery. The diffusion of power through networks is hardly an accident, since the guiding impetus behind the development of the personal computer came from people infused with an idealistic desire to create technologies that would take power and information away from large, centralized, and security-conscious organizations and distribute it instead to "the people." With their roots in the Community Memory electric bulletin board at Berkeley and the People's Computing Company in Menlo Park, the early leaders of what would become the PC industry "sought to transform computers from what they saw as Orwellian instruments of oppression into a liberating force," in the words of the computer historian Frank Rose. These pioneers' common dream of a computer democracy was enshrined in the slogan that inspired Apple in its early days: "One Person, One Computer."

The web-like structure of the network seems almost inevitable, given the continually evolving mesh of informal webs that enabled the invention and fast triumph of personal computers. Those inspired by the dream of decentralizing power through the spread of inexpensive, interactive machines were individualists and improvisers, technology buffs who referred to themselves as hackers. The term "hacker" originated among the systems-minded nonconformists who hung around MIT in the early 1960s. In their personal lingo, a "hack" meant any project undertaken not just in order to fulfill a constructive goal, but rather for the sheer wild pleasure taken in the process of fulfillment. An intense concern for the fulfillment of the individual was thus from the beginning built into the ideology of those who dreamed, before most of us could understand what they were talking about, of vast information networks linking ordinary people.

The hacker ethic, as developed and refined at MIT and in the Bay Area in the late sixties and early seventies, planted the seeds for a radically new approach to organizations—an approach that first took hold in high-tech world. The principles of the hacker ethic are identified by Steven Levy in his study *Hackers*, which traces the effect of the early renegades on the developing industry. Among the beliefs that hackers held sacred:

- Information should flow to whoever can use it.
- No one should need to be authorized to use the tools that get things done.
- No system or program is ever completed—you can always make it better.
- People should always work incrementally on improvements.
- What matters is improving programs, not who owns them.
- Mistrust authority, promote decentralization.
- Hackers should be judged by their hacking, not by criteria such as degrees, age, race, or position.
- Mistakes are a tool for learning, not evidence of failure.
- Above all, honor the "hands-on imperative."

These precepts echo the values and principles that define the web of inclusion, in which information flows freely across levels, teams make their own decisions, work on specific projects evolves in response to needs as they arise, and task is more important than position. An especially strong parallel between the hacker ethic and the web can be found in the injunction to honor the hands-on imperative. This means simply that whatever you imagine, you must also try to produce. In its early days, Apple Computer expressed this principle in its straightforward slogan, "Real Artists Ship."

The hands-on imperative implicit in high technology made instantly obsolete the dichotomy that has prevailed since the dawn of the Industrial Era between thinking and doing, conception and execution. In the words of Don Eastlake, one of the original MIT hackers, "the ideal system can be said to have been both *designer implemented* and *user designed*. The problem of unrealistic software design is greatly diminished when the designer is also the implementor." In other words, complex programs can be successful only when thinking and doing are integrated. This simple principle undermines the basic assumptions upon which most of our organizations are built, and demands the complete dismantling of every variety of structure that isolates decision-making at the top.

Like the team at Nickelodeon responsible for joint ventures with Mattel, the hackers developed a common language. Their vocabulary was abstruse and often impenetrable to outsiders, but it served their purposes and made clear what they considered important. Phrases from hacker lingo have long since entered the general language, so that computer-derived metaphors are now embedded in everyday speech. Most of us now use phrases like "in the loop" or "interface," and describe a particular state as a "mode," without necessarily considering what such terms really express or how they entered our language in the first place.

As functional as the hackers' private language was, its true purpose was to solidify and define the community that shared it. As Liz Sheppard at Nickelodeon observed, "language is really what defines a culture. When you use a common vocabulary, you are defining yourself as belonging to that culture." Tom Ronig, the EVP of Marketing at Mattel, put it this way: "Specific words have a way of bringing back the memory of what you've shared together and what you're trying to achieve. They're a kind of emotional trigger that reminds you of your common purpose." The shared language of the hackers served as just such an emotional trigger, and their distinctive way of using words helped both to define and to spread what was in essence a tribal culture—one that transcended mere geographical borders.

Hackers formulated a philosophy and way of interacting with the world that expressed a fiercely held belief in the need for free-flowing information and the worth of decentralized structures. It is difficult now, when the simple word "bureaucrat" has virtually become an insult, and even corporate executives like to imagine themselves as cowboy entrepreneurs, to remember how radically the hacker ethic departed from attitudes that, not so long ago, were almost universal in mainstream culture. We are really not all that far removed in time from the Organization Man era, when the regimentation that prevailed at a company like IBM was viewed with awe, and assumed to be the ultimate in human efficiency. Our contemporary equation of centralization with clumsiness, our mistrust of anything big—these are a legacy of the hacker ethic. The hackers' obsession with creating a world in which ordinary people might have access to information has transformed us so entirely that we have trouble remembering the presumptions that most of us once held in common.

PERMEABILITY IN THE METAWEB

The meshwork of webs that moved hackers into the mainstream comprised what might be called a metaweb—a flexible and ever evolving weave of structures that keep intersecting at different points, and form new structures as a result. This metaweb was able to take shape because its constituent webs were permeable at the edges, loose in their definition of who was part of them and who was not. Thus metawebs form by means of the organic process known as *syntropy,* which biologists define as the tendency of life to seek ever greater association, communication, cooperation, and awareness—in other words, to reach out. Another organic principle that governs the operation of the metaweb holds that organisms at the higher end of the evolutionary scale have greater freedom to reorganize: consider the freedom humans have compared with that of ants. The flexibility, the inherent structural disequilibrium of the ever changing metaweb, thus identifies it as a system that has evolved to a higher order.

The high-tech metawebs that first began forming around MIT and in the Bay Area not only transformed the nature of our economy, but also its relation to the territory it inhabits. For each of these particular metawebs evolved very specifically within the precincts of a distinctly local region. The events that led to their formation could not have occurred just anywhere. Each metaweb grew where it did because a critical mass of skilled people existed in proximity to a variety of essential tools. This confluence is the defining characteristic of regionally based economies, which before the advent of high tech were considered almost obsolete.

Regions have a long history as hotbeds of innovation and specialized development, stretching back in time to the early medieval guilds that made Florence a center for banking and Bruges the preserve of makers of lace. In the early years of this century, the region found classic expression in the territory around Detroit, where thousands of small machine shops run by individuals fascinated by internal-combustion engines gave rise to the development of the automotive industry. By the early 1960s, however, as the political economist Charles Sabel notes, this decentralized web of enterprises had consolidated into a handful of enormous—and increasingly uncompetitive—corporations.

In the late sixties, as organizations of every variety assumed a multinational scope, they grew less dependent on the resources of the particular locality that had spawned them. The spread of mass production exacerbated the destruction of the region, as large producers sought economies of scale by swallowing up the small subcontractors who were supplying them with specialized parts. These mass producers also sought to contain their costs by standardizing products and routinizing the processes of production. As this happened, their need for skilled labor diminished. This enabled organizations to move at will, loosening their attachment to the regions that gave them birth.

But just as networked technology is bringing in its wake the demise of standardized production, so is it also reversing the multinational trend—in part, by redefining bigness as a liability. Indeed, the pattern of high-tech enterprise heralds a return to the importance of regions, which have increasingly assumed an international visibility and importance. By the early eighties, the new trajectory was becoming clear. Silicon Valley was flourishing for precisely the same reason that small machinists working around Detroit had once thrived: the confluence of specific, indigenous people and events. The hacker idealists from Berkeley played a role, as did the architects of Stanford's Artificial Intelligence Lab, the futurists at Xerox's well-funded Palo

Alto Research Center, and the engineers who had walked out on William Shockley. Even the sweeping flats of Pacific sand that lined the peninsula and the junk shops selling electronic refuse around Moffatt Airforce Base contributed to the creation of an economy strongly rooted in one particular place on the face of the earth, and dependent upon the skills and imaginations of the people who live there.

Charles Sabel notes that few companies today are electing to acquire their subcontractors, but are rather trying to work out long-term relationships with them. The need for smaller, more specialized production runs is in part responsible for this change in the dynamics between large and small companies, which need to work more closely together while also sharing development costs. Also, as large firms try to scale down, they are likely to spin off specialized units, which continue to service them by means of a kind of reciprocal borrowing. As companies become leaner, they depend more on others in their region to provide expertise in fields like marketing and finance, which gives rise to networks of flexible and specialized suppliers. All these trends reinforce one another, causing regional economies to flourish, as they operate on simultaneous principles of decentralization and convergence.

Sabel offers not just Silicon Valley and the area around MIT as examples of thriving regions, but also Rochester, New York, and Austin, Texas. And certainly the concept embraces such diverse regions as those around Bangalore, India, and Guangdong, China. It should be noted that Hollywood has functioned as a regional metaweb all along; even the great corporate mergers of the eighties could not change that. Filmmaking has since its inception relied on a wide variety of people with very specific skills who are hard to find in substantial numbers in other areas of the country.

The principles embedded in networked technologies are returning organizations to ways of operating that survived only where the extremes of mass production never took hold. The manufacturers of fine Italian fabrics, for example, have retained their original cottage industry structures through the course of a century that has until recently been inhospitable to this way of working, regarding it as old-fashioned, too labor-intensive, and inefficient. Nonetheless, these enterprises thrived in specific locations because of the high level of local skills. Remaining small, they made use of a level of inter-industry cooperation that qualifies as a true metaweb. The character of these enterprises is intensely regional, and the regions that support them tend to retain their distinctive cultures—vividness of culture being characteristic of economies based on regions. Only recently considered on the verge of inevitable obsolescence, such industries now provide models for our high-tech future.

TRIBAL VALUES, INCLUSIVE CULTURE

All this emphasis on culture, language, and region puts one inevitably in mind of an ancient institution that is unexpectedly emerging as one of the most significant in our surprising post-Cold War world—the tribe. Like regions, tribes were until very recently considered vestiges of a past that the human race was rapidly outgrowing; we assumed that as the world got smaller, we would lose our particularized identities and become more like one another. Of course, just the opposite has happened.

Joel Kotkin, in his recent book *Tribes*, studies the characteristics of specific ethnic groups that have been particularly successful in doing business on a global scale. Most of these groups are ancient in origin—Jews, overseas Indians, overseas Chinese—and have long been dispersed around the world, which has forced them to function in a state of permanent diaspora. These "global tribes," as Kotkin calls them, nevertheless exhibit strong group loyalties, and cling tenaciously to the traditions that define their cultures. Their identification with the group enables them to form what Kotkin views as "highly consensual business forms," such as Japanese *keiretsu* and Chinese family networks. Inspired by a concern for the clan, they are particularly adept at taking the long-term approach to business—a notable weakness of many American organizations in recent years.

It might be argued that the Chinese family network's ability to focus on the long term can hardly serve as a model for American enterprise. Yet the secret of the family network, as Kotkin is quick to point out, is its absolute and unyielding emphasis on *values*. There are thousands of examples—some of them in this book—that show what people are capable of achieving when their work is a reflection of strongly held values. Web-like organizations are especially apt to be driven by clearly articulated values, since a tight focus on mission is the glue that holds their flowing structures together. Also, the people in webs of inclusion are more likely to take their organization's values seriously, since they play a role in helping to define them.

Gerry Laybourne speaks of the excitement she felt last year when starting Nickelodeon in the U.K.: "We had these meetings in this kind of bunker near Heathrow Airport. It was a real dump. We didn't even have chairs; we all sat on the floor. Just sat there for *hours,* planning everything, all of us together. It brought me back to the old days in this company, when it was just a small group, planning everything as we went. There we were again, this little band, determined to do what everyone assured us could not be done. We worked half the night—it was just *thrilling.*"

That's the kind of enthusiasm that money cannot buy. And it doesn't come from Gerry Laybourne being the boss. Ric Giardina expressed the same sentiments when he described his trademarking work for Intel; so did Vic Bubnow when talking about the *Herald*'s diversity committee. When people are this focused on achievement, they are able to use all their talents, one of the most gratifying experiences a human being can know. Organizations that engage their people by instilling an almost tribal sense of values can get them to focus on what's best for the company in the long term. That's what the risk of enterprise is all about.

Of course, if America's companies are to work this way, some changes will have to be made in how their shares are traded, so the market will not penalize them every time they fail to put the quarterly profits earned by their investors above everything else. Our mechanisms for financing business do not always support the changes in structure that we need to put in place; this is becoming more widely recognized. Corporate boards groping for ways to address the problem are finding new merit in the idea of employee ownership of significant proportion. Financial institutions and economists are also addressing the problem. Michael Porter of Harvard, among others, has recently outlined a number of simple steps that would reform a system that has begun to undermine our organizations.

Capitalism is evolving, like any living system. It needs to find ways of rejuvenating itself to get past inefficiencies that have become apparent. The web of inclusion offers us a way for Americans, with their ingrained respect for the individual freedoms, to integrate the more group-oriented approach to doing business that is so significant an aspect of Asia's success on the global stage. The web provides us with a means for adapting the Meiji Restoration strategy for opening Japan to the wider world: *"Western technology, Eastern spirit."*

Eastern spirit seeks to live in harmony with the principles of life as expressed in the timeless precepts of the Tao. Those principles demand that we keep our organizations open and flowing. In the Tao, this is called "knowing the collective origin"—the origin, that is, of every form of life. The Nobelist Ilya Prigogine's term for open systems is "dissipative structures," which he observes always exhibit a flowing wholeness. The more developed a dissipative structure, the more energy it needs to maintain all its interconnections, which makes it vulnerable to internal fluctuations. Thus it is said to be "far from equilibrium." In the physical sciences, a state of equilibrium does not imply a healthy balance, but refers rather to random dispersal of energy—a kind of death. The more coherent or rigid the structure, the tighter and more "organized," the more immune it is to the living energies of transformation.

Being far from equilibrium enables a structure to attain the state of dynamic growingness—the aforementioned syntropy—appropriate to our profoundly interconnected world. This growingness is a gift of the Eastern spirit. But the very structure of Western technology has now come also to reflect the principles of life rather than reinforcing the image of the world as simply a giant machine governed by rigid and predictable laws. The confluence between East and West is something that the Meijis could not have dreamed of; indeed, most of us could not have until the last decade or so. It promises to alter the way we view our possibilities for living in the world, and leads us on to the next stage in our own evolution.

Notes

CHAPTER ONE

Page 9. Sally Helgesen. *The Female Advantage: Women's Ways of Leadership*. New York: Doubleday/Currency, 1990.

Page 12. Peter Drucker. *Post-Capitalist Society*. New York: Harper Business, 1993. The nature of the evolving knowledge economy is the theme of this book.

Page 12. Margaret Wheatley. *Leadership and the New Science: Learning About Organization from an Orderly Universe*. San Francisco: Berrett-Koehler, 1992, p. 17.

Page 14. Stanley Davis. *Future Perfect*. Reading, Mass.: Addison-Wesley, 1987, pp. 87–89.

Page 14. Henry Mintzberg. Organigraphs: Organization Charts for Real. Working Paper #94-03-06. Faculty of Management, McGill University, Montreal. Unpublished, pp. 2–3.

Page 15. Charles Handy. *The Age of Unreason.* Cambridge, Mass.: Harvard Business School Press, 1989, p. 89.

Page 15. Davis, p. 5.

Page 15. Erich Jantsch quoted in Wheatley, p. 23.

Page 16. Fritjof Capra. *The Tao of Physics.* London: Flamingo Press, 1983 edition, pp. 151–55.

CHAPTER TWO

Page 23. Mintzberg, pp. 1–5.

Pages 24–25. Nancy Singer, conversation with the author. A version of the story is also quoted by Nancy Austin. "Now About This Female Management Style . . ." *Executive Female,* September–October 1992, pp. 48–51.

Pages 27–29. Frank Rose. *West of Eden: The End of Innocence at Apple Computer.* New York: Penguin, 1989. My synopsis of IBM's response to Apple's rise is taken from this book.

Pages 30–31. Eric Utne, conversation with the author.

Page 31. See especially Al Ries and Jack Trout. *Bottom-Up Marketing.* New York: Plume, 1990. See also Gary Hamel and C. K. Prahald. "Corporate Imagination and Expeditionary Marketing." *Harvard Business Review,* July–August 1991.

Pages 33–35. Alton F. Doody and Ron Bingaman. *Reinventing the Wheels: Ford's Spectacular Comeback.* Cambridge, Mass.: Ballinger, 1988. The whole book is essentially a discussion of the role Team Taurus played in turning Ford around in the late 1980s. See also David Halberstam's brilliant history *The Reckoning,* New York: Avon, 1986, for an extended discussion of where Ford went wrong in the first place.

Pages 35–36. James P. Womack, Daniel T. Jones, and Daniel Roos. *The Machine That Changed the World.* New York: Rawson Associates, 1990. For NUMMI, see especially pp. 77–84. See also Maryann Keller, *Rude Awakening: The Rise, Fall, and Struggle for Recovery of General Motors,* New York: Harper Perennial, 1989, for more insight into GM's refusal to learn from its competition.

Page 36. Christopher Alexander et al. *A Pattern Language: Towns, Buildings, Construction.* New York: Oxford University Press, 1977. The discussion of scale permeates the book, but see especially pp. 11–68.

Page 37. Sally Helgesen. *Wildcatters: A Story of Texans, Oil and Money.* New York: Doubleday, 1981, pp. 77–83, "To Hell with the Herd Laws."

Page 38. Stanley Crouch. "Blues to Be There." From the program notes for *The One Hundred Years of Jazz and Blues Festival.* Brooklyn, N.Y.: Kings Majestic Corporation. 1992.

Pages 40ff. John Pfeiffer. "The Secret of Life at the Limits: Cogs Become Big Wheels." *The Smithsonian Magazine,* Spring 1993.

PART II INTRODUCTION TO STUDIES

Page 49. John Naisbitt. *The Global Paradox.* New York: William Morrow, 1994.

CHAPTER THREE

Page 51. Regis McKenna. "Marketing is Everything." *Harvard Business Review,* January–February 1991, p. 68.

Pages 52–53. McKenna, pp. 65–79. For a discussion of McKenna's role in the development of both Apple and Intel, see Rose, especially pp. 33–36.

Page 54. Andrew Grove quoted in "Inside Intel." *Business Week,* July 1, 1992. Figures on Intel from 1993 Annual Report.

Pages 58–60. For discussion of Intel's rise in the early days of Silicon Valley, see Rose, especially pp. 23–48. Re Moore's Law, p. 31.

CHAPTER FOUR

Page 93. "The age of redefinition" is Stanley Crouch's phrase. Conversation with the author.

Page 94. Henry Mintzberg, conversation with the author.

Pages 96–97. Figures on the *Miami Herald* from Dave Lawrence.

CHAPTER FIVE

Page 125. Peter Drucker. "The Coming of the New Organization." *Harvard Business Review,* January–February 1988, p. 47.

Page 125. Alvin Toffler. *Power Shift: Knowledge, Wealth, and Violence at the Edge of the Twenty-first Century.* New York: Bantam, 1990, p. 210.

Pages 126–27. For development of hierarchy in the Catholic Church, see Thomas Bokenkotter. *A Concise History of the Catholic Church.* New York: Doubleday, 1979.

Page 128. Toffler, p. 209.

Pages 129–30. For a discussion of the effect of early twentieth-century reforms on medicine in the United States, see Barbara Ehrenreich and Deirdre English. *For Her Own Good: 150 Years of the Experts' Advice to Women.* New York: Anchor/Doubleday, 1978, especially pp. 110–39.

Pages 131–32. This summary of change in the nursing profession is derived from Joyce Clifford. "The Future of Nursing Practice," in *The Nursing Profession.* St. Louis: C. V. Mosby Company, 1992, pp. 617–22.

Page 160–61. Shoshonna Zuboff. *In the Age of the Smart Machine: The Future of Work and Power.* New York: Basic Books, 1988, p. 169. See also pp. 97–128 and 156–72 for a broader discussion.

CHAPTER SIX

Page 164. Davis, p. 178.

Pages 165–66. Nancy Badore, conversation with the author.

Page 167. Zuboff, pp. 36–46.

Page 170. Anixter's figures from 1993 Annual Report.

CHAPTER EIGHT

Pages 254–55. Badore, interview with the author.

Page 257. Quotes and observations taken from Museum of Modern Art exhibition of the work of Louis Kahn. June 14–August 18, 1992.

Page 257. Helgesen, *The Female Advantage,* pp. 143–56.

Page 264. Stewart Brand. From work-in-progress, delivered as a lecture at the Third Annual Technology, Entertainment, and Design Conference, Monterey, California, March 1992. Brand traces in particular the history of DEC's Building 20.

Pages 265–66. Phil Patton. "The Virtual Office." *New York Times,* October 28, 1993.

Pages 266–67. Nancy Foy. *The Yin and Yang of Organizations.* Quoted in Ginette Paris. *Pagan Meditations: Aphrodite, Hestia, Artemis.* Dallas: Spring Publications, 1986, p. 172.

Page 267. Paris, p. 173.

Pages 267–68. Handy, pp. 109–13.

Pages 269–70. Material on Fitch RichardsonSmith is from Tom Peters's newsletter "On Achieving Excellence," March 1990, pp. 2–5.

Page 271. Peter Calthorpe, in conversation with the author.

CHAPTER NINE

Pages 274–75. Kelly Morgan. *Beyond Potential.* Unpublished manuscript.

Page 277. Paul Hawken. *Growing a Business.* New York: Fireside, 1987, p. 61.

Page 278. Marilyn Ferguson. *The Aquarian Conspiracy.* Los Angeles: J. P. Tarcher Co., 1980, p. 214.

Pages 279–81. For background on the early role of community memory and the People's Computing Company, see Steven Levy, *Hackers,* New York: Dell, 1989, pp. 156ff.

Page 283. For an account of the role of machine shops around Detroit in the development of the U.S. auto industry, see Halberstam, pp. 72–76.

Page 284. On the notion of a return to early ways of organizing labor markets in the post-industrial economy, see Charles F. Sabel, "Flexible Specialisation and the Re-emergence of Regional Economies," essay published in *Reversing Industrial Decline? Industrial Structure and Policy in*

Britain and Her Competitors, eds. Paul Hirst and Jonathan Zeitlin, London: Oxford University Press, 1989, pp. 17ff.

Page 284. Sabel, pp. 21–25 and ff. This idea is now being more widely recognized.

Page 284. The notion of Hollywood as the prototypical metaweb is from a conversation with Laurence Wilkinson of the Global Business Network.

Pages 285–86. Joel Kotkin. *Tribes.* New York: Random House, 1993, pp. 3–13.

Page 287. Michael E. Porter. "Capital Disadvantage: America's Failing Capital Investment System." *Harvard Business Review,* September–October 1992, p. 65.

Index

Printed in the United States
44094LVS00005B/39